A-Z EDINBU

D0550863

CONTENTS

Key to Map Pages	2-3
Large Scale City Centre	4-5
Map Pages	6-50
Guide to Selected Places of Interest	51-57
Index to Streets, Towns, Villages, Hospitals and Selected Places of Interest	58-84

REFERENCE

Motorway	M8	Car Park (Selected)	P
A Road	A702	Church or Chapel	†
B Road	B701	Fire Station	■
Dual Carriageway		Hospital	H
One-way Street		House Numbers A & B Roads only	122 68
Traffic flow on A Roads is also indicated by a heavy line on the driver's left.	→	Information Centre	i
Junction Name	GOGAR JUNCTION	National Grid Reference	575
Restricted Access		Park & Ride	Ingliston P+
Pedestrianized Road		Police Station	▲
Track / Footpath		Post Office	★
Residential Walkway		Safety Camera with Speed Limit Fixed cameras and long term road works cameras Symbols do not indicate camera direction	30 Fixed Speed Limit
Cycleway		Toilet:	
Railway	Level Crossing / Station / Tunnel	without facilities for the disabled	▽
		with facilities for the disabled	▽
NET (New Edinburgh Tramways) (Under Construction Due to open 2011) The boarding of trams at stops may be limited to a single direction, indicated by the arrow	Stop	Viewpoint	⁂ ☀
Built-up Area	MILL LA	Educational Establishment	
Local Authority Boundary	—··—··—	Hospital or Hospice	
Posttown Boundary		Industrial Building	
Postcode Boundary within Posttown		Leisure or Recreational Facility	
		Place of Interest	
Map Continuation	8 / Large Scale Centre 4	Public Building	
		Shopping Centre or Market	
Airport	✈	Other Selected Buildings	

SCALE

Map Pages 6-50	1:19000	3.33 inches to 1 mile	Map Pages 4-5	1:9500	6.7 inches to 1 mile
0	¼	½ Mile	0	⅛	¼ Mile
0 250 500 750 Metres			0 125 250 375 Metres		
5.26cm to 1km 8.47cm to 1 mile			10.52cm to 1km 16.94 cm to 1 mile		

Copyright of Geographers' A-Z Map Company Limited

Fairfield Road, Borough Green, Sevenoaks, Kent TN15 8PP
Telephone: 01732 781000 (Enquiries & Trade Sales)
01732 783422 (Retail Sales)
www.a-zmaps.co.uk

Copyright © Geographers' A-Z Map Co. Ltd.

Edition 5 2009

Ordnance Survey® This product includes mapping data licensed from Ordnance Survey® with the permission of the Controller of Her Majesty's Stationery Office.

© Crown Copyright 2008. All rights reserved. License number 100017302

Safety camera information supplied by www.PocketGPSWorld.com
Speed Camera Location Database Copyright 2008 © PocketGPSWorld.com

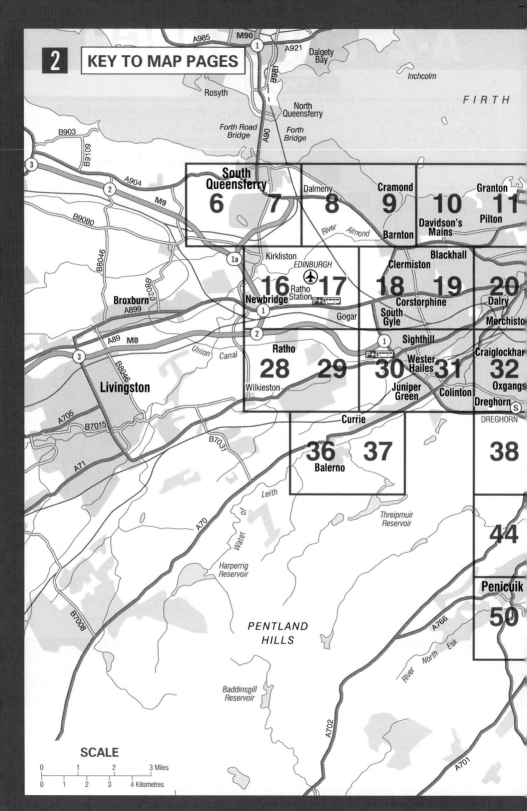

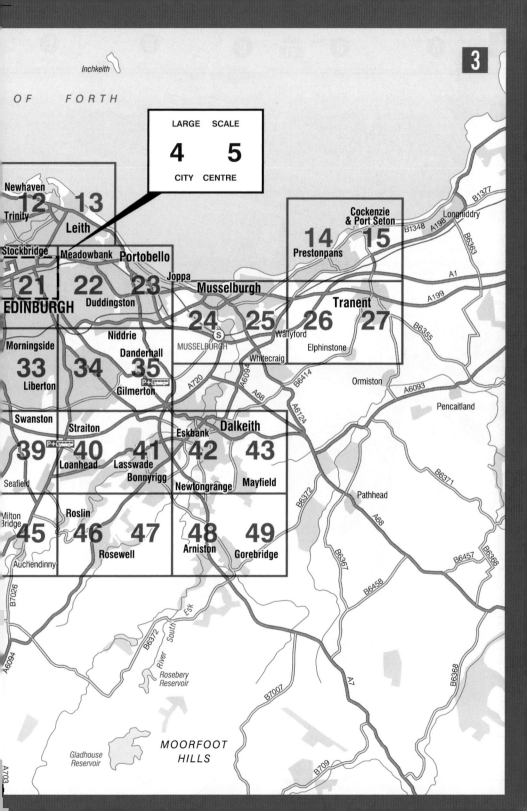

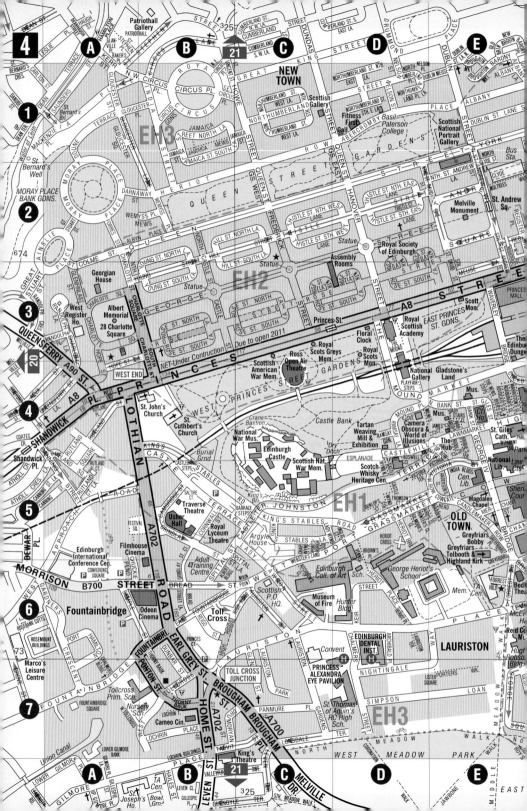

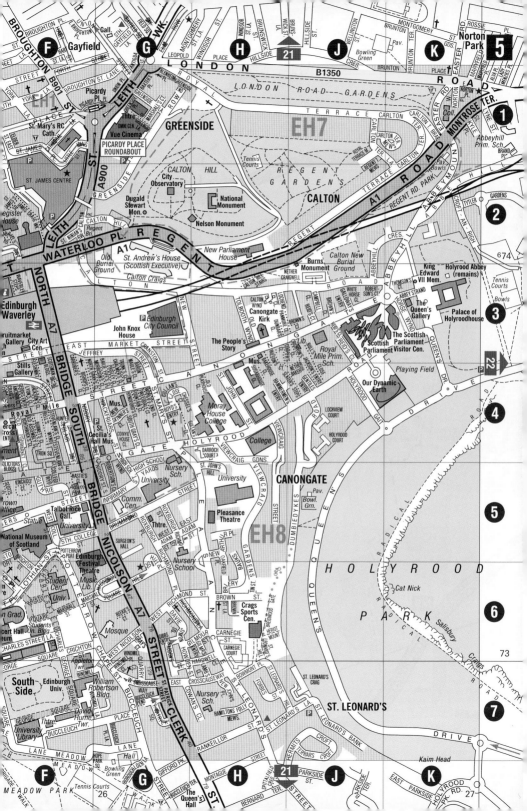

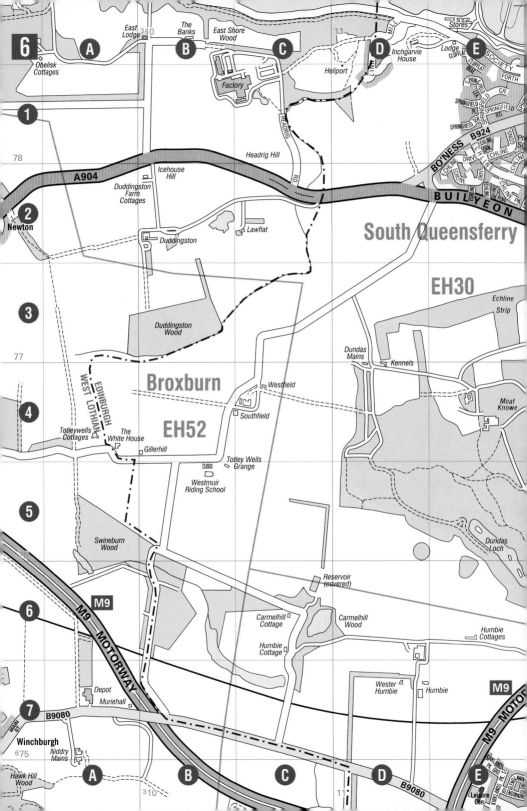

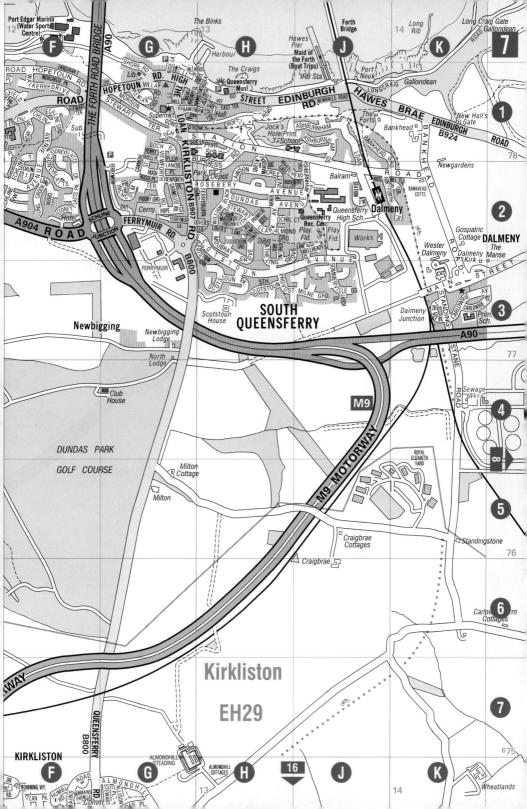

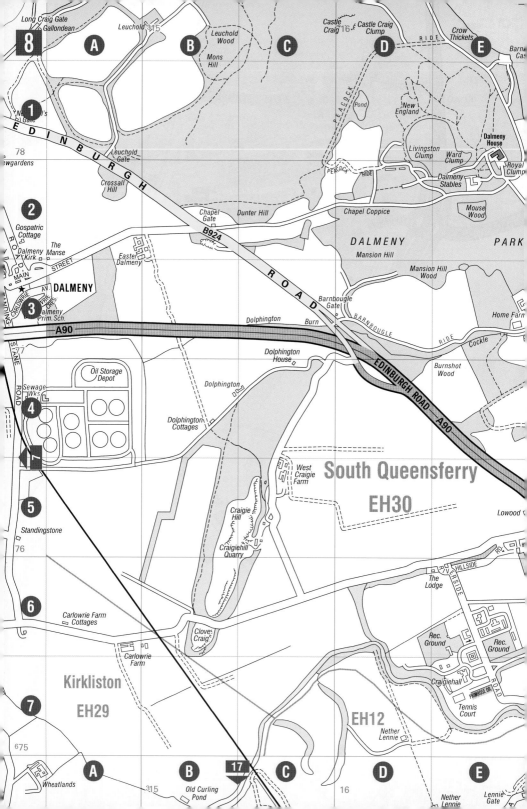

8

A · **B** · **C** · **D** · **E**

Long Craig Gate
Gallondean
Leuchold 315
Leuchold Wood
Mons Hill
Castle Craig 16
Castle Craig Clump
Crow Thickets
Barn
Cas

1
EDINBURGH
78
ewgardens
Leuchold Gate
Crossall Hill
Chapel Gate
Dunter Hill
PEACOCK RIDE
Pond
New England
Livingston Clump
Ward Clump
Dalmeny House
Royal Clump
Dalmeny Stables
Mouse Wood

2
Gospatric Cottage
The Manse
Dalmeny Kirk
Easter Dalmeny
STREET
MAIN
DALMENY
Chapel Coppice
PEACOCK RIDE
Barnbougle Gate
D A L M E N Y   P A R K
Mansion Hill
Mansion Hill Wood
Home Farm

3
Dalmeny Prim. Sch.
CARLOWRIE
VINE
AV.
★
B924
ROAD
Dolphington Burn
Barnbougle
RIDE
Cockle

A90
77
STANE
Dolphington House
EDINBURGH ROAD   A90
Burnshot Wood

4
ROAD
Sewage Wks
Oil Storage Depot
Dolphington
Dolphington Cottages

7

5
Standingstone
76
West Craigie Farm
South Queensferry
EH30
Lowood

6
Carlowrie Farm Cottages
Craigie Hill
Craigiehill Quarry
RIVERSIDE
HILLSIDE
RD
The Lodge

7
Kirkliston
EH29
675
Carlowrie Farm
Cloves Craig
Rec. Ground
Rec. Ground
Craigiehall
PRIMROSE DR
Tennis Court
ROAD
EH12
Nether Lennie

A · **B** · **17** · **C** · **D** · **E**

Wheatlands
315
Old Curling Pond
16
Nether Lennie
Lennie Gate

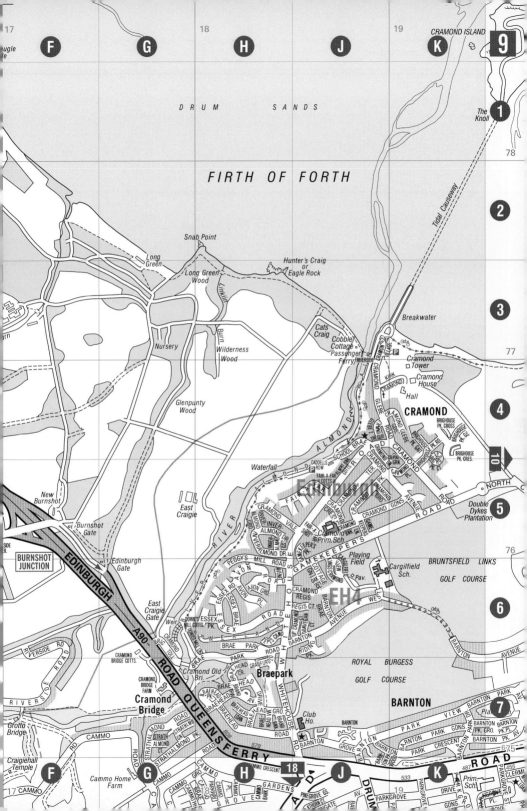

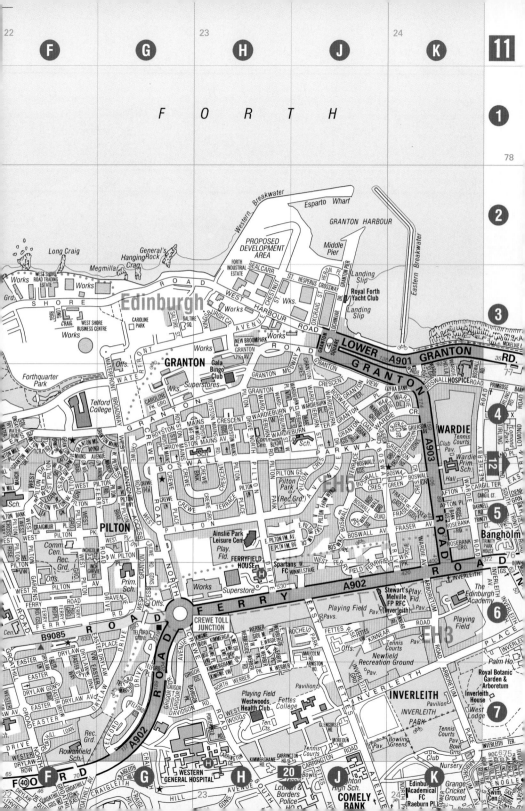

FIRTH OF

PRESTONPANS

Jetty

The Humlocks

Cocke
Gener
Stati

Slideaway
Rocks

Mathew Rocks

Hepburn Rocks

Mackie Rocks

New
Cemetery

Girdle Rocks

Football
Grd.

Ox Rocks

Playground

Inf. Sch.

Cuthill Rocks

Miners'
Welfare Institute

Preston
Athletic
FC

Rugby
Grd.

Preston
High

Comm
Cen

Big Ox

Preston
Twr

Playing
Fields

Preston

PRESTON

Prestonpans

B1348

MORRISON'S
HAVEN

Exhibition
Hall

Visitor
Cen.

CUTHILL

Club
House

Prestonrange Industrial
Heritage Museum

B1361

MID ROAD
IND. EST.

Wks.

ROYAL MUSSELBURGH

GOLF COURSE

South
Lodge

26

Drummohr
Caravan

East Lodge

RIGLEY HILL

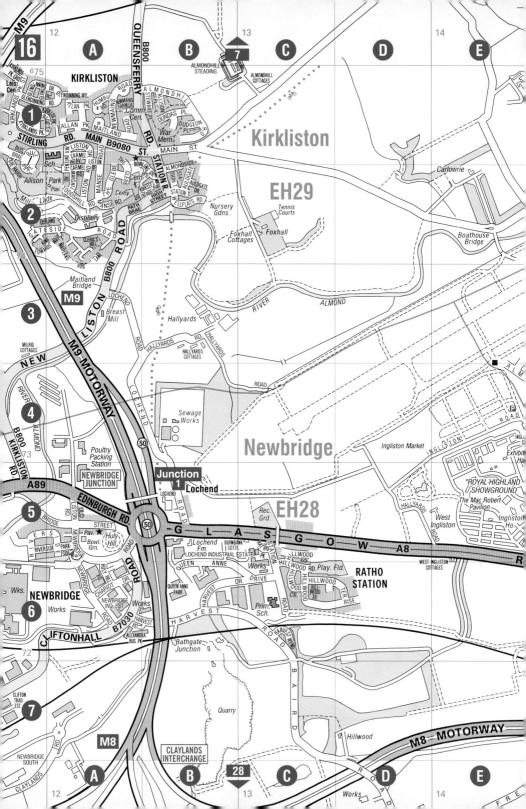

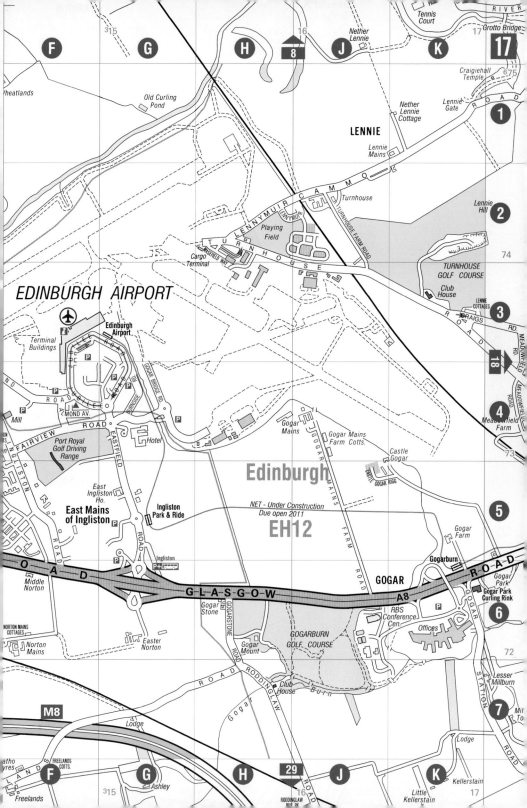

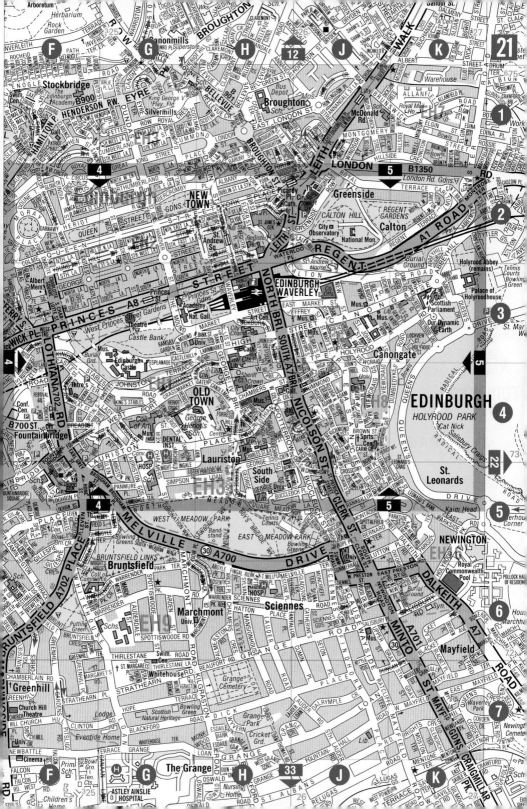

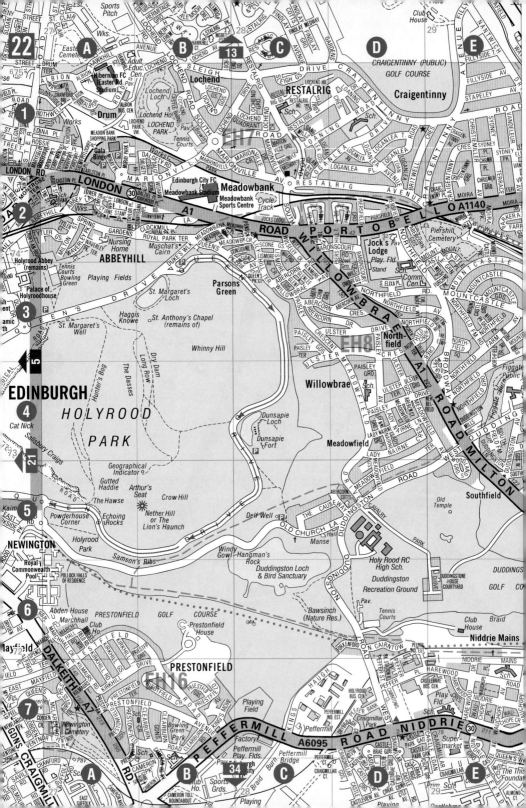

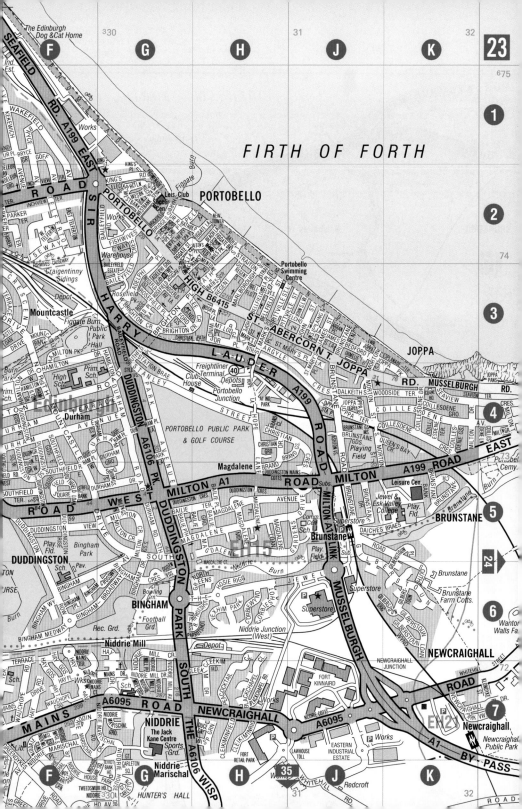

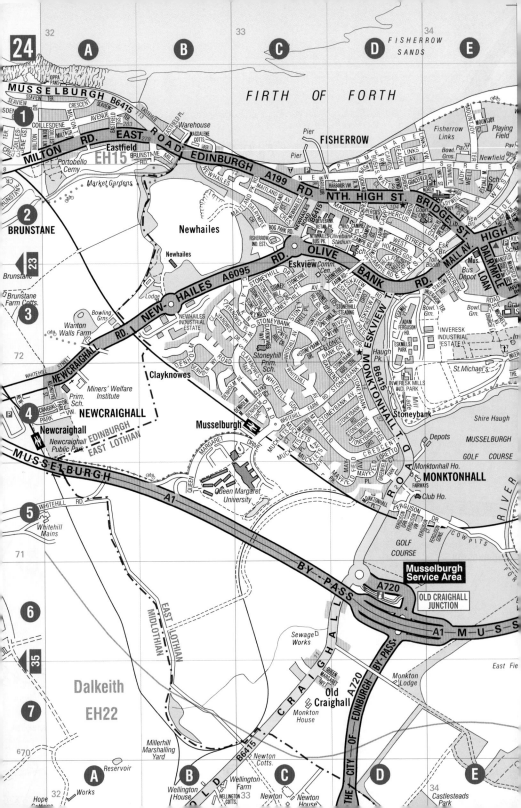

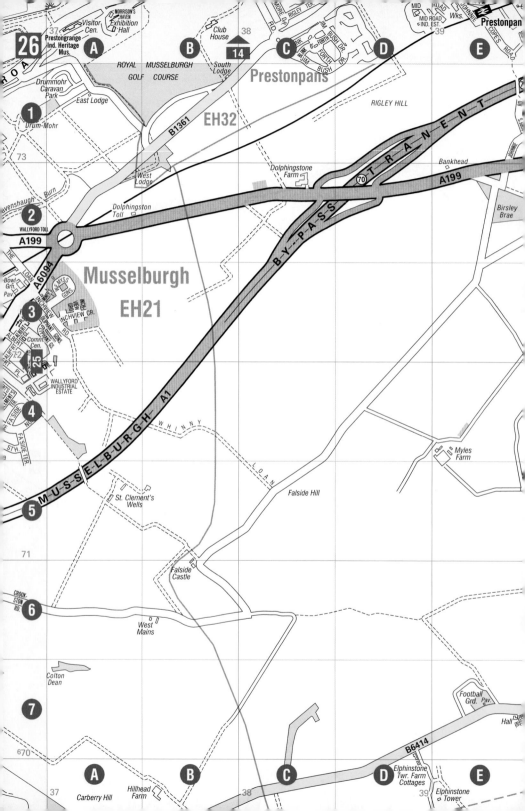

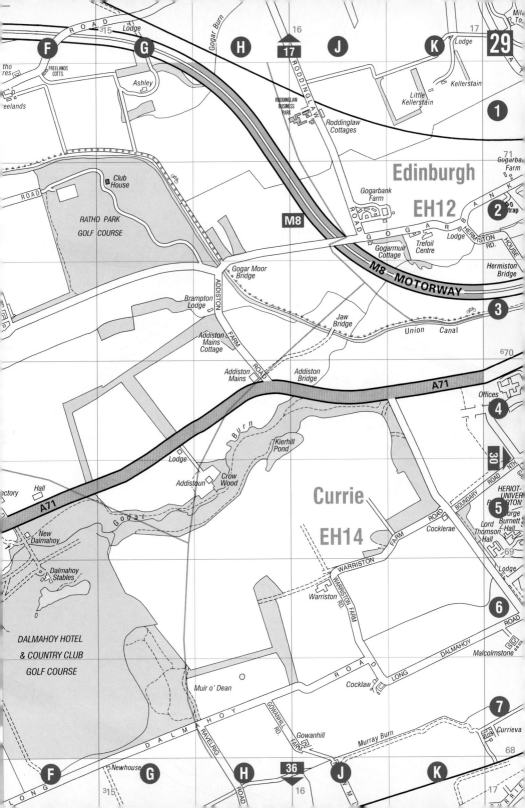

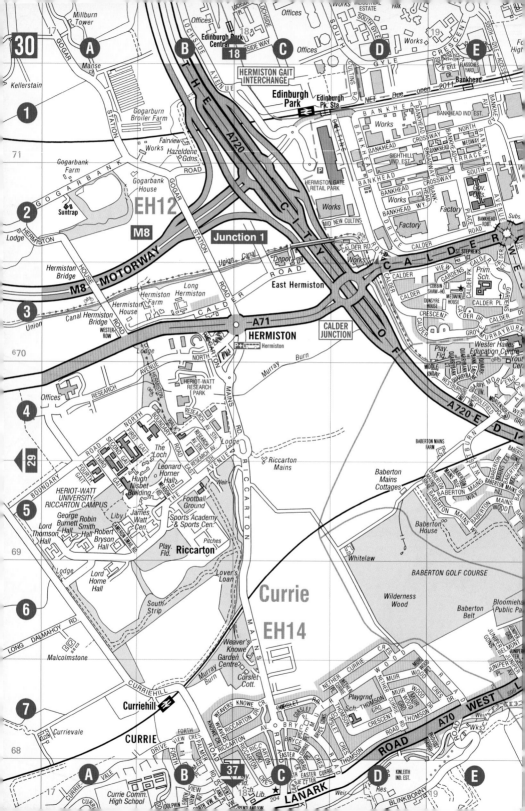

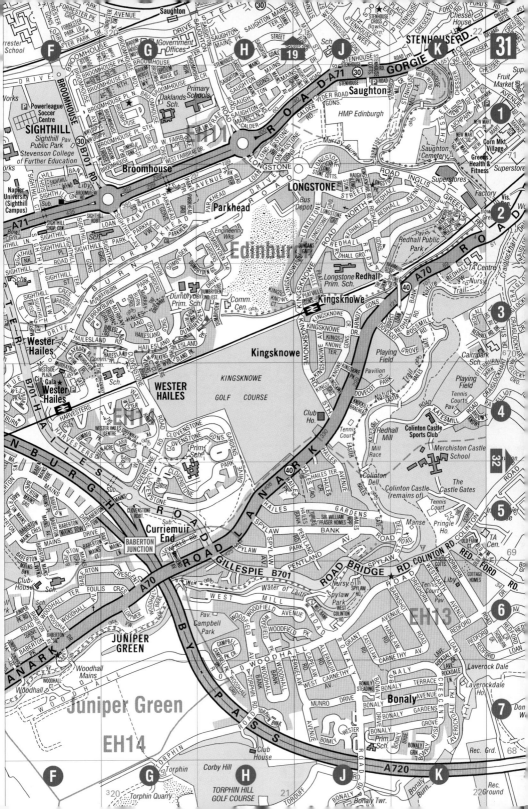

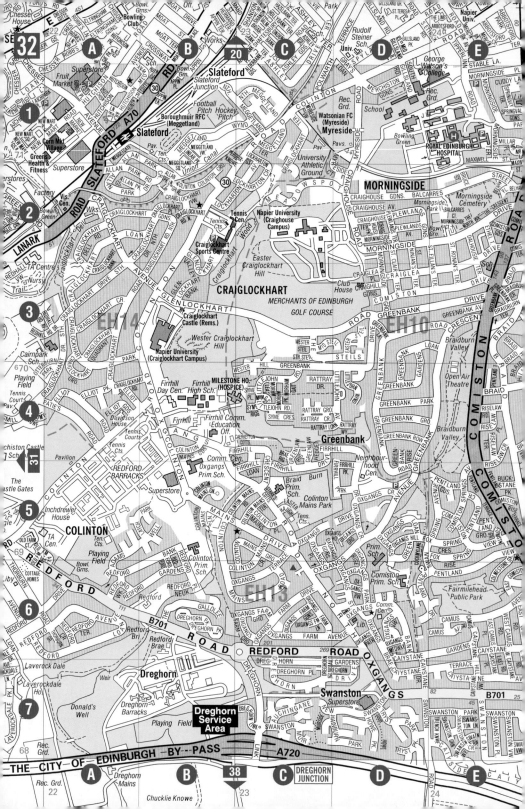

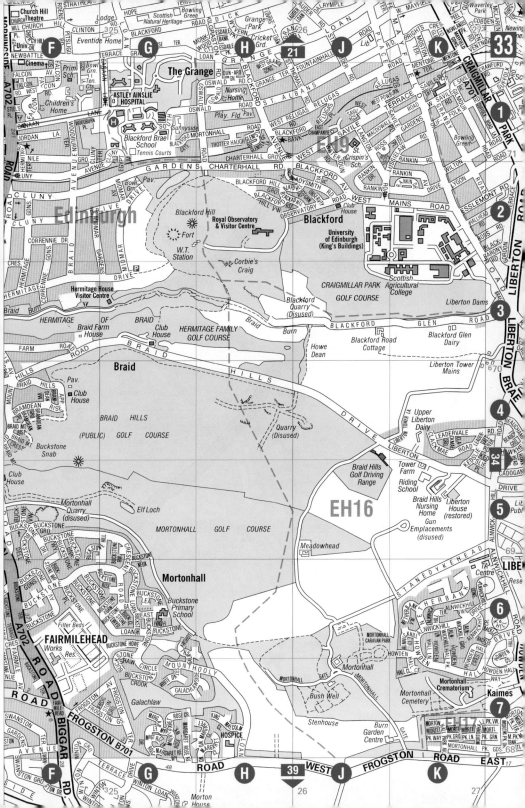

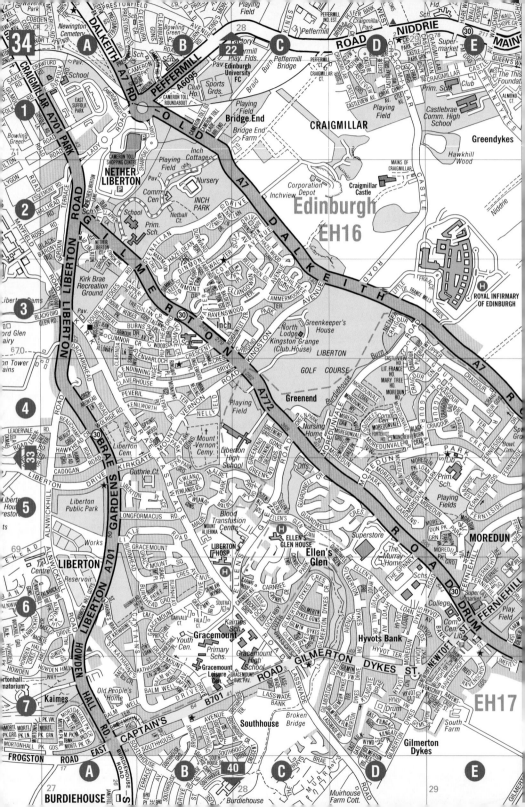

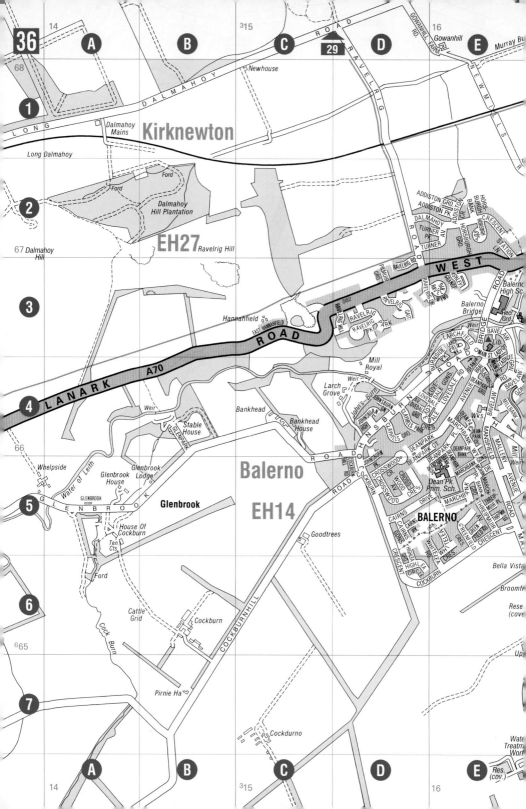

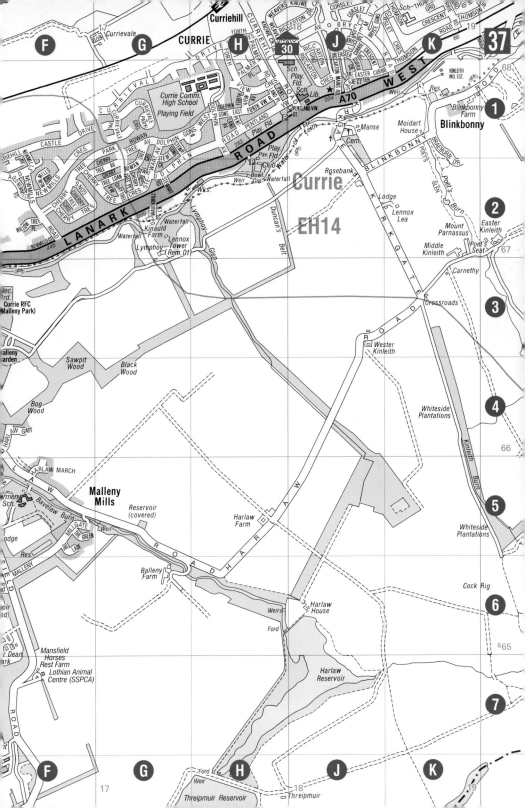

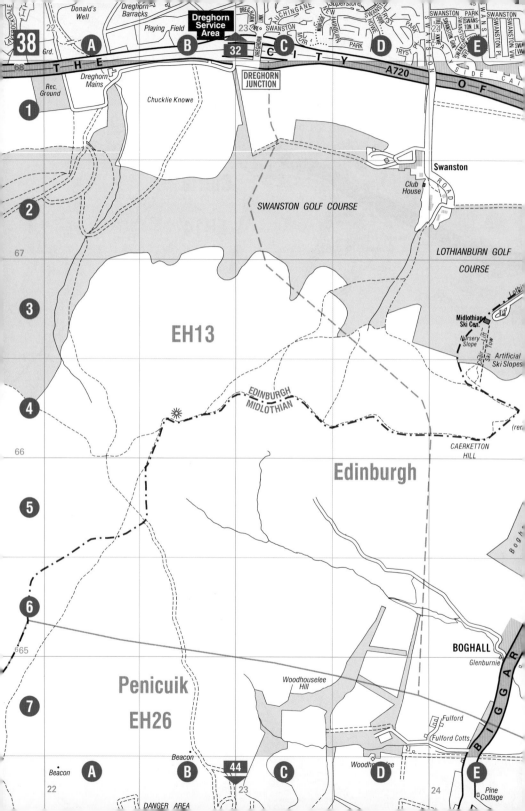

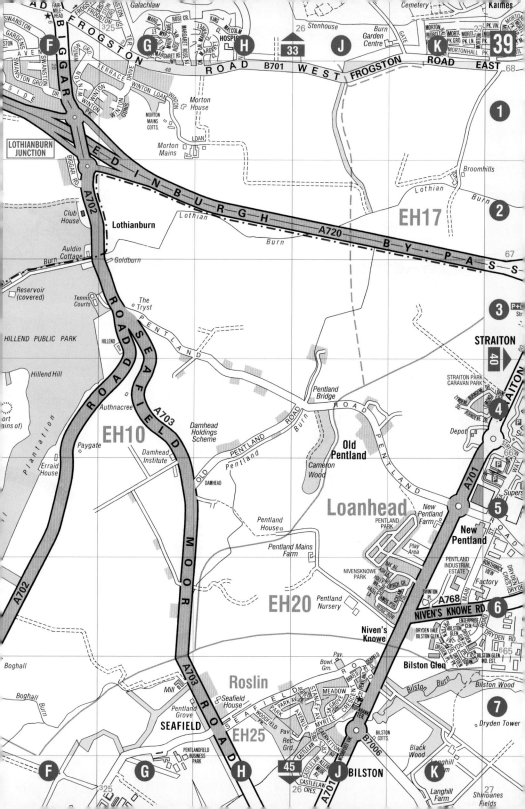

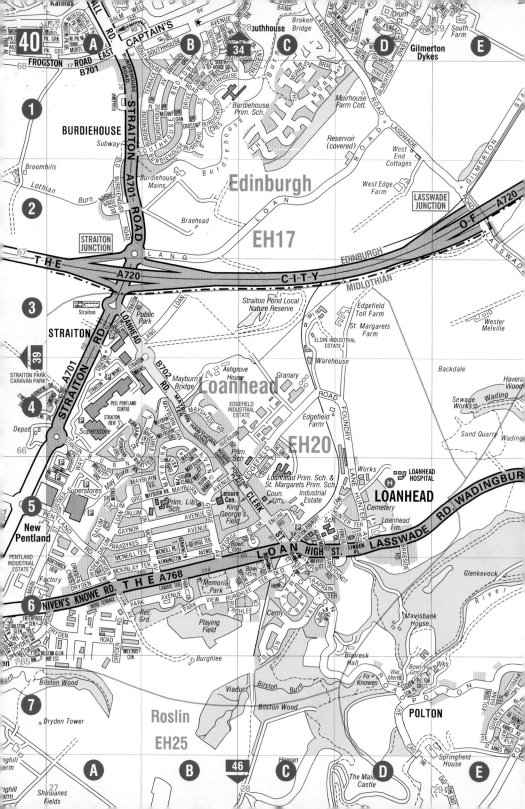

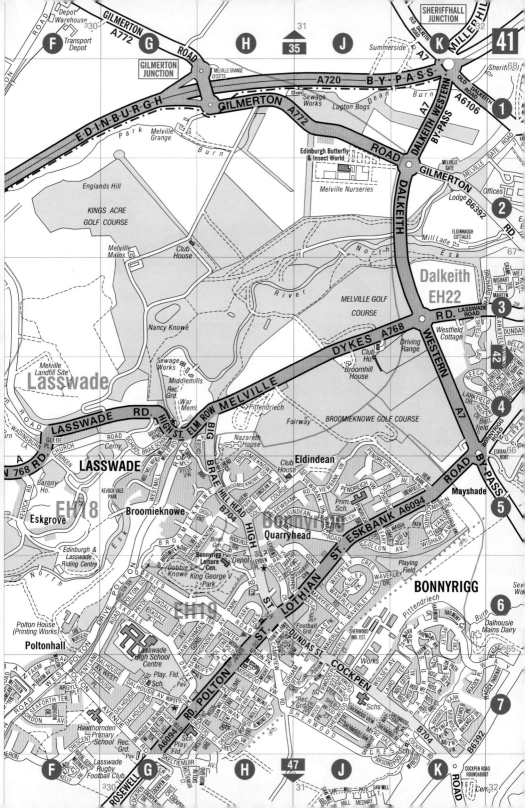

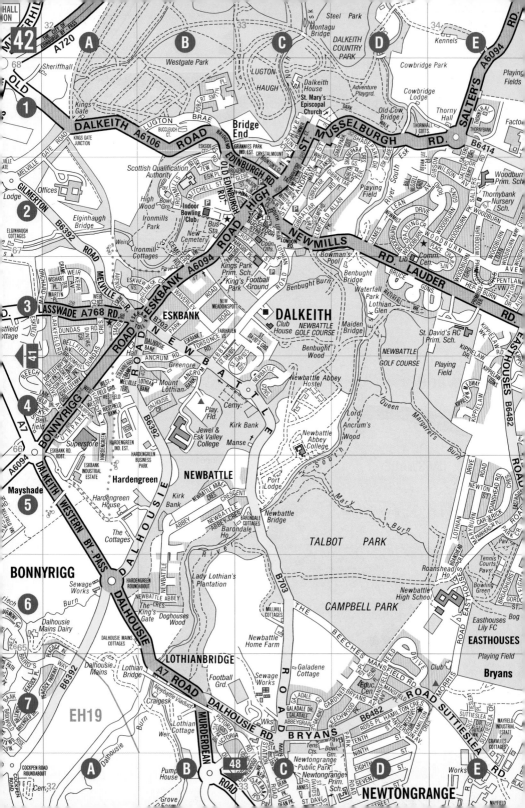

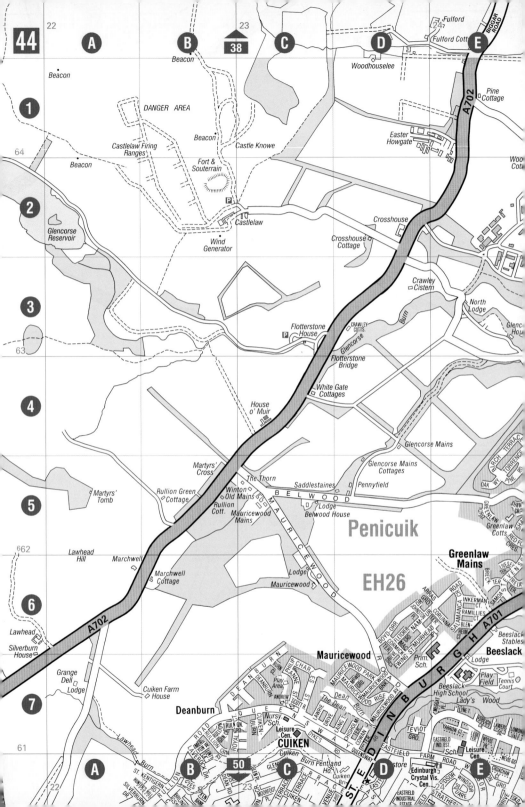

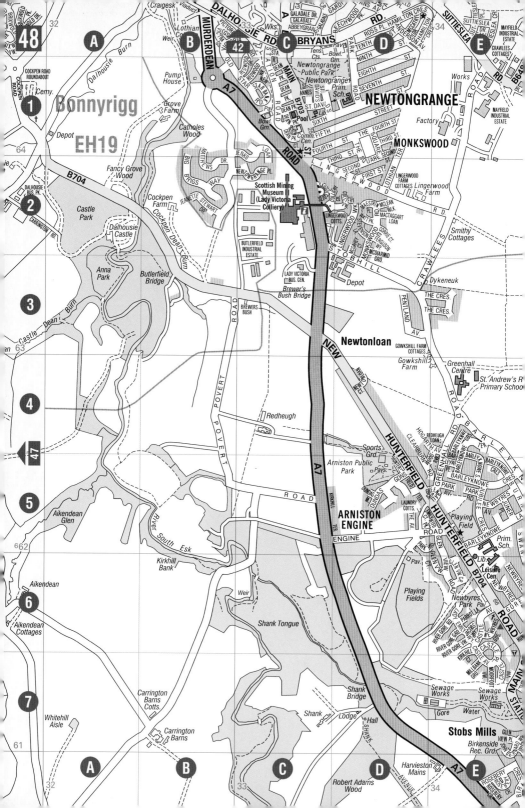

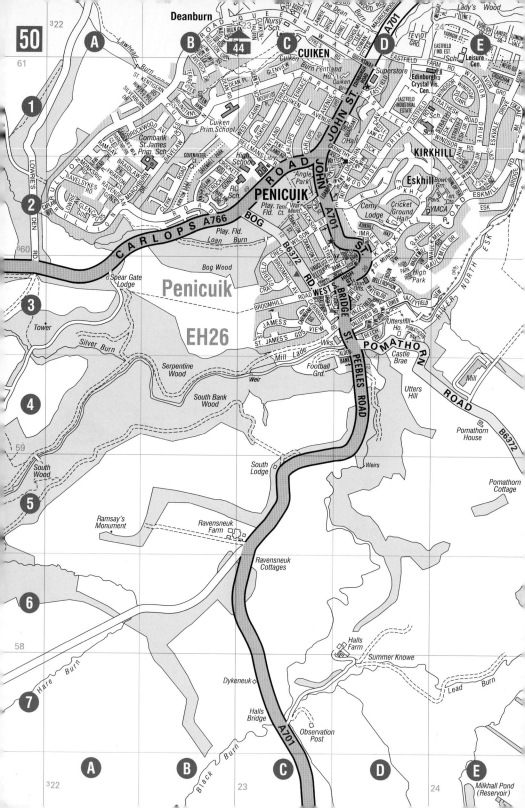

GUIDE TO SELECTED PLACES OF INTEREST

HOW TO USE THE GUIDE

Opening times for places of interest vary considerably depending on the season, day of the week or the ownership of the property. Please check opening times before starting your journey.

The index reference is to the square in which the place of interest appears. e.g. **Arthur's Seat** 5B **22**, is to be found in square 5B on page 22.

HS, Historic Scotland - Always open.
HS, Historic Scotland - Restricted opening.
NTS, National Trust of Scotland - Always open.
NTS, National Trust of Scotland - Restricted opening.

EDINBURGH

Referred to as the 'Athens of the North', Edinburgh is a flourishing city renowned for its history, style, diversity, and prestigious annual festival, which is considered to be the most important and successful event of its kind in Britain. During the month of August, the city becomes a magnet for thousands of people from around the world intent on participating in the festival scene.

Edinburgh divides itself between the Old and New Town areas. The Old Town includes the ancient city centre, where the famous Royal Mile links the Castle and Holyrood, and the historical districts of Grassmarket and Greyfriars. The New Town, dating mainly from the 18th century extends north from Princes Street, Edinburgh's main shopping street, and comprises a continuous development of grand streets, squares, circuses and green spaces regarded as a masterpiece of urban architecture.

Edinburgh Castle

 Tourist Information Centre (All year):

Edinburgh & Scotland Information Centre, 3 Princes Street. Tel: 0845 22 55 121

www.edinburgh.org

Arthur's Seat   5B 22

The remnant of a volcanic eruption dating back to the Carboniferous period, this natural attraction is a prominent and celebrated landmark of the city skyline. Positioned within Holyrood Park to the east of the city centre, it stands at just 250m (823 feet) and is easily surmountable in an hour by way of its gentle slopes. A breath-taking panoramic view of Edinburgh's magnificent cityscape awaits those who reach the summit, and if attempted on a clear day, the mountains of the Trossachs can be seen.

Brass Rubbing Centre
(Chalmers Close)   4G 5

Housed in Trinity Apse, the only remaining part of the collegiate church founded in 1462. The centre holds a fine collection of replica brasses and Pictish stones from which rubbings can be made.

Burns Monument   2J 5

A monument dedicated to Scotland's most beloved poet Robert Burns (1759-1796) built in 1830 by architect Thomas Hamilton.

Butterfly and Insect World
1J **41**

A popular attraction housed in a vast indoor rainforest. Visitors experience the free-flying butterflies first-hand, while the daily 'Meet the Beasties' sessions allow for close handling of the more friendlier creatures. Tarantulas, leaf-cutting ants, scorpions, pythons and chameleons are also part of the experience.

Calton Hill
2G **5**

Although Calton Hill may not be the highest of the city's hills, it still enjoys the most spectacular outlook with views stretching to Leith and the Firth of Forth to the north, and Holyrood Park to the south. The most distinguishing feature by far must be the unusual assortment of buildings and monuments dotted about the vicinity, in particular, the National Monument - a tribute to the Parthenon, and the Nelson Monument - built in the shape of a telescope.

Camera Obscura & World of Illusions
4D **4**

This Victorian 'Eye in the Sky' has fascinated visitors for 150 years with its live moving panorama of the city. Spy on people and even pick them up in your hand, enjoy access to free telescopes showing a spectacular 360° rooftop panorama and listen to your guide recount tales of Edinburgh's exciting past. In World of Illusions you can immerse yourself in three floors of mind-boggling hands-on exhibits from shadow walls to bendy mirrors, seeing in 3D to shaking hands with your ghost.

City Art Centre
(2 Market Street)
3F **5**

A rich collection of fine art, almost entirely by Scottish artists, is housed within the City Art Centre. Since opening in 1980, the six exhibition galleries have displayed work dating from the 17th century, and encompasses a wide range of media, including painting, drawing, print, sculpture, tapestry and photography.

Collective Gallery
4F **5**

Established in 1984, this gallery supports new contemporary artists through exhibitions and new commissions.

Craigmillar Castle HS
2D **34**

A beautifully preserved medieval castle seated 3 miles south east from the city centre. Its historical significance is undoubtedly linked to Mary, Queen of Scots who sought refuge in its walls after the infamous murder of her secretary, David Rizzio, at

Holyrood Palace. The castle also bore witness to the plot to assassinate Mary's second husband, the brutish Lord Darnley.

Dalmeny House
1E **8**

The stately home of the Earls of Rosebery for nearly 200 years, Dalmeny House is an interesting mix of Tudor revival, with its octagonal towers and carved chimneys, gothic flourishes of stained glass and fan vaulted corridors, and lavish rooms in typical Regency style. Paintings by Gainsborough, Raeburn, Reynolds and Lawrence adorn the walls of the Dining room, while Scotland's premier collection of French tapestries, porcelain and furniture occupy other rooms. A notable hallmark of this house is the collection of Napoleonic accoutrements, from paintings of the Emperor, to personal furniture and mementoes amassed by Prime Minister Archibald Philip Primrose, 5th Earl of Rosebery.

Dean Gallery
3D **20**

Noted for its impressive collections of Dada and Surrealism, the Dean Gallery also boasts an extensive body of work by Edinburgh-born sculptor Sir Eduardo Paolozzi including drawings, prints, plaster maquettes, and artefacts from his studio donated by the artist himself. Located opposite the Scottish National Gallery of Modern Art, the gallery's grounds play host to sculpture by Bourdelle, Hamilton Finlay, Turnbull, Rickey and Paolozzi. Visitors can also view items from the gallery library and archive by appointment.

Edinburgh Castle HS
4C **4**

The imposing fortress of Edinburgh Castle has dominated the cityscape since the Middle Ages, defiantly rooted to the ancient volcanic outcrop upon which it stands. Far from being a quaint romantic vision of a castle, its strategic positioning and defensive structure have withstood countless sieges, and provided successive Kings and Queens with refuge in times of peril. Mary, Queen of Scots, chose to give birth to James VI of Scotland (James I of England upon the death of Elizabeth I) within its safe confines, and the tiny room in which this took place can be seen by visitors today. It was James IV that commissioned the hammerbeam roof in the Great Hall, with the castle's principal courtyard, the Crown Square, developed in the 16th century. Of particular note is the remarkable St Margaret's Chapel, which has remained perfectly intact for 900 years, making it Edinburgh's oldest surviving building. Unearthed in 1818 by Sir Walter Scott, the crown jewels lay dormant for over a hundred years in a locked room in the depths of the castle. These treasured symbols of

royalty, known as the Honours of Scotland, comprising the Crown, Sceptre and Sword of State, are now viewable by the public, together with the Stone of Destiny, the One o'clock Gun and the famous 15th century siege gun Mons Meg.

Edinburgh Dungeon   3E 4

Experience life in barbaric times with reconstructions, exhibits and special effects that evoke the horrific aspects of Scotland's past. Relive the devastation of the plague, inspect gruesome torture devices and discover the brutal reality of clan warfare.

Edinburgh Zoo   4H 19

In the Corstorphine area of Edinburgh lies one of Scotland's top tourist attractions. The zoo is inhabited by 1,000 animals from over 150 species ranging from Meer Cats and Snow Leopards, to King Penguins and Dwarf Crocodiles. Watch out for the daily Penguin parade and activities such as Sealion training and the hilltop safari. Close Encounters allows visitors to handle some smaller, friendlier animals. Recent additions to the Zoo include the Budongo Trail, a world class chimpanzee enclosure, and Rainbow Landings, an exciting interactive walk-through aviary exhibiting rainbow lorikeets.

Floral Clock   3D 4

In 1903, John McHattie, the city's park superintendent, conceived the idea of the Floral Clock. Imitated by many cities around the world, the face and hands of the working clock are carpeted with thousands of small plants, all of which are replanted in Spring & Autumn, each time adopting a topical theme publicising a particular event or organisation. Be sure to arrive in time for the quaint cuckoo that announces every quarter past the hour.

Forth Bridge   1J 7

The imposing cantilever bridge, spanning 1.5 miles, stands as testament to robust engineering from the Industrial Age. It remains one of the most distinctive landmarks in Scotland, carrying trains over the Firth of Forth.

Fruitmarket Gallery, The   3F 5

Exhibiting contemporary art of the highest quality, the gallery is committed to bringing the work of artists with both established & emerging international reputation to Scotland & presenting the work of Scottish artists in an international context.

Edinburgh Festival

Every year, for three weeks in August, the city throws open its doors and streets to host a myriad of cultural events, comprising theatre, comedy, music, literature and military expertise. Recognised the world-over as one of the most acclaimed celebrations of the arts, it is certainly a most stimulating and enjoyable experience for both participant and visitor alike.
Founded back in 1947, the original line-up of events consisted of the Edinburgh International Festival, the Fringe Festival, and the International Film Festival. It was hoped that in a post war world it would re-unite people and provide some much needed merriment. By 1950, the addition of the Military Tattoo allowed the Army to demonstrate their skill and pageantry, while in more recent times the Edinburgh Book Festival, and Edinburgh Jazz and Blues Festival have emerged as successful events.

Edinburgh International Festival
From its inception in the late 1940's, the International Festival has attracted the world's eminent performing arts companies, from such disciplines as theatre, opera, ballet, and music. Considered to be the more highbrow of the festivals, it is staged in various venues around the city, with the beauty of Edinburgh's architecture enhancing each performance with a most unique atmosphere.

The Fringe Festival
Proud of its all-embracing, avant-garde approach to performance, the Fringe grew out of an impulsive grass roots reaction to the more conventional International Festival. Reflecting its 'open access' principle, the festival showcases the talent of students and professionals alike, from lively amateur productions to stand-up comedy, and small-scale productions to West End dramatics.

Edinburgh Military Tattoo
For over fifty years the tattoo has been an annual event staged in the dramatic setting of the Castle Esplanade. Garnering a reputation for unrivalled pageantry and skill, the programme is timed to coincide with twilight to silhouette the breathtaking backdrop of Edinburgh Castle. Although the performances vary year on year, the show inevitably features the music of the massed Pipes and Drums of the Scottish Regiments and Military Bands and a lone piper performing from the battlements. Televised in 30 countries amassing 100 million viewers, the event has welcomed international participants from as far afield as Nepal and New Zealand. The finale is naturally an awesome climax to events with the gathering of the performers for the taking of the salute, together with a dazzling fireworks display.

Georgian House, The NTS   3A 4

Situated on the north side of Charlotte Square and designed by Robert Adam in 1791, this house exemplifies the style of Edinburgh's New Town architecture. The rooms of No. 7 (built in 1796) are furnished in period style and there is a video presentation "Living in a Grand Design" that reflects life in the New Town. The "Below Stairs" life of the servants is also illustrated. The National Trust for Scotland also owns numbers 5 and 6 on the north side and 26 to 31 on the south.

Gladstone's Land NTS   4E 4

Built in 1620, this six-storey tenement building in the Old Town is furnished in period style with unusual tempera paintings on the ceilings and walls.

Greyfriars Bobby   5E 4

Statue in memory of Greyfriars Bobby, the Skye terrier who watched over his master's grave for 14 years after his death from 1858 to 1872.

Holyrood Abbey HS   3K 5

The ruined nave is all that remains of this once magnificent Abbey church, founded for Augustinian canons during the late 12th early 13th centuries. A substantial amount of the building was destroyed in the Reformation and, sadly, attempts to restore the ruin in the 18th century were abandoned when the roof collapsed. Beneath the Abbey the Royal Vault is the final resting place for a number of Scottish Kings, including David II (son of Robert the Bruce), James II, James V and Lord Darnley, Mary Queen of Scot's second husband.

Inverleith House   7K 11

Set within the heart of the Royal Botanic Gardens, Inverleith House runs an all-year programme of exhibitions by internationally-acclaimed contemporary artists using the visual arts and botanical science as themes. Within the gallery, there is a permanent sculpture exhibition showing work by Andy Goldsworthy and Barbara Hepworth. Inverleith House also displays work by new artists from within Scotland and abroad, and acts as a venue for the Edinburgh arts Festival.

John Knox House   4G 5
(43-45 High Street)

There is some contention as to whether John Knox, the religious reformer, actually lived in this 15th century town house. It is known, however, that it was once inhabited by James Mossman, goldsmith to Mary, Queen of Scots. Maintained by the Church of Scotland, the house features relics of the Reformation and information regarding Knox's life and influence. Now part of the adjacent Storytelling Centre.

Lauriston Castle   5B 10

Near to the southern side of the Firth of Forth stands this 16th century Tower House. Much altered in the 19th century to include Jacobean style features, in 1926 Lauriston Castle was left in trust to the nation by its last private owners Mr and Mrs William Robert Reid. The original Edwardian interiors remain, and showcase some fine examples of period furniture, Flemish tapestries and Derbyshire Blue John ware.

Malleny Garden NTS   3F 37

Maintained by the National Trust for Scotland, this pleasant walled garden allows visitors to enjoy the beautiful collection of old-fashioned roses and herbaceous borders. Of particular note is the quartet of clipped yew trees that date back 400 years. Additionally, the National Bonsai Collection for Scotland is located here.

Museum of Childhood   4G 5

This museum houses an extensive collection of childhood memorabilia including toys, games, books and dolls. For the adult visitor there are exhibitions relating to the history of child welfare including health, education and upbringing.

Museum of Edinburgh, The   3H 5

Huntly House, a beautifully well-preserved 16th century building, provides the setting for exhibitions devoted to the local history of Edinburgh. The diverse range of artefacts include pottery, silverware, street signs and treasures of national importance, such as the National Covenant and articles relating to Field Marshal Earl Haig.

Museum of Fire   6C 4

Displays illustrate the history of the oldest municipal fire brigade in the UK. Other exhibits include fire engines dating from 1806 and information relating to the development of fire fighting.

Museum on the Mound   4E 4

Based in the headquarters of Scotland's oldest bank, the museum illustrates why the bank was founded, with displays on the history of money, banks and building societies and the people who work in them.

National Gallery of Scotland   4D **4**

Located in the heart of the city, the gallery has been open to the public since 1859. The collection comprises a comprehensive catalogue of work from the Renaissance era to the Post Impressionist period.

Nelson Monument

National Library of Scotland   4E **4**

Founded in 1682, the library is one of the largest in Britain and since 1710 has been able to claim a copy of every book published in Britain.

National Monument   2H **5**

Built in 1822 to honour the Scottish who perished in the Napoleonic wars, this monument was designed to emulate the Parthenon, (temple dedicated to Athena, the Greek goddess of War). Unfortunately, it was never completed due to a collapse in funding and remains today unfinished.

National Museum of Scotland   5F **5**

Formerly the Museum of Scotland and the neighbouring Royal Museum, the National Museum of Scotland is a work in progress. Until 2011 parts of the former Royal Museum are closed in preparation for full integration. Meanwhile the visitable parts of the

National Museum trace the history of the Scottish people from prehistory, through Scotland as a separate nation to becoming part of the Union, Scotland and industry, social history, and sport in Scotland. There are interactive galleries on science and technology, and the story of human communication.

National War Museum of Scotland   4C **4**
(Edinburgh Castle)

The history of Scotland cannot be told without reference to war and military service, and its effect on its people and their land. This absorbing museum reflects the experience of war, sourced from personal diaries, photographs and official documents. Other exhibits include uniforms, insignia, equipment, medals, decorations, weapons, paintings, ceramics and silverware.

Nelson Monument   2H **5**

Built between 1807 and 1815, this was one of the first monuments to Admiral Nelson and is shaped like an upturned telescope. The climb to the top is rewarded with splendid panoramic views across the city.

Newhailes NTS   2B **24**

An outstanding 17th century house characterised by its original rococo interiors and curious landscape. Built in 1686 and added to in the 18th century, the building once held an impressive collection of books in its library (later moved to the National Library of Scotland) and was described by Dr Samuel Johnson as "the most learned room in Europe". Now in the hands of The National Trust for Scotland, the grounds have undergone archaeological investigations, which have revealed some remarkable features - a raised walkway, water garden with cascades and a rococo shell grotto.

Our Dynamic Earth   4J **5**

Discover our planet's past, present and future. Be shaken by volcanoes, fly over glaciers, feel the chill of polar ice, get caught in a tropical rainstorm and debate the planet's future in the Futuredome.

Palace of Holyroodhouse   3K **5**
& Holyrood Park

At the opposite end of the Royal Mile, providing a 'bookend' with Edinburgh Castle, stands the fine baroque Palace of Holyroodhouse, and its adjoining royal parkland. Steeped in history, with its origins dating back to 1128, it is most commonly associated with Mary, Queen of Scots, who spent six tumultuous

years within its walls from 1561. Subsequent Kings and Queens, including Queen Elizabeth II, have used the palace as their official Royal residence in Scotland. Today, tourists can visit the Royal apartments, the Throne room, the Royal Dining Room and the Great Gallery to experience the grandeur of this historical address. Holyrood Park, some 630 acres of unique landscape, contains an array of wonders; from the panoramic vista of the ancient Arthur's Seat, to the numerous holy wells dotted around the park. Within the Palace complex stands the Queen's Gallery, showing a programme of changing exhibitions from the Royal Collection.

People's Story, The   3H 5

Housed in the 16th century Tolbooth, this museum reflects working class life in Edinburgh since the 18th century. Sounds, sights, smells and reconstructed rooms combine to evoke an atmosphere of a bygone era. Complementing the reconstructions are displays of everyday objects and rare artifacts, including an impressive collection of trade union banners.

Real Mary King's Close   4E 4
(Warriston Close)

Beneath the City Chambers on the Royal Mile stands a warren of narrow streets with houses either side, where folk lived and died between the 16th and 19th centuries. Ravaged by the plague in the 17th century and built over in the 18th, Mary King's Close has an atmosphere of mystery and eeriness, where the visitor may view the well preserved tenements and hear stories of those who lived in them.

Reid Concert Hall Museum of Instruments 6E 4

An outstanding and diverse collection of over 1000 musical instruments from around the world chronicling the art of instrument making over the past 400 years. On display are some fine examples of wind, string, brass and percussion instruments.

Royal Botanic Garden   7A 12

Established in 1670, the garden is considered to be one of the finest in the world, covering over 6% of the plant kingdom. "The Botanics", as it is locally known, covers seventy acres with features such as the Temperate Palm House, arranged into ten climate zones and, at 23 metres high, is the UK's tallest Palm House - a definite must-see. A visit to the Peat and Rock House showcases the world's largest collection of Vireya Rhododendrons, while the tranquil setting of the Chinese Hillside provides visitors with the chance to see some historic Chinese species. A thoroughly rewarding and exhilarating experience.

Royal Scottish Academy   3D 4

Presenting the cream of Scottish contemporary art through an ongoing programme of exciting exhibitions including painting, sculpture, printmaking, installation, photography, architecture, new media, film and performance art.

Royal Yacht Britannia   3E 12

The decommissioning of Britannia as a working royal yacht has allowed visitors an insight into the

© Olga van de Veer. image from BigStockPhoto.com

        Royal Botanic Garden

splendour of life aboard this illustrious vessel. The Visitor Centre in Ocean Terminal sets the scene before stepping aboard for the self-guided tour through the decks. Highlights include the bridge - the hub of the ship, the Admiral's cabin and quarters, the Sun Lounge - reputed to be one of the Queen's favourite places onboard, the State dining and drawing rooms, and the Queen and Duke of Edinburgh's bedrooms. A fascinating glimpse into a piece of royal history.

St Cecilia's Hall Museum of Instruments   4G 5

St Cecilia's Hall was built in 1763 and is the oldest concert hall in Scotland. It also houses a museum displaying 50 highly important and well-preserved early keyboard instruments. There is also a display of harps, lutes, citterns and guitars.

St. Giles' Cathedral   4E 4

Founded in 1120, most of the remaining architecture dates from the 14th and 15th centuries, including the famous crown spire that dominates the city skyline. Also known as the High Kirk of Edinburgh, it contains the Chapel of the Order of the Thistle (Scotland's chivalric company of Knights) and is also noted for its stained glass windows that date from the 1870's onwards.

St. Mary's RC Cathedral   1F 5

The Cathedral church of St Mary was designed by Gillespie Graham and dates from 1814 and 1890. The St Andrews Altar contains the National Shrine to Scotland's patron saint.

Scotch Whisky Experience, The   5D 4

An award winning attraction that takes the visitor on a ride through history in a whisky barrel to discover the ancient traditions and origins of the "water of life" and its production.

Scottish National Gallery of Modern Art   3C 20

A fine collection of 19th and 20th century artwork resides in this exceptional gallery set in parkland to the west of the city centre. Treasured work by such notable figures as Matisse, Picasso, Bacon, Hockney, Warhol, Moore, Hirst and Emin sit comfortably amid light and spacious surroundings. A deserving aspect of the gallery is the presence of work by Scottish artists Mackintosh, the Scottish Colourists, Gillies, Maxwell and Eardley, to name but a few.

Scottish Parliament   3K 5

Standing boldly at the eastern end of the historic Royal Mile, the new parliament building allows visitors to explore its public galleries of the chamber and committee rooms, watch proceedings from information screens in the main hall and discover the history behind the Scottish Parliament through exhibitions.

Scott Monument   3E 4

One of Edinburgh's most famous landmarks, this monument to Sir Walter Scott was designed by George Kemp and erected between 1840 and 1844. The statue itself depicts Scott with his dog and incorporates characters from his novels.

Scottish National Portrait Gallery   1E 4

Visual history of Scotland from the 16th century to the present day depicted through portraits of figures that shaped it: royalty, philosophers, poets and rebels are included. The gallery also houses the National Collection of Photography.

Stills Gallery   4F 5

Scotland's premier photographic gallery exhibits a generous collection of contemporary images.

Talbot Rice Gallery   5F 5

The gallery exhibits Edinburgh University's 'Old Master' collection alongside a changing programme of temporary displays.

Tartan Weaving Mill and Exhibition   4D 4

Housed in the former Castlehill Reservoir Cistern, this working mill allows visitors to view the entire production process of tartan from sheep to shop.

Water of Leith Visitors Centre   2A 32
(24 Lanark Road)

Once serving as a power supply to a series of mills dating from the 13th century, the Water of Leith flows from its source in the Pentland Hills, winding through the centre of Edinburgh to its mouth at the Firth of Forth, covering 35km in all. A walkway trails the course of river over 19km from Balerno to Leith, with this well-equipped visitor centre located halfway at Slateford. Visitors can learn more about the heritage and wildlife associated with this charming waterway through interactive exhibitions.

INDEX

Including Streets, Places & Areas, Hospitals etc., Industrial Estates,
Selected Flats & Walkways, Junction Names & Service Areas, Stations and Selected Places of Interest.

HOW TO USE THIS INDEX

1. Each street name is followed by its Postcode District, then by its Locality abbreviation(s) and then by its map reference;
e.g. **Abbey Rd.** EH22: Dalk . . . .**3B 42** is in the EH22 Postcode District and the Dalkeith Locality and is to be found in square 3B on page **42**.
The page number is shown in bold type.

2. A strict alphabetical order is followed in which Av., Rd., St., etc. (though abbreviated) are read in full and as part of the street name;
e.g. **Beechgrove Rd.** appears after **Beech Gro. Av.** but before **Beech Loan**

3. Streets and a selection of flats and walkways too small to be shown on the maps, appear in the index with the thoroughfare to which it is connected shown in brackets; e.g. **Abbeyhill Ind. Est.** EH8: Edin . . . .**2A 22** (off Abbey La.)

4. Addresses that are in more than one part are referred to as not continuous.

5. Places and areas are shown in the index in BLUE TYPE and the map reference is to the actual map square in which the town centre or area is located and not to the place name shown on the map; e.g. **BALERNO** **4E 36**

6. An example of a selected place of interest is **Craigmillar Castle** **2D 34**

7. An example of a station is **Brunstane Station (Rail)** . . . .**5J 23**. Included are Rail **(Rail)**, New Edinburgh Tramways **(NET)** and Park & Ride
e.g. Hermiston **(Park & Ride)** **3C 30**

8. Junction names and Service Areas are shown in the index in BOLD CAPITAL TYPE; e.g. **BABERTON JUNC.** **5G 31**

9. An example of a Hospital or Hospice is **ASTLEY AINSLIE HOSPITAL** **1G 33**

10. Map references for entries that appear on large scale pages **4** & **5** are shown first, with small scale map references shown in brackets;
e.g. **Abbeyhill** EH8: Edin . . . .**3K 5 (3K 21)**

GENERAL ABBREVIATIONS

App. : Approach	**Ct.** : Court	**Junc.** : Junction	**Rd.** : Road
Arc. : Arcade	**Cres.** : Crescent	**La.** : Lane	**Rdbt.** : Roundabout
Av. : Avenue	**Cft.** : Croft	**Lit.** : Little	**Shop.** : Shopping
Bk. : Back	**Dr.** : Drive	**Lwr.** : Lower	**Sth.** : South
Bri. : Bridge	**E.** : East	**Mnr.** : Manor	**Sq.** : Square
Blvd. : Boulevard	**Est.** : Estate	**Mkt.** : Market	**Sta.** : Station
B'way. : Broadway	**Fld.** : Field	**Mdw.** : Meadow	**St.** : Street
Bldgs. : Buildings	**Gdn.** : Garden	**M.** : Mews	**Ter.** : Terrace
Bus. : Business	**Gdns.** : Gardens	**Mt.** : Mount	**Trad.** : Trading
Cvn. : Caravan	**Ga.** : Gate	**Mus.** : Museum	**Up.** : Upper
C'way. : Causeway	**Gt.** : Great	**Nth.** : North	**Va.** : Vale
Cen. : Centre	**Grn.** : Green	**Pde.** : Parade	**Vw.** : View
Chu. : Church	**Gro.** : Grove	**Pk.** : Park	**Vs.** : Villas
Circ. : Circle	**Hgts.** : Heights	**Pav.** : Pavilion	**Vis.** : Visitors
Cir. : Circus	**Ho.** : House	**Pl.** : Place	**Wlk.** : Walk
Cl. : Close	**Ho's.** : Houses	**Quad.** : Quadrant	**W.** : West
Cnr. : Corner	**Ind.** : Industrial	**Res.** : Residential	**Yd.** : Yard
Cotts. : Cottages	**Info.** : Information	**Ri.** : Rise	

LOCALITY ABBREVIATIONS

Auch : **Auchendinny**	Edin : **Edinburgh**	May : **Mayfield**	Rat S : **Ratho Station**
Bal : **Balerno**	Edin A : **Edinburgh Airport**	Mil B : **Milton Bridge**	Rose : **Rosewell**
Bil : **Bilston**	Elph : **Elphinstone**	Muss : **Musselburgh**	Rosl : **Roslin**
Bonn : **Bonnyrigg**	Gore : **Gorebridge**	Nbdge : **Newbridge**	S Q'fry : **South Queensferry**
Cock : **Cockenzie**	Ing : **Ingliston**	Newh : **Newhaven**	Tran : **Tranent**
Cram : **Cramond**	J Grn : **Juniper Green**	Newt : **Newtongrange**	Wall : **Wallyford**
Cur : **Currie**	Kltn : **Kirkliston**	Pen : **Penicuik**	Whit : **Whitecraig**
Dalk : **Dalkeith**	Kntn : **Kirknewton**	Port : **Portobello**	Wilk : **Wilkieston**
Dalm : **Dalmeny**	Las : **Lasswade**	Port S : **Port Seton**	Winch : **Winchburgh**
Dan : **Danderhall**	Leith : **Leith**	Pres : **Prestonpans**	
East : **Easthouses**	Loan : **Loanhead**	Rat : **Ratho**	

	Abbey Strand	**Acheson Dr.** EH32: Pres 7C 14	**Ainslie Pk. Leisure Cen.** 5H 11
	EH8: Edin 3K 5 (3K 21)	**Acklam Path** EH20: Loan 6K 39	**Ainslie Pl.** EH3: Edin . . .2A 4 (3E 20)
28 Charlotte Square 3A 4	**Abbey St.** EH7: Edin 2A 22	**Adam Ferguson Ho.**	**Aird's Cl.** EH1: Edin 5D 4
	Abbotsford Ct. EH10: Edin 7E 20	EH21: Muss 3D 24	**Airlie Pl.** EH3: Edin 1G 21
	Abbotsford Cres. EH10: Edin . .7E 20	**Adam Pottery, The** *1F 21*	**Aitchison's Cl.** EH3: Edin 6C 4
	Abbotsford Pk. EH10: Edin 7E 20	*(off Henderson Row)*	**Aitchison's Pl.** EH15: Port 2H 23
A	**Abden Av.** EH24: Rose 5C 46	**Adams Cl.** EH13: Edin 6D 32	**Alan Breck Gdns.** EH4: Edin . . .2F 19
	Abercorn Av. EH8: Edin 3D 22	**Adams Well** EH13: Edin 5A 32	**Albany La.** EH1: Edin 1E 4 (2H 21)
A1 Ind. Pk. EH15: Port 4H 23	**Abercorn Cotts.** EH15: Edin . . .5D 22	**Addiston Cres.** EH14: Bal 2E 36	**Albany St.** EH1: Edin 1E 4 (2H 21)
Abbeygrange	**Abercorn Ct.** EH8: Edin 4D 22	**Addiston Farm Rd.**	**Albany St. La.**
EH22: Newt 7C 42	**Abercorn Cres.** EH8: Edin 3C 22	EH28: Rat 3H 29	EH1: Edin 1E 4 (2H 21)
ABBEYHILL 2A 22	**Abercorn Dr.** EH8: Edin 3C 22	**Addiston Gro.** EH14: Bal 2D 36	**Albert Bldgs.** EH14: Edin 6B 4
Abbeyhill EH8: Edin . . .3K 5 (3K 21)	**Abercorn Gdns.** EH8: Edin 2D 22	**Addiston Pk.** EH14: Bal 2D 36	**Albert Cl.** EH21: Wall 3K 25
Abbeyhill Cres.	**Abercorn Gro.** EH8: Edin 3C 22	**Adelphi Gro.** EH15: Port 3G 23	**Albert Cres.** EH21: Wall 3K 25
EH8: Edin 3J 5 (2K 21)	**Abercorn Rd.** EH8: Edin 3C 22	**Adelphi Pl.** EH15: Port 3G 23	**Albert Memorial**
Abbeyhill Ind. Est.	**Abercorn Ter.** EH15: Port 3H 23	**Admiral Ter.** EH10: Edin 6F 21	Edinburgh 3A 4 (3F 20)
EH8: Edin *2A 22*	**Abercromby Pl.**	**Admiralty St.** EH6: Leith 4E 12	**Albert Pl.** EH7: Edin 1J 21
(off Abbey La.)	EH3: Edin 1D 4 (2G 21)	**Advocate's Cl.** EH1: Edin 4E 4	EH21: Wall 3K 25
Abbey La. EH8: Edin 2A 22	**Abinger Gdns.** EH12: Edin 4B 20	**Affleck Ct.** EH12: Edin 3C 18	*(not continuous)*
Abbeymount	**Academy La.** EH20: Loan 5C 40	**Afton Pl.** EH5: Edin 5K 11	**Albert Rd.** EH6: Leith 5G 13
EH7: Edin 2K 5 (2K 21)	**Academy Pk.** EH6: Edin 6F 13	**Afton Ter.** EH5: Edin 5K 11	*(not continuous)*
Abbey Rd. EH22: Dalk 3B 42	**Academy St.** EH6: Leith 6F 13	**Agnew Ter.** EH6: Edin 5C 12	**Albert St.** EH7: Edin 7E 12

Albert Ter. EH10: Edin 7E 20
   EH21: Muss 2G 25
Albion Bus. Cen. EH7: Edin ...1A 22
Albion Gdns. EH7: Edin 1A 22
Albion Pl. EH7: Edin 1A 22
Albion Rd. EH7: Edin 1A 22
Albion Ter. EH7: Edin 1A 22
Albyn Pl. EH2: Edin 2A 4
Alcorn Rigg EH14: Edin 5G 31
   (off Clovenstone Dr.)
Alcorn Sq. EH14: Edin 5G 31
Alderbank EH26: Pen 3D 50
Alderbank Gdns. EH11: Edin ..7C 20
Alderbank Pl. EH11: Edin 7C 20
Alderbank Ter. EH11: Edin 7C 20
Alder Rd. EH32: Port S 4G 15
Alemoor Cres. EH7: Edin 7G 13
Alemoor Pk. EH7: Edin 7G 13
Alexander Dr. EH11: Edin 6A 20
   EH32: Pres 7C 14
Alexandra Bus. Pk.
   EH28: Nbdge 6A 16
Alfred Pl. EH9: Edin 7K 21
Allanfield EH7: Edin 1K 21
Allanfield Pl. EH7: Edin 1K 21
Allan Pk. EH29: Kltn 1A 16
Allan Pk. Cres. EH14: Edin ...1A 32
Allan Pk. Dr. EH14: Edin 2A 32
Allan Pk. Gdns. EH14: Edin ...2A 32
Allan Pk. Loan EH14: Edin 2B 32
Allan Pk. Rd. EH14: Edin 2A 32
Allan St. EH4: Edin 1E 20
Allan Ter. EH22: Dalk 2D 42
Allermuir Av. EH25: Bil 1J 45
Allermuir Rd. EH13: Edin 6J 31
Allison Pl. EH29: Kltn 1B 16
Alloway Loan EH16: Edin 3A 34
Almond Av. EH12: Edin A 4F 17
Almond Bank Cotts.
   EH4: Cram 5J 9
Almondbank Ter. EH11: Edin ..7C 20
Almond Ct. EH16: Edin 1E 34
Almond Ct. E. EH4: Cram 7H 9
   (off Braehead Pk.)
Almond Ct. W. EH4: Cram 7H 9
   (off Braehead Pk.)
Almond Dr. EH19: Bonn 7H 41
Almond Grn. EH12: Edin 3C 18
Almond Gro. EH30: S Q'fry 2H 7
Almondhill Cotts. EH29: Kltn ..1C 16
Almondhill Rd. EH29: Kltn 1B 16
Almondhill Steading
   EH29: Kltn 1B 16
Almond Rd. EH12: Edin A 4E 16
Almondside EH29: Kltn 2B 16
Almond Sq. EH12: Edin 3C 18
Alnwickhill Ct. EH16: Edin 6K 33
Alnwickhill Cres. EH16: Edin ..6K 33
Alnwickhill Dr. EH16: Edin 6K 33
Alnwickhill Gdns.
   EH16: Edin 6K 33
Alnwickhill Gro. EH16: Edin ..6K 33
Alnwickhill Loan EH16: Edin ..6K 33
Alnwickhill Rd. EH16: Edin ...6A 34
Alnwickhill Ter. EH16: Edin ...6K 33
Alnwickhill Vw. EH16: Edin ...6K 33
Alvanley Ter. EH9: Edin 6F 21
Alva Pl. EH7: Edin 1K 5 (2A 22)
Alva St. EH2: Edin 4A 4 (3E 20)
Ambassador Ct. EH21: Muss ..2F 25
Amos Path EH20: Loan 6J 39
Anchor Cl. EH1: Edin 4F 5
Anchorfield EH6: Newh 4C 12
   (not continuous)
Ancrum Bank EH22: Dalk 4B 42
Ancrum Rd. EH22: Dalk 4B 42
Anderson Av. EH22: Newt 7D 42
Anderson Pl. EH6: Edin 5D 12
Anderson's Cl. EH1: Edin 5E 4
Andrew Ct. EH26: Pen 7C 14
Andrew Dodds Av.
   EH22: May 6F 43
Andrew Wood Ct.
   EH6: Newh 4B 12
Andy Kelly Ct EH19: Bonn ...1F 47
Andy Kelly Vw. EH19: Bonn ..1F 47
Angle Pk. Ter. EH11: Edin 6D 20
Angres Ct. EH22: Dan 4J 35

Annandale St. EH7: Edin 7C 12
Annandale St. La.
   EH7: Edin 1J 21
Anne St. EH26: Pen 7C 44
Annfield EH6: Newh 4C 12
Annfield St. EH6: Newh 4C 12
Ann St. EH4: Edin 2E 20
Ann Ter. EH8: Edin 2A 22
Antigua St. EH1: Edin 1G 5
Appin Dr. EH32: Pres 5E 14
Appin La. EH14: Edin 1B 32
Appin Pl. EH14: Edin 1B 32
Appin St. EH14: Edin 1B 32
Appin Ter. EH14: Edin 7B 20
Arboretum Av. EH4: Edin 1E 20
Arboretum Pl. EH3: Edin 7K 11
Arboretum Rd. EH3: Edin 6K 11
Arbuthnot Rd. EH20: Loan ...6C 40
Archibald Pl.
   EH3: Edin 6D 4 (4G 21)
Arden St. EH9: Edin 6G 21
Ardmillan Pl. EH11: Edin 6D 20
Ardmillan Ter. EH11: Edin 6C 20
Ardmillan Ter. La.
   EH11: Edin 6D 20
Ardshiel Av. EH4: Edin 2E 18
Argyle Cres. EH15: Port 3H 23
Argyle Pk. Ter. EH9: Edin 6H 21
Argyle Pl. EH9: Edin 6H 21
   EH19: Bonn 7F 41
Argyle St. EH6: Newh 4D 12
Argyll Ter. EH11: Edin 4E 20
Armine Pl. EH26: Pen 7F 45
ARNISTON ENGINE 5D 48
Arniston Ho. EH4: Edin 7J 11
Arniston Pl. EH19: Bonn 6H 41
Arnott Gdns. EH14: Edin 3J 31
Arnprior Rd. EH23: Gore 6F 49
Arran Pl. EH15: Port 3J 23
Arras Gro. EH26: Pen 6D 44
Arrol Pl. EH30: S Q'fry 2H 7
Arthur's Seat 5A 22
Arthur St. EH6: Edin 7E 12
Arthur St. La. EH6: Edin 7D 12
Arthur Vw. Cres. EH22: Dan ..4H 35
Arthur Vw. Ter. EH22: Dan ...4H 35
Ashburnham Gdns.
   EH30: S Q'fry 1J 7
Ashburnham Loan
   EH30: S Q'fry 1J 7
Ashburnham Rd.
   EH30: S Q'fry 2J 7
Ash Gro. EH22: May 6G 43
Ashgrove EH21: Muss 2G 25
Ashgrove Pl. EH21: Muss 2H 25
Ashgrove Vw. EH21: Muss ...2G 25
Ash La. EH20: Loan 6J 39
Ashley Dr. EH11: Edin 1C 32
Ashley Grange EH14: Bal 3E 36
Ashley Gdns. EH11: Edin 1C 32
Ashley Pl. EH11: Edin 7C 20
Ashley Pl. EH6: Edin 6D 12
Ashley Ter. EH11: Edin 7C 20
Ashton Gro. EH16: Edin 3B 34
Ashton Vs. EH15: Port 4J 23
Ashville Ter. EH6: Edin 7G 13
Assembly Rooms
   Edinburgh 2D 4
Assembly St. EH6: Leith 5F 13
Assynt Bank EH26: Pen 1E 50
ASTLEY AINSLIE HOSPITAL ...1G 33
Atheling Gro. EH30: S Q'fry ...2H 7
Atholl Cres.
   EH3: Edin 5A 4 (4E 20)
Atholl Cres. La.
   EH3: Edin 5A 4 (4E 20)
Atholl Pl. EH3: Edin 4E 20
Atholl Ter. EH11: Edin 4E 20
Atholl Vw. EH32: Pres 5E 14
Attlee Cres. EH22: May 1G 49
AUCHENDINNY 6G 45
Auchingane EH10: Edin 7C 32
Auchinleck Brae EH6: Newh ...4C 12
   (off Park Rd.)
Auchinleck Ct. EH6: Newh 4B 12
Auldgate EH29: Kltn 2B 16
Auld Orchard EH19: Bonn 6J 41
Avenel EH4: Cram 6H 9

Avenue, The EH14: Cur 5B 30
   EH23: Gore 5D 48
Avenue Rd. EH22: Dalk 3A 42
   EH32: Cock 4G 15
Avenue Vs. EH4: Edin 1D 20
Avondale Pl. EH3: Edin 7A 12
Avon Gro. EH4: Cram 6H 9
   EH26: Pen 1E 50
Avon Pl. EH4: Cram 6H 9
Avon Rd. EH4: Cram 6H 9
Ayres Wynd EH32: Pres 6D 14

B

Baberton Av. EH14: J Grn 6F 31
Baberton Cres. EH14: J Grn ..6F 31
BABERTON JUNC. 5G 31
Baberton Loan EH14: J Grn ...4F 31
Baberton Mains Av.
   EH14: Edin 5F 31
Baberton Mains Bank
   EH14: Edin 5F 31
Baberton Mains Brae
   EH14: Edin 5E 30
Baberton Mains Ct.
   EH14: Edin 5F 31
Baberton Mains Cres.
   EH14: Edin 5F 31
Baberton Mains Dell
   EH14: Edin 5E 30
Baberton Mains Dr.
   EH14: Edin 5E 30
Baberton Mains Farm
   EH14: Edin 4D 30
Baberton Mains Gdns.
   EH14: Edin 4E 30
Baberton Mains Grn.
   EH14: Edin 5F 31
Baberton Mains Gro.
   EH14: Edin 5F 31
Baberton Mains Hill
   EH14: Edin 5E 30
Baberton Mains Lea
   EH14: Edin 5E 30
Baberton Mains Loan
   EH14: Edin 5G 31
Baberton Mains Pk.
   EH14: Edin 5F 31
Baberton Mains Pl.
   EH14: Edin 5F 31
Baberton Mains Ri.
   EH14: Edin 5E 30
Baberton Mains Row
   EH14: Edin 5F 31
Baberton Mains Ter.
   EH14: Edin 5F 31
Baberton Mains Vw.
   EH14: Edin 5E 30
Baberton Mains Way
   EH14: Edin 5E 30
Baberton Mains Wood
   EH14: Edin 5E 30
Baberton Mains Wynd
   EH14: Edin 5F 31
Baberton Pk. EH14: J Grn 6F 31
Baberton Sq. EH14: J Grn 6F 31
Back Dean EH4: Edin 3D 20
Backdean Rd. EH22: Dan 4G 35
Backlee EH16: Edin 6A 34
   (not continuous)
Bk. Station Rd. EH16: Edin ...7D 22
Baileyfield Cres. EH15: Port ..3G 23
Baileyfield Est. EH15: Port ...3G 23
Baileyfield Rd. EH15: Port 2G 23
   (Fishwives' Causeway)
   EH15: Port 3G 23
   (Southfield Pl.)
Bailie Fife's Cl. EH1: Edin 4G 5
Bailie Gro. EH15: Port 5G 23
Bailie Path EH15: Port 5G 23
Bailie Pl. EH15: Port 5H 23
Bailie Ter. EH15: Port 5G 23
Bainfield Bowling and Social Club
   ....7A 20
Baird Av. EH12: Edin 5A 20
Baird Dr. EH12: Edin 6K 19
Baird Gdns. EH12: Edin 5A 20
Baird Gro. EH12: Edin 5A 20

Baird Rd. EH28: Rat 7C 16
Baird's Way EH19: Bonn 7K 41
   (not continuous)
Baird Ter. EH12: Edin 5A 20
Bakehouse Cl. EH8: Edin 4H 5
Balbirnie Pl. EH12: Edin 4C 20
Balcarres Ct. EH10: Edin 2E 32
Balcarres Pl. EH21: Muss 1F 25
Balcarres Rd. EH21: Muss 1F 25
Balcarres St. EH10: Edin 2D 32
Balderston Gdns.
   EH16: Edin 3B 34
Balderston Gdns. Nth.
   EH16: Edin 3B 34
Baldwin Ct. EH26: Pen 3C 50
BALERNO 4E 36
Balfour Ct. EH12: Edin 2D 18
Balfour Pl. EH6: Edin 7D 12
Balfour Sq. EH33: Tran 2H 27
   (not continuous)
Balfour St. EH6: Edin 6E 12
Balfour Street Stop (NET)
   (Due to open 2011) 7E 12
Balfour Ter. EH26: Pen 5F 45
Balfron Loan EH4: Edin 2E 18
Balgreen Av. EH12: Edin 5J 19
Balgreen Gdns. EH12: Edin ..5J 19
Balgreen Rd. EH12: Edin 5K 19
Balgreen Rd. EH11: Edin 5K 19
   EH12: Edin 5K 19
Balgreen Stop (NET)
   (Due to open 2011) 6K 19
Ballantyne La. EH6: Edin 5E 12
Ballantyne Rd. EH6: Edin 5D 12
Balmoral Pl. EH3: Edin 7A 12
Balm Well Av. EH16: Edin 7B 34
Balm Well Gro. EH16: Edin ...7B 34
Balm Well Pk. EH16: Edin 7B 34
Balm Well Ter. EH16: Edin ...7A 34
Baltic St. EH6: Leith 5F 13
BANGHOLM 5A 12
Bangholm Av. EH5: Edin 5A 12
Bangholm Bower Av.
   EH5: Edin 5A 12
Bangholm Gro. EH5: Edin 5B 12
Bangholm Loan EH5: Edin ...5B 12
Bangholm Pk. EH5: Edin 5A 12
Bangholm Pl. EH5: Edin 5A 12
Bangholm Rd. EH5: Edin 5A 12
Bangholm Ter. EH3: Edin 6A 12
Bangholm Vw. EH5: Edin 5B 12
Bangholm Vs. EH5: Edin 5B 12
   (off Ferry Rd.)
Bangor Rd. EH6: Edin 5D 12
Bankfoot EH32: Pres 6B 14
Bankhead Av. EH11: Edin 1E 30
Bankhead B'way.
   EH11: Edin 1D 30
Bankhead Cotts. EH30: Dalm ..2K 7
Bankhead Crossway Nth.
   EH11: Edin 1D 30
Bankhead Crossway Sth.
   EH11: Edin 2D 30
Bankhead Dr. EH11: Edin 1D 30
Bankhead Gro. EH30: Dalm ..1J 7
Bankhead Ind. Est.
   EH11: Edin 1E 30
Bankhead Medway
   EH11: Edin 1E 30
Bankhead Pl. EH11: Edin 1E 30
Bankhead Rd. EH30: Dalm ...1K 7
Bankhead Rdbt. EH11: Edin ..2E 30
Bankhead Stop (NET)
   (Due to open 2011) 1E 30
Bankhead St. EH11: Edin 2D 30
Bankhead Ter. EH11: Edin ...2D 30
Bankhead Way EH11: Edin ...2D 30
Bankmill EH26: Pen 3D 50
   (off Bridge St.)
Bankmill Vw. EH26: Pen 3D 50
   (not continuous)
Bankpark Brae EH33: Tran ...1F 27
Bankpark Cres. EH33: Tran ...1F 27
Bankpark Grange EH33: Tran .1F 27
Bank St. EH1: Edin 4E 4 (3H 21)
   EH26: Pen 3D 50
Bankton Ct. EH33: Tran 2H 27

BANKTON INTERCHANGE 7H 15
Bankton Ter. EH32: Pres 7F 15
Barclay Pl. EH10: Edin 5F 21
Barclay Ter. EH10: Edin 6F 21
Barley Ct. EH22: East 5F 43
Barleyknowe Cres.
 EH23: Gore 5E 48
Barleyknowe Gdns.
 EH23: Gore 4E 48
Barleyknowe La. EH23: Gore ..5E 48
Barleyknowe Pl. EH23: Gore ..4E 48
Barleyknowe Rd.
 EH23: Gore 4E 48
Barleyknowe St. EH23: Gore ..4E 48
Barleyknowe Ter.
 EH23: Gore 5E 48
Barnbougle Ride
 EH30: S Q'fry 3D 8
Barn Pk. EH14: Edin 4G 31
Barn Pk. Cres. EH14: Edin ...4G 31
Barnshot Rd. EH13: Edin 6K 31
Barntalloch Ct. EH12: Edin ...4D 18
 (off Craigievar Wynd)
BARNTON 7J 9
Barnton Av. EH4: Edin 6K 9
Barnton Av. W. EH4: Cram ...6J 9
Barnton Brae EH4: Cram 6J 9
Barnton Ct. EH4: Edin 7J 9
Barnton Gdns. EH4: Edin 6B 10
Barntongate Av. EH4: Edin ...1D 18
Barntongate Dr. EH4: Edin ...1D 18
Barntongate Ter. EH4: Edin ..1D 18
Barnton Gro. EH4: Cram, Edin ..7J 9
BARNTON JUNC. 1D 18
Barnton Loan EH4: Edin 6B 10
Barnton Pk. EH4: Edin 6B 10
Barnton Pk. Av. EH4: Edin ...7K 9
Barnton Pk. Cres. EH4: Edin ..7J 9
Barnton Pk. Dell EH4: Edin ...7A 10
Barnton Pk. Dr. EH4: Edin ...7K 9
Barnton Pk. Gdns. EH4: Edin ..7K 9
Barnton Pk. Gro. EH4: Edin ...7K 9
Barnton Pk. Pl. EH4: Edin 7A 10
Barnton Pk. Vw. EH4: Edin ...7J 9
Barnton Pk. Wood EH4: Edin ..1D 18
Barnton Ter. EH4: Edin 6B 10
Barondale Cotts. EH22: Dalk ...5C 42
Baron Maule's Cl. EH1: Edin ...4G 5
Baronscourt Rd. EH8: Edin ...2C 22
Baronscourt Ter. EH8: Edin ...2D 22
Barony Pl. EH3: Edin ...1E 4 (1H 21)
Barony St. EH3: Edin ...1E 4 (1H 21)
Barony Ter. EH12: Edin 4F 19
Barrace Steps EH1: Edin 5C 4
Barracks St. EH32: Port S ...3H 15
Bathfield EH6: Newh 4D 12
Bath Pl. EH15: Port 2H 23
Bath Rd. EH6: Leith 5G 13
Bath St. EH15: Port 3H 23
Bath St. La. EH15: Port 3H 23
Bavelaw Cres. EH26: Pen 1B 50
Bavelaw Gdns. EH14: Bal 4E 36
Bavelaw Grn. EH14: Bal 3E 36
Bavelaw Rd. EH14: Bal 4E 36
Bawsinch (Nature Reserve) ...6C 22
Baxter's Pl. EH1: Edin 1G 5
Bayview EH32: Port S 3H 15
Beach La. EH15: Port 3G 23
 (not continuous)
 EH21: Muss 1D 24
Beauchamp Gro. EH16: Edin ..4A 34
Beauchamp Rd. EH16: Edin ..4A 34
Beaufort Rd. EH9: Edin 7H 21
Beaverbank Office Pk.
 EH7: Edin 7B 12
 (off Beaverbank Pl.)
Beaverbank Pl. EH7: Edin 7B 12
Beaverhall Rd. EH7: Edin 7C 12
Bedford Ct. EH4: Edin 1E 20
Bedford St. EH4: Edin 1E 20
Bedford Ter. EH15: Port 3J 23
Bedlam Theatre 6E 4
Beeches, The EH22: Newt ...6C 42
Beech Gro. Av. EH22: Dalk ...4K 41
Beechgrove Rd. EH22: May ...7G 43
Beech Loan EH19: Bonn 7H 41
Beechmount Cres.
 EH12: Edin 4K 19
Beechmount Pk. EH12: Edin ..5K 19
Beech Pl. EH26: Pen 3D 50

Beechwood Mains
 EH12: Edin 4K 19
Beechwood Pk. EH22: Newt ..7D 42
Beechwood Ter. EH6: Edin ...6G 13
BEESLACK 7E 44
Begbie Vw. EH26: Mil B 4F 45
Belford Av. EH4: Edin 2C 20
Belford Bri. EH4: Edin 3D 20
Belford Gdns. EH4: Edin 2B 20
Belford M. EH4: Edin 3D 20
Belford Pl. EH4: Edin 3D 20
Belford Rd. EH4: Edin 3D 20
Belford Ter. EH4: Edin 3D 20
Belgrave Cres. EH4: Edin 2D 20
Belgrave Cres. La.
 EH4: Edin 2D 20
Belgrave Gdns. EH12: Edin ...4G 19
Belgrave M. EH4: Edin 2D 20
Belgrave Pl. EH4: Edin 2D 20
 EH12: Edin 5G 19
Belgrave Rd. EH12: Edin 4G 19
Belgrave Ter. EH12: Edin 5G 19
Belhaven Pl. EH10: Edin 2E 32
Belhaven Ter. EH10: Edin 2E 32
Bellenden Gdns. EH16: Edin ..3C 34
Bellerophon Dr. EH26: Pen ...3D 50
Bellevue EH7: Edin 1H 21
Bellevue Cres. EH3: Edin 1H 21
Bellevue Gdns. EH7: Edin 7C 12
Bellevue Gro. EH7: Edin 1H 21
Bellevue Pl. EH7: Edin 1H 21
Bellevue Rd. EH7: Edin 1H 21
Bellevue St. EH7: Edin 1H 21
Bellevue Ter. EH7: Edin 1H 21
Bellfield Av. EH21: Muss 2D 24
 EH22: Dalk 3A 42
Bellfield Ct. EH21: Muss 3D 24
Bellfield La. EH15: Port 3H 23
Bellfield Sq. EH32: Pres 7C 14
Bellfield St. EH15: Port 3H 23
Bellfield Ter. EH15: Port 3H 23
Bellfield Vw. EH19: Bonn 5K 41
Bellmans Rd. EH26: Pen 1C 50
Bells Brae EH4: Edin 3E 20
BELL'S MILLS 3D 20
Bell's Mills EH4: Edin 3D 20
Bell Stane EH30: S Q'fry 1G 7
 (off High St.)
Bell's Wynd EH1: Edin 4F 5
Bellyford Rd. EH33: Elph 7E 26
Belmont Av. EH12: Edin 4K 19
Belmont Cres. EH12: Edin ...4K 19
Belmont Dr. EH12: Edin 4K 19
Belmont Gdns. EH12: Edin ...4K 19
Belmont Pk. EH12: Edin 4K 19
Belmont Rd. EH14: J Grn 6E 30
Belmont Ter. EH12: Edin 4K 19
Belmont Vw. EH12: Edin 4K 19
Belvedere Pk. EH6: Newh 4B 12
Belwood Cres. EH26: Mil B ...5F 45
Belwood Rd. EH26: Pen 5C 44
Benbow Av. EH5: Edin 4B 12
Beresford Gdns. EH5: Edin ...5B 12
Beresford Pl. EH5: Edin 5A 12
Beresford Ter. EH5: Edin 4B 12
Bernard St. EH6: Leith 4F 13
Bernard Street Stop (NET)
 (Due to open 2011) 5F 13
Bernard Ter.
 EH8: Edin 7H 5 (5J 21)
Bethlehem Way EH7: Edin ...7G 13
Beulah EH21: Muss 2G 25
Bevan Lee Ct. EH22: Dalk ...2D 42
Bevan Rd. EH22: May 1F 49
Beveridge Av. EH22: May 2G 49
Beveridge Cl. EH22: May 1G 49
Big Brae EH18: Las 4H 41
Big Brigs Way EH22: Newt ...2B 48
Biggar Rd. EH10: Edin 7F 33
 EH26: Edin 7E 38
Bill Russell Gro. EH22: Dalk ...2D 42
Bilston Cotts. EH25: Bil 7J 39
BILSTON GLEN 6K 39
Bilston Glen EH20: Loan 6K 39
Bilston Glen Ind. Est.
 EH20: Loan 6K 39

BINGHAM 6G 23
Bingham Av. EH15: Edin 6F 23
Bingham B'way. EH15: Edin ..6F 23
Bingham Cres. EH15: Edin ...6G 23
Bingham Crossway
 EH15: Edin 6F 23
Bingham Dr. EH15: Edin 6G 23
Bingham Medway
 EH15: Edin 6F 23
Bingham Pl. EH15: Edin 6F 23
Bingham Way EH15: Edin 6F 23
Biocampus EH26: Pen 2G 45
Birch Cl. EH4: Edin 1D 18
Birch Cres. EH20: Loan 6K 39
Birch Ter. EH26: Mil B 5E 44
Birkenside EH23: Gore 7E 48
Birnies Ct. EH4: Edin 5D 10
Birsley Rd. EH33: Tran 2G 27
Bishops Cl. EH1: Edin 4F 5
Bishop's Wlk. EH3: Edin 4E 20
Blackadder Pl. EH5: Edin 4H 11
Blackbarony Rd. EH16: Edin ..2A 34
Blackburn Crag EH17: Edin ..4J 35
Blackchapel Cl. EH15: Edin ..7H 23
Blackchapel Rd. EH15: Edin ..7H 23
BLACKFORD 2J 33
Blackford Av. EH9: Edin 1H 33
Blackford Bank EH9: Edin ...1H 33
Blackford Ga. EH9: Edin 1G 33
Blackford Glen Rd.
 EH16: Edin 3J 33
Blackford Hill Gro.
 EH9: Edin 2H 33
Blackford Hill Ri. EH9: Edin ..2H 33
Blackford Hill Vw. EH9: Edin ..2H 33
Blackford Rd. EH9: Edin 7G 21
Blackfriars St.
 EH1: Edin 4G 5 (3J 21)
BLACKHALL 1J 19
Blackhall Ter. EH26: Mil B ...5E 44
Blackie Rd. EH6: Edin 6G 13
Blackthorn Ct. EH4: Edin 1D 18
Blackwood Cres. EH9: Edin ..6J 21
Blaeberry Gdns. EH4: Edin ...1D 18
Blair St. EH1: Edin 4F 5 (3H 21)
Blandfield EH7: Edin 7C 12
 (not continuous)
Blantyre Ter. EH10: Edin 7E 20
Blawearie Rd. EH33: Tran ...2H 27
Bleachfield EH6: Edin 6C 12
Blenheim Ct. EH26: Pen 6E 44
Blenheim Pl. EH7: Edin 1G 5
BLINKBONNY 1K 37
Blinkbonny Av. EH4: Edin ...2B 20
Blinkbonny Cres. EH4: Edin ..2A 20
Blinkbonny Gdns. EH4: Edin ..2B 20
Blinkbonny Gro. EH4: Edin ...2B 20
Blinkbonny Gro. W.
 EH4: Edin 2A 20
Blinkbonny Rd. EH4: Edin ...2B 20
 EH14: Cur 2J 37
Blinkbonny Ter. EH4: Edin ...2A 20
Blink o' Forth EH32: Pres 7C 14
Boat Grn. EH3: Edin 7B 12
BOGHALL 7E 38
Bog Pk. Rd. EH21: Muss 2C 24
Bog Rd. EH26: Pen 2C 50
Bogsmill Rd. EH14: Edin 3K 31
Bogwood Ct. EH22: May 6F 43
Bogwood Rd. EH22: May 6F 43
BONALY 7K 31
Bonaly Av. EH13: Edin 7J 31
Bonaly Brae EH13: Edin 7K 31
Bonaly Cres. EH13: Edin 7K 31
Bonaly Dr. EH13: Edin 7J 31
Bonaly Gdns. EH13: Edin 7J 31
Bonaly Gro. EH13: Edin 7J 31
Bonaly Ri. EH13: Edin 7K 31
Bonaly Rd. EH13: Edin 6J 31
Bonaly Steading EH13: Edin ..7J 31
Bonaly Ter. EH13: Edin 7J 31
Bonaly Wester EH13: Edin ...7J 31
Bonar Pl. EH6: Edin 5C 12

Bo'ness Rd. EH30: S Q'fry 1E 6
BONNINGTON 5C 12
Bonnington Av. EH6: Edin ...5C 12
Bonnington Bus. Cen.
 EH6: Edin 6E 12
 (off Bonnington Rd.)
Bonnington Gait EH6: Edin ...6D 12
Bonnington Gro. EH6: Edin ...5C 12
Bonnington Ind. Est.
 EH6: Edin 6D 12
Bonnington Rd. EH6: Edin ...6D 12
 EH27: Wilk 6A 28
Bonnington Rd. La.
 EH6: Edin 6D 12
Bonnington Ter. EH6: Edin ...5C 12
Bonnybank Ct. EH23: Gore ...6F 49
Bonnybank Rd. EH23: Gore ..6F 49
Bonnyhaugh EH6: Edin 6C 12
Bonnyhaugh La. EH6: Edin ...6C 12
BONNYRIGG 6K 41
Bonnyrigg Leisure Cen. 5H 41
Bonnyrigg Rd. EH22: Dalk ...4A 42
Boothacre Cotts. EH6: Edin ..6H 13
Boothacre La. EH6: Edin 6H 13
Boroughloch
 EH8: Edin 7G 5 (5J 21)
Boroughloch Sq. EH8: Edin ..5J 21
Boroughmuir RFC 1B 32
Borthwick Pl. EH12: Edin 4C 20
Borthwick's Cl. EH1: Edin ...4F 5
Borthwick Vw. EH20: Loan ...6A 40
Boswall Av. EH5: Edin 5J 11
Boswall Cres. EH5: Edin 5J 11
Boswall Dr. EH5: Edin 4J 11
Boswall Gdns. EH5: Edin 5J 11
Boswall Grn. EH5: Edin 5K 11
Boswall Gro. EH5: Edin 5J 11
Boswall Loan EH5: Edin 4J 11
Boswall Parkway EH5: Edin ..5G 11
Boswall Pl. EH5: Edin 5J 11
Boswall Quad. EH5: Edin 5J 11
Boswall Rd. EH5: Edin 4K 11
Boswall Sq. EH5: Edin 5J 11
Boswall Ter. EH5: Edin 5J 11
Boswell's Cl. EH1: Edin 4D 4
Bothwell St. EH7: Edin 1A 22
Boundary Rd. E. EH14: Cur ..4B 30
Boundary Rd. Nth.
 EH14: Cur 5K 29
Bowie's Cl. EH6: Leith 5F 13
 (off Shore Pl.)
Bowling Grn., The EH6: Edin ..5E 12
Bowling Grn. Rd. EH29: Kltn ..2B 16
Bowling La. EH6: Edin 5E 12
 (off The Bowling Grn.)
Bowmans Vw. EH22: Dalk ...2C 42
 (off Newmills Rd.)
Bowmont Pl.
 EH8: Edin 7H 5 (5J 21)
Boyd-Orr Dr. EH26: Pen 6D 44
Boyd's Entry
 EH1: Edin 4G 5 (3J 21)
Boy's Brigade Wlk.
 EH3: Edin 7E 4 (5H 21)
Brae, The EH26: Auch 6G 45
Braehead Av. EH4: Cram 7H 9
Braehead Bank EH4: Cram ...7H 9
Braehead Cres. EH4: Cram ...7H 9
Braehead Dr. EH4: Cram 7H 9
Braehead Gro. EH4: Cram ...7H 9
Braehead Loan EH4: Cram ...7H 9
Braehead Pk. EH4: Cram 7H 9
Braehead Rd. EH4: Cram 7H 9
Braehead Row EH4: Cram ...7H 9
Braehead Vw. EH4: Cram 7H 9
BRAEPARK 7H 9
Brae Pk. EH4: Cram 6H 9
Brae Pk. Rd. EH4: Cram 7H 9
Braeside Rd. EH20: Loan 5D 40
Braeside Rd. Nth.
 EH23: Gore 6F 49
Braeside Rd. Sth.
 EH23: Gore 6F 49
BRAID 4F 33
Braid Av. EH10: Edin 3F 33
Braidburn Cres. EH10: Edin ..3E 32

Braidburn Ter.—Burnhead Path E.

Braidburn Ter. EH10: Edin 3E 32
Braid Cres. EH10: Edin 3E 32
Braid Farm Rd. EH10: Edin 3E 32
Braid Hills App. EH10: Edin 4F 33
Braid Hills Av. EH10: Edin 3E 32
Braid Hills Cres. EH10: Edin . . .4E 32
Braid Hills Dr. EH10: Edin 3G 33
EH16: Edin 3G 33
Braid Hills Rd. EH10: Edin 4E 32
Braidlaw Pk. EH26: Pen 2A 50
Braid Mt. EH10: Edin 4E 32
Braid Mt. Crest EH10: Edin 4F 33
Braid Mt. Ri. EH10: Edin 4F 33
Braid Mt. Vw. EH10: Edin 4F 33
Braid Rd. EH10: Edin 3E 32
Bramble Dr. EH4: Edin 1D 18
Brambles, The EH22: Dalk 4H 43
Bramdean Gro. EH10: Edin 4F 33
Bramdean Pl. EH10: Edin 4F 33
Bramdean Ri. EH10: Edin 4F 33
Bramdean Vw. EH10: Edin 4F 33
Brand Dr. EH15: Port 5H 23
Brandfield St. EH3: Edin 5E 20
Brand Gdns. EH15: Port 4J 23
Brandon St. EH3: Edin 1G 21
Brandon Ter. EH3: Edin 1G 21
Brand Pl. EH8: Edin 1K 5 (2A 22)
Brass Rubbing Cen., The *4G 5*
(off Chalmer's Cl.)
Breadalbane St. EH6: Edin 5D 12
Breadalbane Ter. EH11: Edin . . .5E 20
Bread St. EH3: Edin 6B 4 (4F 21)
Bread St. La. EH3: Edin 6B 4
Breck Ter. EH26: Pen 6E 44
Breidwood Ga.
EH8: Edin 6H 5 (4J 21)
Brewers Bush EH19: Bonn 3C 48
Brewery Cl. EH30: S Q'fry 1G 7
Briarbank Ter. EH11: Edin 7C 20
Brickfield EH15: Port 2G 23
Brickworks Rd. EH33: Tran 1F 27
BRIDGE END
EH16 . . . . .1C 34
EH22 . . . . .1C 42
Bridge End EH16: Edin 1B 34
Bridgend EH22: Dalk 1B 42
Bridgend Ct. EH22: Dalk 2B 42
Bridge Pl. EH3: Edin 1E 20
Bridge Rd. EH13: Edin 6J 31
EH14: Bal 3E 36
Bridge St. EH15: Port 2G 23
EH21: Muss 2E 24
EH26: Pen 3D 50
EH28: Nbdge 5A 16
EH33: Tran 2G 27
Bridge St. La. EH15: Port 2G 23
Briery Bauks
EH8: Edin 6H 5 (4J 21)
Brighouse Pk. Ct. EH4: Cram . . .5K 9
Brighouse Pk. Cres.
EH4: Cram 4K 9
Brighouse Pk. Cross
EH4: Cram 4K 9
Brighouse Pk. Dr. EH4: Cram . . .5K 9
Brighouse Pk. Gait
EH4: Cram 4K 9
Brighouse Pk. Gdns.
EH4: Cram 4K 9
Brighton Pl. EH15: Port 3G 23
Brighton St.
EH1: Edin 5F 5 (4H 21)
Brights Cres. EH9: Edin 7K 21
Bright Ter. EH11: Edin 4E 20
Bristo Pl. EH1: Edin 6E 4 (4H 21)
Bristo Port EH1: Edin . . .5F 5 (4H 21)
Bristo Sq. EH8: Edin . . .6F 5 (4H 21)
Britannia 3E 12
Britannia Vis. Cen. 3E 12
Britwell Cres. EH7: Edin 2D 22
Brixwold Bank EH19: Bonn 7K 41
Brixwold Dr. EH19: Bonn 7K 41
Brixwold Neuk EH19: Bonn 7K 41
Brixwold Pk. EH19: Bonn 7K 41
Brixwold Ri. EH19: Bonn 7K 41
Brixwold Vw. EH19: Bonn 7K 41
Broadhurst Rd. EH22: East 6E 42
Broadway Pk. EH12: Edin 7D 18
Broad Wynd EH6: Leith 5F 13
Brockwood Av. EH26: Pen 1A 50
Brodie's Cl. EH1: Edin 4E 4
Brookfield Ter. EH25: Bil 7J 39
Broombank Ter. EH12: Edin 7F 19
Broomburn Gro. EH12: Edin . . .6G 19
Broomfield Cres.
EH12: Edin 6G 19
Broomhall Av. EH12: Edin 7F 19
Broomhall Bank EH12: Edin 6F 19
Broomhall Cres. EH12: Edin 6F 19
Broomhall Dr. EH12: Edin 6E 18
(not continuous)
Broomhall Gdns. EH12: Edin . . .6F 19
Broomhall Loan EH12: Edin 6F 19
Broomhall Pk. EH12: Edin 6F 19
Broomhall Pl. EH12: Edin 6F 19
Broomhall Rd. EH12: Edin 6E 18
Broomhall Ter. EH12: Edin 6F 19
Broomhill Av. EH26: Pen 3C 50
Broomhill Dr. EH22: Dalk 4A 42
Broomhill Pk. EH22: Dalk 4A 42
Broomhill Rd. EH26: Pen 3C 50
BROOMHOUSE 1G 31
Broomhouse Av. EH11: Edin . . .1F 31
Broomhouse Bank
EH11: Edin 1G 31
Broomhouse Cotts. E.
EH11: Edin 1G 31
Broomhouse Cotts. W.
EH11: Edin 1F 31
Broomhouse Ct. EH11: Edin . . .1G 31
Broomhouse Cres.
EH11: Edin 1G 31
Broomhouse Dr. EH11: Edin . . .7F 19
Broomhouse Gdns. E.
EH11: Edin 7G 19
Broomhouse Gdns. W.
EH11: Edin 7F 19
Broomhouse Gro.
EH11: Edin 1G 31
Broomhouse Loan
EH11: Edin 1G 31
Broomhouse Mkt.
EH11: Edin 1G 31
(off Broomhouse Pl. Nth.)
Broomhouse Medway
EH11: Edin 7G 19
Broomhouse Pk. EH11: Edin . . .1F 31
Broomhouse Path
EH11: Edin 1F 31
(off Broomhouse Av.)
Broomhouse Pl. Nth.
EH11: Edin 1F 31
Broomhouse Pl. Sth.
EH11: Edin 1G 31
Broomhouse Rd. EH11: Edin . . .7F 19
EH12: Edin 7F 19
Broomhouse Row
EH11: Edin 7G 19
Broomhouse Sq. EH11: Edin . . .1G 31
Broomhouse St. Nth.
EH11: Edin 1F 31
Broomhouse St. Sth.
EH11: Edin 2G 31
Broomhouse Ter. EH11: Edin . . .7G 19
Broomhouse Wlk.
EH11: Edin 1G 31
Broomhouse Way
EH11: Edin 1G 31
Broomhouse Wynd
EH11: Edin 1G 31
(off Broomhouse Cres.)
BROOMIEKNOWE 5G 41
Broomieknowe EH18: Las 5G 41
Broomieknowe Gdns.
EH19: Bonn 5H 41
Broomieknowe Pk.
EH19: Bonn 5H 41
Broomlea Cres. EH12: Edin 6F 19
Broompark Bus. Pk.
EH5: Edin 3H 11
(off New Broompark)
Broompark Rd. EH12: Edin 6F 19
Broomside Ter. EH12: Edin 6G 19
Broomview Ho. EH11: Edin 2F 31
Broomyknowe EH14: Edin 4K 31
Brotherstone's Way
EH33: Tran 4H 27
Brougham Pl.
EH3: Edin 7C 4 (5G 21)
Brougham St.
EH3: Edin 7B 4 (5F 21)
BROUGHTON 1H 21
Broughton Mkt.
EH3: Edin 1E 4 (2H 21)
Broughton Pl.
EH1: Edin 1F 5 (1H 21)
Broughton Pl. La. EH1: Edin . . .1H 21
Broughton Rd. EH7: Edin 7C 12
Broughton St.
EH1: Edin 1F 5 (1H 21)
Broughton St. La.
EH1: Edin 1F 5 (2H 21)
Brown's Cl. EH8: Edin . . .3J 5 (3K 21)
Brown's Ct. EH8: Edin 3J 5
Brown's Pl. EH1: Edin 5D 4
Brown St. EH8: Edin 6H 5 (4J 21)
Brown St. La. EH8: Edin 6H 5
Bruce Gdns. EH22: Dalk 3D 42
Bruce St. EH10: Edin 2E 32
BRUNSTANE 5K 23
Brunstane Bank EH15: Port 5K 23
Brunstane Cres. EH15: Port . . .5K 23
Brunstane Dr. EH15: Port 5J 23
Brunstane Gdns. EH15: Port . . .4J 23
EH26: Pen 1B 50
Brunstane Gdns. M.
EH15: Port 4J 23
Brunstane Mill Rd.
EH15: Port 1B 24
Brunstane Rd. EH15: Port 4J 23
Brunstane Rd. Nth.
EH15: Port 3J 23
Brunstane Rd. Sth.
EH15: Edin, Port 5J 23
Brunstane Station (Rail) 5J 23
Brunswick Pl. *EH7: Edin 1J 21*
(off Leith Wlk.)
Brunswick Rd. EH7: Edin 1J 21
Brunswick St.
EH7: Edin 1H 5 (1J 21)
Brunswick St. La.
EH7: Edin 1H 5 (1J 21)
Brunswick Ter. EH7: Edin 1K 21
Brunton Ct. EH21: Muss 2E 24
Brunton Gdns.
EH7: Edin 1K 5 (1K 21)
Brunton Pl. EH7: Edin . . .1J 5 (1K 21)
Brunton's Cl. EH22: Dalk 2C 42
Brunton Ter.
EH7: Edin 1K 5 (1K 21)
Brunton Theatre 2E 24
BRUNTSFIELD 6G 21
Bruntsfield Av. EH10: Edin 6F 21
Bruntsfield Cres. EH10: Edin . . .6F 21
Bruntsfield Gdns.
EH10: Edin 7F 21
Bruntsfield Pl. EH10: Edin 6F 21
Bruntsfield Ter. EH10: Edin 6F 21
BRYANS 7D 42
Bryans Av. EH22: Newt 7D 42
Bryans Rd. EH22: Newt 7C 42
Bryce Av. EH7: Edin 1F 23
Bryce Cres. EH14: Cur 7C 30
Bryce Gdns. EH14: Cur 7C 30
Bryce Gro. EH7: Edin 1F 23
Bryce Pl. EH14: Cur 7C 30
Bryce Rd. EH14: Cur 7C 30
Bryson Rd. EH11: Edin 6D 20
Buccleuch Ct. EH22: Dalk 1B 42
Buccleuch Pend EH8: Edin 7G 5
Buccleuch Pl.
EH8: Edin 7F 5 (5H 21)
Buccleuch St.
EH8: Edin 7G 5 (5J 21)
EH22: Dalk 2C 42
Buccleuch Ter.
EH8: Edin 7G 5 (5J 21)
Buccleugh Pl. La. EH8: Edin 7G 5
Buchanan St. EH6: Edin 7E 12
Buckie Rd. EH22: May 7G 43
Buckingham Ter. EH4: Edin 2D 20
Buckstane Pk. EH10: Edin 5E 32
Buckstone Av. EH10: Edin 6F 33
Buckstone Bank EH10: Edin 5F 33
Buckstone Circ. EH10: Edin 6G 33
Buckstone Cl. EH10: Edin 6G 33
Buckstone Ct. EH10: Edin 6F 33
Buckstone Cres. EH10: Edin . . .5F 33
Buckstone Crook EH10: Edin . . .7G 33
Buckstone Dell EH10: Edin 5F 33
Buckstone Dr. EH10: Edin 5F 33
Buckstone Gdns. EH10: Edin . . .6F 33
Buckstone Ga. EH10: Edin 6G 33
Buckstone Grn. EH10: Edin 6G 33
Buckstone Gro. EH10: Edin 5F 33
Buckstone Hill EH10: Edin 5F 33
Buckstone Howe EH10: Edin . . .6G 33
Buckstone Lea EH10: Edin 6G 33
Buckstone Loan EH10: Edin 6F 33
Buckstone Loan E.
EH10: Edin 6G 33
Buckstone Neuk EH10: Edin . . .5G 33
Buckstone Pl. EH10: Edin 6F 33
Buckstone Ri. EH10: Edin 6G 33
Buckstone Rd. EH10: Edin 6F 33
Buckstone Row EH10: Edin 5G 33
Buckstone Shaw EH10: Edin . . .7G 33
Buckstone Ter. EH10: Edin 6F 33
Buckstone Vw. EH10: Edin 5F 33
Buckstone Way EH10: Edin 5F 33
Buckstone Wood EH10: Edin . . .6F 33
Buckstone Wynd EH10: Edin . . .6G 33
BUGHTLIN 3D 18
Bughtlin Dr. EH12: Edin 2C 18
Bughtlin Gdns. EH12: Edin 3C 18
Bughtlin Grn. EH12: Edin 2C 18
Bughtlin Loan EH12: Edin 3C 18
Bughtlin Mkt. EH12: Edin 3D 18
Bughtlin Pk. EH12: Edin 3D 18
Bughtlin Pl. EH12: Edin 2C 18
Buie Brae EH29: Kltn 1A 16
Buie Haugh EH29: Kltn 1A 16
Buie Rigg *EH29: Kltn 1A 16*
(off Buie Brae)
Builyeon Rd. EH30: S Q'fry 2E 6
Bull's Cl. EH8: Edin 3J 5 (3K 21)
BURDIEHOUSE 1B 40
Burdiehouse Av. EH17: Edin . . .1B 40
Burdiehouse Cres.
EH17: Edin 1B 40
Burdiehouse Crossway
EH17: Edin 1B 40
Burdiehouse Dr. EH17: Edin . . .1B 40
Burdiehouse Loan
EH17: Edin 1B 40
Burdiehouse Medway
EH17: Edin 1B 40
Burdiehouse Pl. EH17: Edin . . .1B 40
Burdiehouse Rd. EH17: Edin . . .7A 34
Burdiehouse Sq. EH17: Edin . . .2A 40
Burdiehouse St. EH17: Edin . . .1B 40
Burdiehouse Ter. EH17: Edin . . .1B 40
Burgess Rd. EH30: S Q'fry 1H 7
Burgess St. EH6: Leith 5F 13
Burgess Ter. EH9: Edin 7A 22
Burghlee Cres. EH20: Loan 6B 40
Burghlee Ter. EH20: Loan 6B 40
Burghtoft EH17: Edin 7E 34
Burlington St. EH6: Edin 5E 12
Burnbank EH20: Loan 5A 40
Burnbank Cotts.
EH28: Nbdge 5B 16
Burnbank Cres.
EH20: Loan 4A 40
Burnbank Gro. EH20: Loan 4A 40
Burnbank Ter. EH25: Bil 7J 39
Burnbrae EH12: Edin 3C 18
Burnbrae Av. EH19: Bonn 2J 47
Burnbrae Cres. EH19: Bonn 1J 47
(not continuous)
Burnbrae Dr. EH12: Edin 3C 18
Burnbrae Gdns. EH19: Bonn . . .1J 47
Burnbrae Loan EH19: Bonn 1J 47
Burnbrae Pend EH19: Bonn 1J 47
Burnbrae Pl. EH12: Edin 3C 18
EH19: Bonn 1J 47
Burnbrae Rd. EH19: Bonn 1H 47
Burnbrae Ter. EH19: Bonn 1J 47
Burnbrae Vw. EH19: Bonn 2J 47
Burnbrae Wlk. EH19: Bonn 1J 47
Burndene Dr. EH20: Loan 4K 39
Burnet's Cl. EH1: Edin 4F 5
Burnhead Cres. EH16: Edin 5A 34
Burnhead Gro. EH16: Edin 6B 34
Burnhead Loan EH16: Edin 6B 34
Burnhead Path E.
EH16: Edin 6B 34

Burnhead Path W.
EH16: Edin 6A 34
BURNSHOT JUNC. 5F 9
Burnside EH11: Edin 1J 31
EH12: Edin 3C 18
EH32: Pres 6C 14
Burnside Av. EH22: East ..6F 43
Burnside Cres. EH22: East ..6F 43
Burnside Pk. EH14: Bal ...4E 36
Burnside Rd. EH12: Edin A ..4G 17
EH23: Gore 5E 48
Burns Monument 2J 5
Burns Pl. EH6: Leith 6C 12
(off Newhaven Rd.)
Burns St. EH6: Edin 6F 13
Bush Est., The EH26: Pen 3F 45
BUSH LOAN 2G 45
Bush St. EH21: Muss 2D 24
Bush Ter. EH21: Muss 2D 24
Butlerfield Ind. Est.
EH19: Bonn 2C 48
Butts, The EH33: Tran 2G 27
(off Market Vw.)
Buxley Rd. EH33: Elph 7F 27
Byer's Cl. EH1: Edin 4E 4

C

Cables Wynd EH6: Leith 5E 12
Cables Wynd Ho.
EH6: Leith 5E 12
Caddells Row EH4: Cram 5J 9
Cadell Pl. EH32: Cock 3G 15
Cadell Sq. EH33: Tran 2H 27
Cadiz St. EH6: Leith 5F 13
Cadogan Rd. EH16: Edin 5A 34
Cadzow Pl. EH7: Edin 2A 22
Caerketton Av. EH25: Bil ...7J 39
Caerketton Cotts.
EH13: Edin 4C 32
Caerlaverock Ct. EH12: Edin ..4D 18
(off Craigievar Wynd)
Caesar Rd. EH33: Tran 2G 27
Caesar Way EH33: Tran 2G 27
Cairds Row EH21: Muss 1D 24
Cairnbank Gdns. EH26: Pen ..3C 50
Cairnbank Rd. EH26: Pen 3C 50
Cairnmuir Rd. EH12: Edin ...3G 19
Cairns Dr. EH14: Bal 5D 36
Cairns Gdns. EH14: Bal 5D 36
Cairntows Cl. EH16: Edin ...7D 22
Caithness Pl. EH5: Edin 5A 12
Caiyside EH10: Edin 7E 32
Caiystane Av. EH10: Edin ...7E 32
Caiystane Cres. EH10: Edin ..6E 32
Caiystane Dr. EH10: Edin ...7D 32
Caiystane Gdns. EH10: Edin ..6D 32
Caiystane Hill EH10: Edin ...6E 32
Caiystane Ter. EH10: Edin ...7D 32
Caiystane Vw. EH10: Edin ...7E 32
Calder Ct. EH11: Edin 2E 30
Calder Cres. EH11: Edin 3D 30
Calder Dr. EH11: Edin 3E 30
Calder Gdns. EH11: Edin 3D 30
Calder Gro. EH11: Edin 3D 30
CALDER JUNC. 3D 30
Calder Pk. EH11: Edin 3E 30
Calder Pl. EH11: Edin 3E 30
Calder Rd. EH11: Edin 2D 30
(not continuous)
Calder Rd. Gdns. EH11: Edin ..1J 31
Calder Vw. EH11: Edin 3D 30
EH14: Cur 3B 30
Caledonia Ho. EH12: Edin ...7C 18
Caledonian Cres.
EH11: Edin 5D 20
Caledonian Pl. EH11: Edin ..5D 20
Caledonian Rd. EH11: Edin ..5E 20
CALTON 1K 5 (2K 21)
Calton Hill 2G 5 (2J 21)
Calton Hill EH1: Edin ..2F 5 (2J 21)
EH7: Edin 2G 5 (2J 21)
Calton Hill Stairs EH8: Edin ..3H 5
Calton Rd. EH1: Edin ..2F 5 (2H 21)
EH7: Edin 3F 5 (3H 21)
EH8: Edin 3F 5 (3H 21)
Calton Wynd EH8: Edin 3H 5
Cambridge Av. EH6: Edin ...7D 12

Cambridge Gdns. EH6: Edin ..7D 12
Cambridge St.
EH1: Edin 5B 4 (4F 21)
Cambusnethan St.
EH7: Edin 2B 22
Camera Obscura & World of Illusions
.................4D 4
Cameron Cres. EH16: Edin ..1B 34
EH19: Bonn 1E 46
Cameron Ho. Av. EH16: Edin ..7B 22
Cameron March EH16: Edin ..1A 34
Cameron Pk. EH16: Edin ...1B 34
Cameron Smail Rd.
EH14: Cur 5A 30
Cameron Ter. EH16: Edin ...1B 34
Cameron Toll Gdns.
EH16: Edin 1B 34
Cameron Toll Lade
EH16: Edin 1B 34
Cameron Toll Rdbt.
EH16: Edin 1B 34
Cameron Toll Shop. Cen.
EH16: Edin 1A 34
Cameron Way EH32: Pres ...5E 14
CAMMO 1B 18
Cammo Bank EH4: Cram 1C 18
Cammo Brae EH4: Cram 1C 18
Cammo Cres. EH4: Cram 1C 18
Cammo Gdns. EH4: Cram 1C 18
Cammo Gro. EH4: Cram 1B 18
Cammo Hill EH4: Cram 1B 18
Cammo Parkway EH4: Cram ..1C 18
Cammo Pl. EH4: Cram 1C 18
Cammo Rd. EH4: Cram, Edin ..2J 17
EH12: Edin 2J 17
Cammo Wlk.
EH4: Cram, Edin 1B 18
Campbell Av. EH12: Edin ...4A 20
Campbell Pk. Cres.
EH13: Edin 6H 31
Campbell Pk. Dr.
EH13: Edin 6H 31
Campbell Rd. EH12: Edin ...3A 20
Campbell's Cl.
EH8: Edin 3J 5 (3K 21)
Campie Ct. EH21: Muss 2D 24
Campie Gdns. EH21: Muss ..2D 24
(not continuous)
Campie La. EH21: Muss 2D 24
Campie Rd. EH21: Muss 3D 24
Campview EH22: May 6G 43
Campview Av. EH22: Dan ...5H 35
Campview Cres. EH22: Dan ..5H 35
Campview Gdns. EH22: Dan ..5H 35
Campview Gro. EH22: Dan ...5J 35
Campview Rd. EH19: Bonn ..6H 41
Campview Ter. EH22: Dan ...5H 35
Camp Wood Vw.
EH22: May 1G 49
Camus Av. EH10: Edin 6E 32
Camus Pk. EH10: Edin 6E 32
Canaan La. EH10: Edin 1F 33
Candlemaker Row
EH1: Edin 5E 4 (4H 21)
Candlemaker's Cres.
EH17: Edin 6F 35
Candlemakers Pk.
EH17: Edin 6F 35
Canmore St. EH30: S Q'fry ...2G 7
Canning St. EH3: Edin ..4A 4 (4F 21)
Canning St. La. EH3: Edin ...5A 4
CANONGATE 3H 5 (3J 21)
Canongate EH8: Edin ..4G 5 (3J 21)
Canongate Kirk 3H 5
Canon La. EH3: Edin 1G 21
CANONMILLS 7B 12
Canonmills EH3: Edin 7B 12
Canonmills Bri. EH3: Edin ...7B 12
(off Huntly St.)
Canon St. EH3: Edin 7B 12
Capelaw Rd. EH13: Edin 7J 31
Caplaw Way EH26: Pen 2A 50
Caponhall Ct. EH33: Tran ...3G 27
Caponhall Dr. EH33: Tran ...3G 27
Caponhall Rd. EH33: Tran ...3G 27
Caponhall Way EH33: Tran ...2G 27
Captain's Dr. EH16: Edin ...6A 34

Captain's Loan EH16: Edin ..6B 34
Captain's Rd. EH17: Edin ...7A 34
Captain's Row EH16: Edin ...7B 34
Carberry Cl. EH21: Muss 5F 25
Carberry Ct. EH21: Whit 7G 25
Carberry Gro. EH21: Muss ..5F 25
Carberry Pl. EH12: Edin 4C 20
Carberry Rd. EH21: Muss ...4F 25
Carfrae Gdns. EH4: Edin 1J 19
Carfrae Gro. EH4: Edin 1J 19
Carfrae Pk. EH4: Edin 1J 19
Carfrae Rd. EH4: Edin 1J 19
Cargil Ct. EH5: Edin 5A 12
Cargilfield Vw. EH4: Cram ...6J 9
Cargil Ter. EH5: Edin 5K 11
Carlaverock Cl. EH33: Tran ..4J 27
Carlaverock Ct. EH33: Tran ..3J 27
Carlaverock Cres.
EH33: Tran 3H 27
Carlaverock Dr. EH33: Tran ..3H 27
Carlaverock Gro. EH33: Tran ..3H 27
Carlaverock Ter. EH33: Tran ..3H 27
Carlaverock Vw. EH33: Tran ..4H 27
Carlaverock Wlk.
EH33: Tran 3H 27
Carlops Av. EH26: Pen 1C 50
Carlops Cres. EH26: Pen 1C 50
Carlops Rd. EH26: Pen 2A 50
Carlowrie Av. EH30: Dalm ...3K 7
Carlowrie Cres. EH30: Dalm ..3K 7
Carlowrie Pl. EH23: Gore ...5F 49
Carlton St. EH4: Edin ..1A 4 (2E 20)
Carlton Ter.
EH7: Edin 1K 5 (2K 21)
Carlton Ter. Brae
EH7: Edin 1K 5 (2K 21)
Carlton Ter. La.
EH7: Edin 1J 5 (2K 21)
Carlton Ter. M.
EH7: Edin 1J 5 (2K 21)
Carlyle Pl. EH7: Edin 2A 22
EH21: Muss 2E 24
Carmel Av. EH29: Kltn 1A 16
Carmelite Rd. EH30: S Q'fry ..2G 7
Carmel Rd. EH29: Kltn 2A 16
Carnbee Av. EH16: Edin 6C 34
Carnbee Cres. EH16: Edin ..6C 34
Carnbee Dell EH16: Edin ...6C 34
Carnbee End EH16: Edin ...6C 34
Carnbee Pk. EH16: Edin 6C 34
Carnegie Ct. EH8: Edin 6H 5
Carnegie St.
EH8: Edin 6H 5 (4J 21)
Carnethie St. EH24: Rose ...6D 46
Carnethy Av. EH13: Edin ...6J 31
EH26: Pen 1C 50
Carnethy Ct. EH26: Pen 2D 50
Caroline Gdns. EH12: Edin ..4G 19
Caroline Pk. EH5: Edin 3G 11
Caroline Pk. Av.
EH5: Edin 4G 11
Caroline Pk. Gro.
EH5: Edin 4G 11
Caroline Pl. EH12: Edin 4G 19
Caroline Ter. EH12: Edin ...3E 18
Carpet La. EH6: Leith 5F 13
Carrick Cres. EH22: East ...5E 42
CARRICK KNOWE 6H 19
Carrick Knowe Av.
EH12: Edin 5H 19
Carrick Knowe Dr.
EH12: Edin 6H 19
Carrick Knowe Gdns.
EH12: Edin 6H 19
Carrick Knowe Gro.
EH12: Edin 6H 19
Carrick Knowe Hill
EH12: Edin 6G 19
Carrick Knowe Loan
EH12: Edin 6G 19
Carrick Knowe Parkway
EH12: Edin 6G 19
Carrick Knowe Pl.
EH12: Edin 6H 19
Carrick Knowe Rd.
EH12: Edin 7G 19
Carrick Knowe Ter.
EH12: Edin 6H 19
Carrington Cres. EH4: Edin ..7H 11
Carrington Ho. EH4: Edin ...7H 11

Carrington Rd. EH4: Edin ...1C 20
EH19: Bonn 2K 47
Carron Pl. EH6: Leith 5G 13
Carruber's Cl. EH1: Edin 3F 5
Casselbank St. EH6: Edin ...6E 12
Cassel's La. EH6: Edin 6E 12
Castle, The EH18: Las 7D 40
Castle Av. EH12: Edin 6F 19
EH23: Gore 6E 48
EH32: Port S 3J 15
Castlebarns Steps EH1: Edin ..5B 4
Castlebrae Av. EH16: Edin ..1D 34
Castlebrae Bus. Cen.
EH16: Edin 7D 22
Castlebrae Glebe
EH16: Edin 7D 22
Castlebrae Gro. EH16: Edin ..1D 34
Castlebrae Pl. EH16: Edin ..1D 34
Castlebrae Rigg
EH16: Edin 1D 34
Castlebrae Wynd
EH16: Edin 1D 34
Castle Gogar Rigg
EH12: Edin 5J 17
Castlehill EH1: Edin ..4D 4 (3G 21)
EH33: Elph 7F 27
(off Main St.)
Castlelaw Ct. EH26: Pen 1D 50
Castlelaw Cres. EH25: Bil ...1J 45
Castlelaw Rd. EH13: Edin ...6J 31
Castlepark Gait EH16: Edin ..7D 22
Castlepark Glade
EH16: Edin 1D 34
Castle Pk. Grn. EH16: Edin ..7D 22
Castle Pl. EH23: Gore 6E 48
Castle Rd. EH32: Port S 3J 15
EH33: Tran 4G 27
Castle St. EH2: Edin ..3B 4 (3F 21)
EH3: Edin 5C 4 (4G 21)
EH32: Port S 3J 15
Castle Vw. EH23: Gore 7E 48
EH32: Port S 3J 15
Castleview Dr. EH16: Edin ..1D 34
Castleview Gro. EH16: Edin ..1D 34
Castleview Ho. EH17: Edin ..3D 34
Castleview Ter. EH16: Edin ..7D 22
Castle Wlk. EH32: Port S 3J 15
Castle Wynd Nth. EH1: Edin ..5D 4
Castle Wynd Sth. EH1: Edin ..5D 4
Cathcart Pl. EH11: Edin 5D 20
Cathedral La.
EH1: Edin 1F 5 (2H 21)
Catriona Ter. EH26: Pen 5F 45
Cauldcoats Cotts.
EH22: Dalk 2H 35
Causeway, The EH15: Edin ..5C 22
Causewayside EH9: Edin 6J 21
Cavalry Pk. Dr. EH15: Edin ..5D 22
Cedar Dr. EH32: Port S 4G 15
Cedar Rd. EH20: Loan 6J 39
Cedars, The EH13: Edin 5K 31
Cemetery Rd. EH22: Dalk ...2B 42
EH32: Pres 5D 14
Chalmers Bldgs. EH3: Edin ..7A 4
Chalmer's Cl. EH1: Edin 4G 5
Chalmers Cres. EH9: Edin ...6H 21
Chalmers St.
EH1: Edin 6D 4 (4G 21)
Chamberlain Rd. EH10: Edin ..7F 21
Chambers St.
EH1: Edin 5E 4 (4H 21)
Champigny Ct. EH21: Muss ..3G 25
Chancelot Cres. EH6: Edin ..5B 12
Chancelot Gro. EH5: Edin ...5B 12
Chancelot Ter. EH6: Edin ...5B 12
Chapel Ct. EH16: Edin 7E 22
Chapel La. EH6: Leith 5F 13
(off Carpet La.)
Chapel Loan EH25: Rosl 3A 46
Chapel St. EH8: Edin ..6G 5 (4J 21)
Chapel Wynd EH1: Edin 5C 4
Chariot Dr. EH28: Nbdge ...6A 16
Charlesfield
EH8: Edin 6F 5 (4H 21)
Charles St. EH8: Edin ..6F 5 (4H 21)
EH26: Pen 7C 44
Charles St. La.
EH8: Edin 6F 5 (4H 21)

Charlotte La.
EH2: Edin 3A **4** (3F **21**)
Charlotte Sq.
EH2: Edin 3A **4** (3F **21**)
Charlton Gro. EH25: Rosl 3K **45**
Charterhall Gro. EH9: Edin . . .1H **33**
Charterhall Rd. EH9: Edin . . .2H **33**
Cherry La. EH22: May 7G **43**
Cherry Rd. EH19: Bonn 7H **41**
Cherry Tree Av. EH14: Bal . . .2G **37**
Cherry Tree Cres.
EH14: Bal, Cur 2F **37**
Cherry Tree Gdns. EH14: Bal . .2F **37**
Cherry Tree Gro. EH14: Bal . . .2F **37**
Cherry Tree Loan EH14: Bal . .2G **37**
Cherry Tree Pk. EH14: Bal . . .2F **37**
Cherry Tree Pl. EH14: Cur . . .2G **37**
Cherry Tree Vw. EH14: Bal . . .2G **37**
Chessel's Ct.
EH8: Edin 4G **5** (3J **21**)
Chesser Av. EH14: Edin 7K **19**
Chesser Cotts. EH11: Edin . . .7A **20**
Chesser Cres. EH14: Edin . . .1A **32**
Chesser Gdns. EH14: Edin . . .7K **19**
Chesser Loan EH14: Edin . . .1K **31**
Chester Dr. EH22: May 1F **49**
Chesters Ct. EH19: Bonn 7G **41**
Chesters Gro. EH19: Bonn . . .7H **41**
Chester St. EH3: Edin 3E **20**
Chesters Vw. EH19: Bonn . . .7H **41**
Chester Vw. EH22: May 1F **49**
Chestnut Gro. EH19: Bonn . . .7H **41**
EH32: Port S 4H **15**
Chestnut St. EH5: Edin 3H **11**
Cheyne St. EH4: Edin 1E **20**
Childhood Mus. 4G **5** (3J **21**)
Chisholm Ter. EH26: Pen 7D **44**
Christian Cres. EH15: Port . . .4H **23**
Christian Gro. EH15: Port . . .4H **23**
Christian Path EH15: Port . . .3G **23**
Christiemiller Av. EH7: Edin . .1E **22**
Christiemiller Gro.
EH7: Edin 2E **22**
Christiemiller Pl. EH7: Edin . .2E **22**
Chuckie Pend
EH3: Edin 6A **4** (4F **21**)
Church Hill EH10: Edin 7F **21**
Church Hill Dr. EH10: Edin . . .7F **21**
Church Hill Pl. EH10: Edin . . .7F **21**
Church Hill Theatre 7F **21**
Church La. EH21: Muss 3E **24**
Church Rd. EH18: Las 4F **41**
EH22: Dan 5J **35**
Church St. EH20: Loan 6C **40**
EH33: Tran 1G **27**
Church Vw. EH22: Dalk 2B **42**
Cinderhall Pl. EH33: Elph 7F **27**
Cineworld Cinema
Edinburgh 5E **20**
Circle, The EH22: Dan 4H **35**
Circus Gdns.
EH3: Edin 1B **4** (2F **21**)
Circus La. EH3: Edin . . .1B **4** (1F **21**)
Circus Pl. EH3: Edin . . .1B **4** (2F **21**)
Citadel Pl. EH6: Leith 4E **12**
Citadel St. EH6: Leith 4E **12**
City Art Cen. 3F **5** (3H **21**)
City Observatory 2G **5** (2J **21**)
City of Edinburgh By-Pass, The
EH10: Edin 1A **38**
EH12: Edin 6B **18**
EH13: Edin 1A **38**
EH14: Edin 1B **30**
EH14: Edin, J Grn 1B **30**
EH14: J Grn 1B **30**
EH17: Edin 3A **40**
EH18: Las 3A **40**
EH21: Muss 7D **24**
EH22: Dalk, Dan
. . . . .7D **24** & 3A **40**
Civic Sq. EH33: Tran 2H **27**
Clackmae Gro. EH16: Edin . . .4K **33**
Clackmae Rd. EH16: Edin . . .4K **33**
Clanranald Av. EH32: Pres . . .5E **14**
Clan Tartan Cen. 5D **12**
Clapper La. EH16: Edin 2A **34**
Clarebank Cres. EH6: Edin . . .6G **13**
Claremont Bank EH7: Edin . . .1H **21**

Claremont Ct. EH7: Edin 7C **12**
Claremont Cres. EH7: Edin . . .7C **12**
Claremont Gdns. EH6: Edin . . .6G **13**
Claremont Gro. EH7: Edin 7C **12**
Claremont Pk. EH6: Edin 6G **13**
Claremont Rd. EH6: Edin 6G **13**
Clarence St. EH3: Edin 1F **21**
Clarendon Cres. EH4: Edin . . .2E **20**
Clarinda Gdns. EH22: Dalk . . .3F **43**
Clarinda Ter. EH16: Edin 4A **34**
Clark Av. EH5: Edin 5B **12**
Clark Pl. EH5: Edin 5A **12**
Clark Rd. EH5: Edin 5A **12**
Claverhouse Dr.
EH16: Edin 4A **34**
Clayhills Gro. EH14: Bal 4D **36**
Clayhills Pk. EH14: Bal 4D **36**
CLAYKNOWES 3C **24**
Clayknowes Av. EH21: Muss . .3C **24**
Clayknowes Ct. EH21: Muss . .4C **24**
Clayknowes Dr. EH21: Muss . .3B **24**
Clayknowes Pl. EH21: Muss . .3B **24**
Clayknowes Rd.
EH21: Muss 3C **24**
Clayknowes Way
EH21: Muss 3C **24**
CLAYLANDS INTERCHANGE . .7A **16**
Claylands Rd. EH28: Nbdge . .1A **28**
Clearburn Cres. EH16: Edin . .7B **22**
Clearburn Gdns. EH16: Edin . .7B **22**
Clearburn Rd. EH16: Edin . . .7B **22**
EH23: Gore 4D **48**
Cleekim Dr. EH15: Edin 7H **23**
Cleekim Rd. EH15: Edin 7H **23**
Cleikiminfield EH15: Edin . . .7H **23**
Cleikiminrig EH15: Edin 7H **23**
Cleric's Hill EH29: Kltn 2A **16**
Clerk Rd. EH26: Pen 2B **50**
Clerk St. EH8: Edin . . .7G **5** (5J **21**)
EH20: Loan 5C **40**
Clermiston Av. EH4: Edin 1F **19**
Clermiston Cres. EH4: Edin . . .1F **19**
Clermiston Dr. EH4: Edin 2F **19**
Clermiston Gdns. EH4: Edin . .2F **19**
Clermiston Grn. EH4: Edin . . .2F **19**
Clermiston Gro. EH4: Edin . . .2F **19**
Clermiston Hill EH4: Edin 1F **19**
Clermiston Junc. EH4: Edin . .7A **10**
Clermiston Loan EH4: Edin . . .1F **19**
Clermiston Medway
EH4: Edin 1F **19**
Clermiston Pk. EH4: Edin 2F **19**
Clermiston Pl. EH4: Edin 2F **19**
Clermiston Rd. EH12: Edin . . .4G **19**
Clermiston Rd. Nth.
EH4: Edin 1G **19**
Clermiston Ter. EH12: Edin . . .3F **19**
Clermiston Vw. EH4: Edin . . .1G **19**
Clerwood Bank EH12: Edin . . .3F **19**
Clerwood Gdns. EH12: Edin . .3F **19**
Clerwood Gro. EH12: Edin . . .3G **19**
Clerwood Loan EH12: Edin . . .3F **19**
Clerwood Pk. EH12: Edin 3F **19**
Clerwood Pl. EH12: Edin 3G **19**
Clerwood Row EH12: Edin . . .3F **19**
Clerwood Ter. EH12: Edin 3G **19**
Clerwood Vw. EH12: Edin . . .3G **19**
Clerwood Way EH12: Edin . . .3F **19**
Cliftonhall Rd. EH28: Nbdge . .6A **16**
Clifton Ter. EH12: Edin 4D **20**
Clifton Trad. Est.
EH28: Nbdge 7A **16**
Clinton Rd. EH9: Edin 7F **21**
Clockmill La. EH8: Edin 2B **22**
Clocktower Bus. Pk.
EH4: Edin 7E **18**
Close, The EH30: S Q'fry 2E **6**
Clovenstone Dr. EH14: Edin . .5G **31**
Clovenstone Gdns.
EH14: Edin 4G **31**
Clovenstone Pk. EH14: Edin . .5G **31**
Clovenstone Rd. EH14: Edin . .5G **31**
Clovenstone Rdbt.
EH14: Edin 5G **31**
Cloverfoot Cotts. EH14: Edin . .2G **35**
Clufflat EH30: S Q'fry 1E **6**
Clufflat Brae EH30: S Q'fry . . .1E **6**
Cluny Av. EH10: Edin 2F **33**

Cluny Dr. EH10: Edin 2F **33**
Cluny Gdns. EH10: Edin 2F **33**
Cluny Pl. EH10: Edin 1G **33**
Cluny Ter. EH10: Edin 1F **33**
Clyde St. EH1: Edin . . .2E **4** (2H **21**)
Coalgate Av. EH33: Tran 1J **27**
Coalgate Rd. EH33: Tran 1H **27**
Coalhill EH6: Leith 5E **12**
Coal Neuk EH33: Tran 2G **27**
Coal Neuk Ct. EH33: Tran . . .2G **27**
COATES 3D **20**
Coates Cres.
EH3: Edin 4A **4** (4E **20**)
Coates Gdns. EH12: Edin 4D **20**
Coates Pl. EH3: Edin 4E **20**
Coatfield La. EH6: Leith 5F **13**
Cobbinshaw Ho. EH11: Edin . .3E **30**
Cobden Cres. EH9: Edin 7K **21**
Cobden Rd. EH9: Edin 7K **21**
Cobden Ter. EH11: Edin 4E **20**
Coburg St. EH6: Edin 5E **12**
Cochrane Pl. EH6: Edin 6F **13**
Cochran Ter. EH7: Edin 1H **21**
Cochrina Pl. EH24: Rose 4D **46**
Cockburn Cres. EH14: Bal . . .5D **36**
Cockburnhill Rd. EH14: Bal . . .6B **36**
Cockburn St.
EH1: Edin 4E **4** (3H **21**)
COCKENZIE 3G **15**
Cockenzie Bus. Cen.
EH32: Cock 3G **15**
Cockmylane EH13: Edin 5D **32**
Cockpen Av. EH19: Bonn 1G **47**
Cockpen Cres. EH19: Bonn . . .1G **47**
Cockpen Dr. EH19: Bonn 1G **47**
Cockpen Pl. EH19: Bonn 1G **47**
Cockpen Rd. EH19: Bonn 7J **41**
Cockpen Rdbt.
EH19: Bonn 1K **47**
Cockpen Ter. EH19: Bonn . . .1G **47**
Cockpen Vw. EH19: Bonn . . .1G **47**
Cock's Cft. EH12: Edin 6F **19**
Coffin La. EH11: Edin 5D **20**
Coillesdene Av. EH15: Port . . .4K **23**
Coillesdene Cres.
EH15: Port 4K **23**
Coillesdene Dr. EH15: Port . . .4K **23**
Coillesdene Gdns.
EH15: Port 4K **23**
Coillesdene Gro. EH15: Port . .4K **23**
Coillesdene Ho. EH15: Port . . .4K **23**
Coillesdene Loan
EH15: Port 1A **24**
Coillesdene Ter. EH15: Port . .4K **23**
Coinyie Ho. Cl. EH1: Edin 4G **5**
COLINTON 5K **31**
Colinton Castle Sports Club . .4K **31**
Colinton Gro. EH14: Edin . . .2B **32**
Colinton Gro. W. EH14: Edin . .2B **32**
Colinton Mains Cres.
EH13: Edin 6C **32**
Colinton Mains Dr.
EH13: Edin 4B **32**
Colinton Mains Gdns.
EH13: Edin 4B **32**
Colinton Mains Grn.
EH13: Edin 5B **32**
Colinton Mains Gro.
EH13: Edin 5C **32**
Colinton Mains Loan
EH13: Edin 5B **32**
Colinton Mains Pl.
EH13: Edin 5C **32**
Colinton Mains Rd.
EH13: Edin 5B **32**
Colinton Mains Ter.
EH13: Edin 5C **32**
Colinton Rd. EH10: Edin 1C **32**
EH13: Edin 5K **31**
EH14: Edin 3B **32**
Collective Gallery 3H **21**
(off Cockburn St.)
College Wynd
EH1: Edin 5F **5** (4H **21**)
Colliery Cres. EH22: Newt . . .2C **48**
Colliery Vw. EH22: Newt 2D **48**
Collins Pl. EH3: Edin 1F **21**
Colmestone Ga.
EH10: Edin 6E **32**

Colonsay Cl. EH5: Edin 4E **10**
Colonsay Way EH5: Edin 4F **11**
Coltbridge Av. EH12: Edin . . .4B **20**
Coltbridge Gdns. EH12: Edin . .3C **20**
Coltbridge Millside
EH12: Edin 4C **20**
(off Coltbridge Av.)
Coltbridge Ter. EH12: Edin . . .4B **20**
Coltbridge Va. EH12: Edin . . .4C **20**
Columba Av. EH4: Edin 1K **19**
Columba Rd. EH4: Edin 1K **19**
Colville Pl. EH3: Edin 1F **21**
COMELY BANK 1D **20**
Comely Bank EH4: Edin 1D **20**
Comely Bank Av. EH4: Edin . . .1E **20**
Comely Bank Gro. EH4: Edin . .1D **20**
Comely Bank Pl. EH4: Edin . . .1E **20**
Comely Bank Pl. M.
EH4: Edin 1E **20**
Comely Bank Rd. EH4: Edin . .1D **20**
Comely Bank Row EH4: Edin . .1E **20**
Comely Bank St. EH4: Edin . . .1D **20**
Comely Bank Ter. EH4: Edin . .1E **20**
Comely Grn. Cres.
EH7: Edin 2A **22**
Comely Grn. Pl. EH7: Edin . . .2A **22**
Comiston Dr. EH10: Edin 3D **32**
Comiston Gdns. EH10: Edin . .2E **32**
Comiston Gro. EH10: Edin . . .5E **32**
Comiston Pl. EH10: Edin 2E **32**
Comiston Ri. EH10: Edin 5E **32**
Comiston Rd. EH10: Edin 4E **32**
Comiston Springs Av.
EH10: Edin 5E **32**
Comiston Ter. EH10: Edin 2E **32**
Comiston Vw. EH10: Edin 5E **32**
Commercial St.
EH6: Leith, Newh 4E **12**
Commercial Wharf
EH6: Leith 4F **13**
Conference Sq. EH3: Edin 6A **4**
Conifer Rd. EH22: May 6G **43**
Connaught Pl. EH6: Edin 5C **12**
Considine Gdns. EH8: Edin . . .2C **22**
Considine Ter. EH8: Edin 2C **22**
Constitution Pl. EH6: Leith . . .4F **13**
Constitution St. EH6: Leith . . .5F **13**
Cook Cres. EH22: May 1F **49**
Cookies Wynd EH32: Pres . . .6C **14**
(off Rope Wlk.)
Co-operative Bldgs.
EH33: Tran 2H **27**
Cooper's Cl. EH8: Edin 3H **5**
Cope La. EH32: Port S 3G **15**
Corbie Dr. EH22: Dalk 2F **43**
Corbiehill Av. EH4: Edin 7D **10**
Corbiehill Cres. EH4: Edin . . .7C **10**
Corbiehill Gdns. EH4: Edin . . .7D **10**
Corbiehill Gro. EH4: Edin 7D **10**
Corbiehill Pl. EH4: Edin 7C **10**
Corbiehill Rd. EH4: Edin 7C **10**
Corbiehill Ter. EH4: Edin 7C **10**
Corbieshot EH15: Edin 6H **23**
Corbiewynd EH15: Edin 6H **23**
Cornhill Ter. EH6: Edin 6G **13**
Corn Market Village 1A **32**
Cornwallis Pl. EH3: Edin 1G **21**
Cornwall St.
EH1: Edin 5B **4** (4F **21**)
Coronation Pl. EH22: May 6F **43**
EH33: Tran 2G **27**
Coronation Wlk.
EH3: Edin 7D **4** (5G **21**)
Corrennie Dr. EH10: Edin 2F **33**
Corrennie Gdns. EH10: Edin . .3F **33**
Corrie Ct. EH22: Newt 2D **48**
Corslet Cres. EH14: Cur 7C **30**
Corslet Pl. EH14: Cur 7C **30**
Corslet Rd. EH14: Cur 7C **30**
CORSTORPHINE 5F **19**
Corstorphine Bank Av.
EH12: Edin 4E **18**
Corstorphine Bank Dr.
EH12: Edin 4E **18**
Corstorphine Bank Ter.
EH12: Edin 4E **18**
Corstorphine High St.
EH12: Edin 5F **19**

Corstorphine Hill Av.
EH12: Edin 4G **19**
Corstorphine Hill Cres.
EH12: Edin 4G **19**
Corstorphine Hill Gdns.
EH12: Edin 4G **19**
Corstorphine Hill Rd.
EH12: Edin 4G **19**
CORSTORPHINE HOSPITAL . . .5H **19**
Corstorphine Ho. Av.
EH12: Edin 5G **19**
Corstorphine Ho. Ter.
EH12: Edin 5G **19**
Corstorphine Pk. Gdns.
EH12: Edin 5G **19**
Corstorphine Rd.
EH12: Edin 5H **19**
Cortleferry Dr. EH22: Dalk 4A **42**
Cortleferry Gro. EH22: Dalk 4A **42**
Cortleferry Pk. EH22: Dalk 4A **42**
Cortleferry Ter. EH22: Dalk 4A **42**
Corunna Pl. EH6: Edin 5E **12**
Corunna Ter. EH26: Pen 6E **44**
Costkea Way EH20: Loan 5A **40**
Cotlaws EH29: Kltn 2A **16**
Cottage Grn. EH4: Cram 6J **9**
Cottage Homes EH13: Edin . . .6K **31**
Cottage La. EH21: Muss 3G **25**
Cottage Pk. EH4: Edin 2J **19**
County Rd. EH32: Pres 6C **14**
County Sq. EH32: Pres 6C **14**
Couperfield EH6: Leith 4E **12**
Couper St. EH6: Leith 4E **12**
Cousland Rd. EH22: Dalk 1F **43**
Covenanter Cl. EH26: Pen . . .1B **50**
Covenanters La.
EH30: S Q'fry 1G **7**
(off High St.)
Cowan Rd. EH11: Edin 7C **20**
Cowan's Cl.
EH8: Edin 7G **5** (5J **21**)
Cowan Ter. EH26: Pen 7D **44**
Cowden Cres. EH22: Dalk 2F **43**
Cowden La. EH22: Dalk 2F **43**
Cowden Pk. EH22: Dalk 2E **42**
Cowden Ter. EH22: Dalk 2F **43**
Cowden Vw. EH22: Dalk 2F **43**
Cowgate EH1: Edin 5E **4** (4H **21**)
Cowgatehead
EH1: Edin 5E **4** (4H **21**)
Cowpits EH21: Whit 6F **25**
Cowpits Ford Rd.
EH21: Muss 5E **24**
Cowpits Rd. EH21: Whit 6F **25**
Coxfield EH11: Edin 7A **20**
Coxfield La. EH11: Edin 7A **20**
Crags Sports Cen. 6H **5** (4J **21**)
Craigcrook Av. EH4: Edin 1H **19**
Craigcrook Gdns. EH4: Edin . . .2K **19**
Craigcrook Gro. EH4: Edin 2J **19**
Craigcrook Pk. EH4: Edin 2J **19**
Craigcrook Pl. EH4: Edin 2A **20**
Craigcrook Rd. EH4: Edin 7C **10**
Craigcrook Sq. EH4: Edin 1J **19**
Craigcrook Ter. EH4: Edin 1A **20**
Craigend Rd. EH16: Edin 3C **34**
CRAIGENTINNY 1E **22**
Craigentinny Av. EH7: Edin . . .2E **22**
Craigentinny Av. Nth.
EH6: Edin 6J **13**
Craigentinny Cres.
EH7: Edin 2E **22**
Craigentinny Gro. EH7: Edin . . .2E **22**
Craigentinny Pl. EH7: Edin 2E **22**
Craigentinny Rd. EH7: Edin . . .1D **22**
Craighall Av. EH6: Newh 4B **12**
Craighall Bank EH6: Newh 4B **12**
Craighall Cres. EH6: Newh 4B **12**
Craighall Gdns. EH6: Newh 5B **12**
Craighall Rd. EH6: Newh 4B **12**
Craighall Ter. EH6: Newh 5B **12**
EH21: Muss 2H **25**
Craighill Gdns. EH10: Edin . . .3D **32**
Craighouse Av. EH10: Edin . . .2D **32**
Craighouse Gdns.
EH10: Edin 2D **32**
Craighouse Pk. EH10: Edin . . .2D **32**
Craighouse Rd. EH10: Edin . . .2D **32**

Craighouse Ter. EH10: Edin 2D **32**
Craigiebield Cres.
EH26: Pen 3C **50**
Craigievar Ho. EH12: Edin 3D **18**
Craigievar Sq. EH12: Edin 3C **18**
Craigievar Wynd EH12: Edin . . .4C **18**
Craiglea Dr. EH10: Edin 3D **32**
Craiglea Pl. EH10: Edin 3D **32**
CRAIGLEITH 1B **20**
Craigleith Av. Nth.
EH4: Edin 3A **20**
Craigleith Av. Sth.
EH4: Edin 3A **20**
Craigleith Bank EH4: Edin 2B **20**
Craigleith Cres. EH4: Edin 2A **20**
Craigleith Dr. EH4: Edin 2A **20**
Craigleith Gdns. EH4: Edin . . .2A **20**
Craigleith Gro. EH4: Edin 2A **20**
Craigleith Hill EH4: Edin 2B **20**
Craigleith Hill Av. EH4: Edin . . .1B **20**
Craigleith Hill Cres.
EH4: Edin 1B **20**
Craigleith Hill Gdns.
EH4: Edin 1B **20**
Craigleith Hill Grn.
EH4: Edin 1B **20**
Craigleith Hill Gro.
EH4: Edin 1B **20**
Craigleith Hill Loan
EH4: Edin 1B **20**
Craigleith Hill Pk. EH4: Edin . . .1B **20**
Craigleith Hill Row
EH4: Edin 1B **20**
Craigleith Retail Pk.
EH4: Edin 1B **20**
Craigleith Ri. EH4: Edin 3A **20**
Craigleith Rd. EH4: Edin 2B **20**
Craigleith Vw. EH4: Edin 3A **20**
CRAIGLOCKHART 3B **32**
Craiglockhart Av.
EH14: Edin 2A **32**
Craiglockhart Bank
EH14: Edin 2A **32**
Craiglockhart Castle (remains)
. . . . .3B **32**
Craiglockhart Cres.
EH14: Edin 3A **32**
Craiglockhart Dell Rd.
EH14: Edin 2A **32**
Craiglockhart Dr. Nth.
EH14: Edin 2A **32**
Craiglockhart Dr. Sth.
EH14: Edin 3A **32**
Craiglockhart Gdns.
EH14: Edin 2A **32**
Craiglockhart Gro.
EH14: Edin 4A **32**
Craiglockhart Loan
EH14: Edin 3A **32**
Craiglockhart Pk.
EH14: Edin 3A **32**
Craiglockhart Pl. EH14: Edin . . .2B **32**
Craiglockhart Quad.
EH14: Edin 3A **32**
Craiglockhart Rd.
EH14: Edin 4A **32**
Craiglockhart Rd. Nth.
EH14: Edin 3B **32**
(not continuous)
Craiglockhart Sports Cen. 2B **32**
Craiglockhart Tennis Cen. 2B **32**
Craiglockhart Ter.
EH14: Edin 2C **32**
Craiglockhart Vw.
EH14: Edin 2B **32**
CRAIGMILLAR 1D **34**
Craigmillar Castle 2D **34**
Craigmillar Castle Av.
EH16: Edin 1D **34**
(not continuous)
Craigmillar Castle Gdns.
EH16: Edin 7D **22**
Craigmillar Castle Loan
EH16: Edin 7E **22**
Craigmillar Castle Rd.
EH16: Edin 7D **22**
Craigmillar Ct. EH16: Edin 1C **34**
Craigmillar Pk. EH16: Edin 1K **33**
Craigmount App. EH12: Edin . . .4E **18**

Craigmount Av. EH12: Edin 4E **18**
Craigmount Av. Nth.
EH4: Edin 2D **18**
EH12: Edin 2D **18**
Craigmount Bank EH4: Edin . . .2D **18**
Craigmount Bank W.
EH4: Edin 2D **18**
Craigmount Brae
EH12: Edin 2D **18**
Craigmount Ct. EH4: Edin 2D **18**
Craigmount Cres.
EH12: Edin 3D **18**
Craigmount Dr. EH12: Edin 3D **18**
Craigmount Gdns.
EH12: Edin 4D **18**
Craigmount Gro. EH4: Edin 4D **18**
Craigmount Gro. Nth.
EH12: Edin 3D **18**
Craigmount Hill EH4: Edin 2D **18**
Craigmount Loan
EH12: Edin 3D **18**
Craigmount Pk. EH12: Edin 4D **18**
Craigmount Pl. EH12: Edin 3D **18**
Craigmount Ter. EH12: Edin . . .4D **18**
Craigmount Vw. EH12: Edin 3D **18**
Craigmount Way EH12: Edin . . .2E **18**
Craigmuir Pl. EH4: Edin 5F **11**
Craigour Av. EH17: Edin 4E **34**
Craigour Cres. EH17: Edin 4E **34**
Craigour Dr. EH17: Edin 3D **34**
Craigour Gdns. EH17: Edin 4E **34**
Craigour Grn. EH17: Edin 4D **34**
Craigour Gro. EH17: Edin 4E **34**
Craigour Loan EH17: Edin 4E **34**
Craigour Pl. EH17: Edin 4D **34**
Craigour Ter. EH17: Edin 4E **34**
Craigpark Av. EH28: Rat 2C **28**
Craigpark Cres. EH28: Rat 2C **28**
Craigroyston Gro. EH4: Edin . . .6D **10**
Craigroyston Pl. EH4: Edin 5D **10**
Craigs Av. EH12: Edin 5D **18**
Craigs Bank EH12: Edin 4D **18**
Craig's Cl. EH1: Edin 4F **5**
Craigs Cres. EH12: Edin 4D **18**
Craigs Dr. EH12: Edin 4D **18**
Craigs Gdns. EH12: Edin 4D **18**
Craigs Gro. EH12: Edin 5E **18**
Craigs Loan EH12: Edin 4E **18**
Craigs Pk. EH12: Edin 4D **18**
Craigs Rd. EH12: Edin 3K **17**
Crame Ter. EH22: Dalk 3A **42**
CRAMOND 4J **9**
Cramond Av. EH4: Cram 5J **9**
Cramond Bank EH4: Cram 5J **9**
CRAMOND BRIDGE 7G **9**
Cramond Bri. Cotts.
EH4: Cram 6G **9**
Cramond Bri. Farm
EH4: Cram 7G **9**
Cramond Brig Toll EH4: Cram . . .6G **9**
Cramond Cres. EH4: Cram 5J **9**
Cramond Gdns. EH4: Cram 5J **9**
Cramond Glebe Gdns.
EH4: Cram 4K **9**
Cramond Glebe Rd.
EH4: Cram 4J **9**
Cramond Glebe Ter.
EH4: Cram 4J **9**
Cramond Grn. EH4: Cram 4J **9**
Cramond Gro. EH4: Cram 5J **9**
Cramond Pk. EH4: Cram 5J **9**
Cramond Pl. EH4: Cram 5K **9**
Cramond Regis EH4: Cram 6J **9**
Cramond Rd. Nth. EH4: Cram . . .4J **9**
Cramond Rd. Sth. EH4: Edin . . .5A **10**
Cramond Ter. EH4: Cram 5J **9**
Cramond Va. EH4: Cram 5J **9**
Cramond Village EH4: Cram 3J **9**
Cranston St.
EH8: Edin 3G **5** (3J **21**)
EH26: Pen 2C **50**
Crarae Av. EH4: Edin 3B **20**
Craufurdland EH4: Cram 7H **9**
Crawford Bri. EH7: Edin 1A **22**
Crawford Rd. EH16: Edin 1K **33**
Crawlees Cotts. EH26: Newt . . .7E **42**
Crawlees Cres. EH22: May 7G **43**
Crawlees Rd. EH22: Newt 3D **48**
Crawley Cotts. EH26: Pen 3D **44**

Crescent, The EH10: Edin 2E **32**
EH23: Gore 3D **48**
Crewe Bank EH5: Edin 5H **11**
Crewe Cres. EH5: Edin 5G **11**
Crewe Gro. EH5: Edin 5H **11**
Crewe Loan EH5: Edin 5G **11**
Crewe Path EH5: Edin 5G **11**
Crewe Pl. EH5: Edin 5G **11**
Crewe Rd. Gdns. EH5: Edin 5G **11**
Crewe Rd. Nth. EH5: Edin 4G **11**
Crewe Rd. Sth. EH4: Edin 6G **11**
Crewe Rd. W. EH5: Edin 4G **11**
Crewe Ter. EH5: Edin 5G **11**
CREWE TOLL JUNC. 6G **11**
Crichton's Cl. EH8: Edin 3J **5**
Crichton St. EH8: Edin 6F **5** (4H **21**)
Crighton Pl. EH7: Edin 7E **12**
Croall Pl. EH7: Edin 1J **21**
Crockett Gdns. EH26: Pen 2B **50**
Croft-an-Righ
EH8: Edin 2K **5** (2K **21**)
Croft St. EH22: Dalk 2C **42**
EH26: Pen 3C **50**
Cromwell Pl. EH6: Edin 4E **12**
Crookston Ct. EH21: Muss 4G **25**
Crookston Rd. EH21: Muss 4G **25**
(not continuous)
Cross Cotts. EH32: Pres 6E **14**
Crosswood Av. EH14: Bal 5D **36**
Crosswood Cres. EH14: Bal 5D **36**
Crown Pl. EH6: Edin 6E **12**
Crown St. EH6: Edin 6E **12**
Cruachan Ct. EH26: Pen 1E **50**
Crusader Dr. EH25: Rosl 3K **45**
Crystal Mt. EH22: Dalk 1C **42**
Cuguen Pl. EH18: Las 4H **41**
CUIKEN 1C **50**
Cuiken Av. EH26: Pen 1C **50**
Cuiken Bank EH26: Pen 1B **50**
Cuikenburn EH26: Pen 7C **44**
Cuiken Ter. EH26: Pen 1B **50**
Cultins Rd. EH11: Edin 1D **30**
(not continuous)
Cumberland St.
EH3: Edin 1C **4** (1G **21**)
Cumberland St. Nth. E. La.
EH3: Edin 1G **21**
Cumberland St. Nth. W. La.
EH3: Edin 1C **4** (1G **21**)
Cumberland St. Sth. E. La.
EH3: Edin 1C **4** (1G **21**)
Cumberland St. Sth. W. La.
EH3: Edin 1C **4** (1G **21**)
Cumlodden Av. EH12: Edin 3A **20**
Cumnor Cres. EH16: Edin 3A **34**
Cunningham Pl. EH6: Edin 6E **12**
CURRIE 1J **37**
Curriehill Castle Dr.
EH14: Bal 1F **37**
Curriehill Rd. EH14: Cur 7B **30**
Curriehill Station (Rail) 7B **30**
CURRIEMUIR END 5G **31**
Currie RFC 3F **37**
Currievale Dr. EH14: Cur 1G **37**
Currievale Pk. EH14: Cur 1G **37**
Currievale Pk. Gro.
EH14: Cur 1G **37**
CUTHILL 7C **14**
Cuthill EH32: Pres 6C **14**

D

Daiches Braes EH15: Port 5J **23**
Daisy Ter. EH11: Edin 7C **20**
Dalgety Av. EH7: Edin 1B **22**
Dalgety Rd. EH7: Edin 1B **22**
Dalgety St. EH7: Edin 2B **22**
Dalhouse Bank EH22: Dalk 3B **42**
Dalhousie Av. EH19: Bonn 7G **41**
Dalhousie Av. W.
EH19: Bonn 7G **41**
Dalhousie Bus. Pk.
EH19: Bonn 2K **47**
Dalhousie Chesters Ct.
EH19: Bonn 2G **47**
Dalhousie Cres. EH22: Dalk . . .4B **42**

Dalhousie Dr. EH19: Bonn 7G **41**
Dalhousie Gdns.
EH19: Bonn 7G **41**
Dalhousie Mains Cotts.
EH22: Dalk 6A **42**
Dalhousie Pl. EH19: Bonn 7F **41**
Dalhousie Rd.
EH22: Dalk, Newt 6A **42**
Dalhousie Rd. E.
EH19: Bonn 7G **41**
Dalhousie Rd. W.
EH19: Bonn 7G **41**
Dalhousie Ter. EH10: Edin . . .2E **32**
DALKEITH 2C **42**
Dalkeith Country Pk. 1D **42**
Dalkeith Home Farm Cotts.
EH22: Dalk 7F **25**
Dalkeith Northern By-Pass
EH22: Dalk 1H **43**
Dalkeith Rd. EH8: Edin 5K **21**
EH16: Edin 6K **21**
Dalkeith Rd. M. EH9: Edin . . .7A **22**
(off Falkeith Rd.)
Dalkeith St. EH15: Port 4J **23**
Dalkeith Western By-Pass
EH22: Dalk 1K **41**
Dalmahoy Cres. EH14: Bal . . .2D **36**
Dalmahoy Rd. EH27: Kntn . . .2D **28**
EH28: Rat 2D **28**
DALMENY 3K **7**
Dalmeny House 1E **8**
Dalmeny Rd. EH6: Edin 5C **12**
Dalmeny Station (Rail) 2J **7**
Dalmeny St. EH6: Edin 7E **12**
DALRY 5D **20**
Dalry Gait EH11: Edin 4D **20**
Dalrymple Cres. EH9: Edin . . .7J **21**
EH21: Muss 2C **24**
Dalrymple Loan EH21: Muss . .2E **24**
Dalry Pl. EH11: Edin 4E **20**
Dalry Rd. EH11: Edin 5D **20**
Dalry Swimming Cen. 5D **20**
Dalton Ct. EH22: May 1G **49**
Dalum Ct. EH20: Loan 5A **40**
Dalum Dr. EH20: Loan 5A **40**
Dalum Gro. EH20: Loan 5A **40**
Dalum Loan EH20: Loan 5A **40**
Dalziel Pl. EH7: Edin 2B **22**
Dambrae EH21: Muss 2E **24**
(off Kilwinning Pl.)
Damhead EH10: Edin 5H **39**
Damside EH4: Edin 3E **20**
DANDERHALL 5H **35**
Danderhall Cres. EH22: Dan . .5H **35**
Danderhall Leisure Cen. 5J **35**
Dania Ct. EH11: Edin 7H **19**
Danube St. EH4: Edin . . .1A **4** (1E **20**)
D'arcy Cres. EH22: May 6H **43**
D'arcy Rd. EH22: May 7G **43**
D'arcy Ter. EH22: May 6G **43**
Dark Wlk. EH22: Dalk 1D **42**
Darnaway St.
EH3: Edin 2A **4** (2F **21**)
Darnell Rd. EH5: Edin 5K **11**
Darroch Ct. EH8: Edin 4H **5**
David Lloyd Leisure
Edinburgh 6D **18**
David Scott Av. EH22: May . . .6G **43**
Davidson Gdns. EH4: Edin . . .7D **10**
Davidson Pk. EH4: Edin 7G **11**
Davidson Rd. EH4: Edin 7G **11**
DAVIDSON'S MAINS 7C **10**
Davies Row EH12: Edin 5F **19**
(off Corstorphine High St.)
Davie St. EH8: Edin 6G **5** (4J **21**)
Dean Bank La. EH3: Edin 1F **21**
Deanbank Pl. EH23: Gore 7F **49**
Dean Bri. EH3: Edin 2E **20**
EH4: Edin 2E **20**
DEANBURN 7C **44**
Deanburn EH26: Pen 7B **44**
Deanery Cl. EH7: Edin 2C **22**
Dean Gallery 3D **20**
Deanhaugh Path EH4: Edin . . .3E **20**
(off Malta Ter.)
Deanhaugh St.
EH4: Edin 1A **4** (1F **21**)
Dean Pk. EH22: Newt 1C **48**
(not continuous)

Deanpark Av. EH14: Bal 4D **36**
Deanpark Bank EH14: Bal 4E **36**
Deanpark Brae EH14: Bal 4E **36**
Dean Pk. Ct. EH22: Newt 1C **48**
Deanpark Ct. EH14: Bal 5D **36**
Dean Pk. Cres. EH4: Edin 2E **20**
Deanpark Cres. EH14: Bal 4E **36**
Deanpark Gdns. EH14: Bal . . .4E **36**
Deanpark Gro. EH14: Bal 4E **36**
Dean Pk. M. EH4: Edin 1E **20**
Dean Pk. Pl. EH22: Newt 1C **48**
Deanpark Pl. EH14: Bal 4E **36**
Deanpark Sq. EH14: Bal 5E **36**
Dean Pk. St. EH4: Edin 1E **20**
Dean Path EH4: Edin 2D **20**
Dean Path Bldgs. EH4: Edin . . .3E **20**
(off Dean Path)
Dean Pl. EH14: Edin 1B **50**
Dean Rd. EH26: Pen 1B **50**
Dean St. EH4: Edin 1A **4** (1E **20**)
Dean Ter. EH4: Edin . . .1A **4** (2E **20**)
Deantown Av. EH21: Whit 7G **25**
Deantown Dr. EH21: Whit 7G **25**
Deantown Path EH21: Whit . . .7G **25**
DEAN VILLAGE 2D **20**
Dechmont Rd. EH12: Edin 4C **18**
Delhaig EH11: Edin 7A **20**
Dell Rd. EH13: Edin 5K **31**
Delta Av. EH21: Muss 3J **25**
Delta Ct. EH21: Muss 2J **25**
Delta Cres. EH21: Muss 2J **25**
Delta Dr. EH21: Muss 2J **25**
Delta Gdns. EH21: Muss 3J **25**
Delta Pl. EH21: Muss 4F **25**
Delta Rd. EH21: Muss 3J **25**
Delta Vw. EH21: Muss 2J **25**
Denham Grn. Av. EH5: Edin . . .5A **12**
Denham Grn. Pl. EH5: Edin . . .5A **12**
Denham Grn. Ter. EH5: Edin . .5A **12**
Denholm Av. EH21: Muss 4B **24**
Denholm Dr. EH21: Muss 4C **24**
Denholm Rd. EH21: Muss 4B **24**
Denholm Way EH21: Muss 4B **24**
De Quincey Path EH18: Las . . .7E **40**
De Quincey Rd. EH18: Las 7E **40**
Dequincey Wlk. EH33: Tran . . .3G **27**
Derby St. EH6: Newh 4C **12**
Devon Pl. EH12: Edin 4D **20**
Dewar Pl. EH3: Edin . . .5A **4** (4E **20**)
Dewar Pl. La. EH3: Edin 4E **20**
Dick Pl. EH9: Edin 7H **21**
Dicksonfield EH7: Edin 1J **21**
Dickson Gro. EH19: Bonn 6H **41**
Dickson St. EH6: Edin 7E **12**
Dick Ter. EH26: Pen 1D **50**
Dinmont Dr. EH16: Edin 3B **34**
Distillery La. EH11: Edin 4D **20**
(off Dalry Rd.)
Dobbie's Rd. EH18: Las 6G **41**
EH19: Bonn 6G **41**
Dochart Dr. EH4: Edin 2E **18**
Dock Pl. EH6: Leith 4E **12**
Dock St. EH6: Leith 4E **12**
Dolphin Av. EH14: Cur 1H **37**
Dolphin Gdns. E. EH14: Cur . .1H **37**
Dolphin Gdns. W. EH14: Cur . .1G **37**
Dolphin Rd. EH14: Cur 2G **37**
Dominion Cinema 1F **33**
Doo'cot Pl. EH32: Pres 7F **14**
(off Preston Rd.)
Dorset Pl. EH11: Edin 6E **20**
Double Dykes EH21: Muss 4F **25**
Double Hedges Pk.
EH16: Edin 3A **34**
Double Hedges Rd.
EH16: Edin 3A **34**
Dougall Ct. EH22: May 1F **49**
Dougall Pl. EH22: May 1F **49**
Dougall Rd. EH22: May 1F **49**
Douglas Cres. EH12: Edin 3D **20**
EH19: Bonn 6H **41**
Douglas Gdns. EH4: Edin 3D **20**
Douglas Gdns. M. EH4: Edin . .3D **20**
Douglas Ter. EH11: Edin 4C **20**
Doune Ter. EH3: Edin . . .1A **4** (2F **21**)
Dovecot Brae EH33: Tran 1G **27**
Dovecot Gro. EH14: Edin 3J **31**
Dovecot Loan EH14: Edin 3J **31**
Dovecot Pk. EH14: Edin 4J **31**

Dovecot Rd. EH12: Edin 6F **19**
Dow Craig EH32: Pres 6C **14**
Dowie's Mill Cotts.
EH4: Cram 6G **9**
Dowie's Mill La. EH4: Cram . . .6G **9**
Downfield Pl. EH11: Edin 5D **20**
Downie Gro. EH12: Edin 5H **19**
Downie Pl. EH21: Muss 2E **24**
Downie Ter. EH12: Edin 5H **19**
Downing Ct. EH25: Rosl 3A **46**
DREGHORN 6B **32**
Dreghorn Av. EH13: Edin 7C **32**
Dreghorn Dr. EH13: Edin 7C **32**
Dreghorn Gdns. EH13: Edin . . .7C **32**
Dreghorn Gro. EH13: Edin 7C **32**
DREGHORN JUNC. 1C **38**
Dreghorn Link EH13: Edin 7C **32**
Dreghorn Loan EH13: Edin . . .6K **31**
Dreghorn Pk. EH13: Edin 6B **32**
Dreghorn Pl. EH13: Edin 7C **32**
DREGHORN SERVICE AREA . . .7B **32**
DRUM 1A **22**
Drum Av. EH17: Edin 6E **34**
DRUMBRAE 2E **18**
Drum Brae Av. EH12: Edin 3E **18**
Drum Brae Cres. EH12: Edin . .2E **18**
Drum Brae Dr. EH4: Edin 2E **18**
Drum Brae Gdns.
EH12: Edin 3E **18**
Drum Brae Gro. EH4: Edin 2E **18**
Drumbrae Junc. EH12: Edin . . .5E **18**
Drumbrae Leisure Cen. 2E **18**
Drum Brae Neuk EH12: Edin . .3E **18**
Drum Brae Nth. EH4: Edin 1D **18**
Drum Brae Pk. EH12: Edin 3E **18**
Drum Brae Pk. App.
EH12: Edin 3E **18**
Drum Brae Pl. EH12: Edin 3E **18**
Drum Brae Sth. EH12: Edin . . .3E **18**
Drum Brae Ter. EH4: Edin 2E **18**
Drum Brae Wlk. EH4: Edin 2D **18**
(not continuous)
Drum Cotts. EH17: Edin 7F **35**
Drum Cres. EH17: Edin 6F **35**
Drumdryan St. EH3: Edin 7B **4**
Drummohr Av. EH21: Wall 3J **25**
Drummohr Gdns.
EH21: Wall 3K **25**
Drummohr Ter. EH21: Wall . . .3J **25**
Drummond Pl.
EH3: Edin 1D **4** (1G **21**)
Drummond St.
EH8: Edin 5G **5** (4J **21**)
Drummore Dr. EH32: Pres 7C **14**
Drum Pl. EH17: Edin 6F **35**
Drumsheugh Gdns.
EH3: Edin 3E **20**
Drumsheugh Pl. EH3: Edin 3E **20**
(off Drumsheugh Gdns.)
Drum St. EH17: Edin 6E **34**
Drum Ter. EH7: Edin 1A **22**
Drum Vw. Av. EH22: Dan 5H **35**
Drum Woods EH17: Edin 5F **35**
Drybrough Cres. EH16: Edin . . .7D **22**
Dryden Av. EH20: Loan 6A **40**
Dryden Cres. EH20: Loan 6A **40**
Dryden Gait EH7: Edin 7D **12**
Dryden Gdns. EH7: Edin 7D **12**
Dryden Glen EH20: Loan 6K **39**
Dryden Gro. EH25: Rosl 2A **46**
Dryden Loan EH20: Loan 6K **39**
Dryden Pk. EH20: Loan 7K **39**
Dryden Pl. EH9: Edin 6K **21**
EH20: Loan 6K **39**
Dryden Rd. EH20: Loan 6K **39**
Dryden St. EH7: Edin 7D **12**
Dryden Ter. EH7: Edin 7D **12**
EH20: Loan 6A **40**
Dryden Vw. EH20: Loan 6K **39**
Dryden Va. Bilston Glen
EH20: Loan 6A **40**
Dryden Vw. EH20: Loan 6A **40**
DRYLAW 7E **10**
Drylaw Av. EH4: Edin 1K **19**
Drylaw Cres. EH4: Edin 1K **19**
Drylaw Grn. EH4: Edin 7E **10**
Drylaw Grn. EH4: Edin 1K **19**
Drylaw Gro. EH4: Edin 1K **19**
Drylaw Ho. Gdns. EH4: Edin . .7E **10**

Drylaw Ho. Paddock
EH4: Edin 7E **10**
Drylaw Wlk. EH4: Edin 7E **10**
Duart Cres. EH4: Edin 2E **18**
Dublin Meuse
EH3: Edin 1D **4** (2H **21**)
Dublin St. EH1: Edin 1E **4** (2H **21**)
EH3: Edin 1E **4** (2H **21**)
Dublin St. La. Nth.
EH3: Edin 1E **4** (1H **21**)
Dublin St. La. Sth.
EH1: Edin 1E **4** (2H **21**)
DUDDINGSTON 5G **23**
Duddingston Av. EH15: Port . . .5E **22**
Duddingston Cres.
EH15: Port 5G **23**
Duddingston Ho. Courtyard
EH15: Port 6E **22**
Duddingston Gdns. Nth.
EH15: Port 4F **23**
Duddingston Gdns. Sth.
EH15: Port 5F **23**
Duddingston Gro. E.
EH15: Port 4F **23**
Duddingston Gro. W.
EH15: Port 5F **23**
Duddingston Loan
EH15: Port 4E **22**
Duddingston Loch & Bird Sanctuary
. . . . .6C **22**
Duddingston Mains Cotts.
EH15: Port 5H **23**
Duddingston Mills EH8: Edin . .4E **22**
Duddingston Pk. EH15: Edin . .4G **23**
Duddingston Pk. Sth.
EH15: Port 5G **23**
Duddingston Ri. EH15: Edin . . .5F **23**
Duddingston Rd. EH15: Port . . .4E **22**
Duddingston Rd. W.
EH15: Edin 5D **22**
EH16: Edin 6D **22**
Duddingston Row
EH15: Edin 5F **23**
Duddingston Sq. E.
EH15: Port 4F **23**
Duddingston Sq. W.
EH15: Port 4F **23**
Duddingston Vw. EH15: Edin . .5F **23**
Duddingston Yards
EH15: Port 6G **23**
Dudgeon Pl. EH29: Kltn 1B **16**
Dudley Av. EH6: Newh 4C **12**
Dudley Av. Sth. EH6: Newh . . .5D **12**
Dudley Bank EH6: Newh 4C **12**
Dudley Cres. EH6: Newh 4C **12**
Dudley Gdns. EH6: Newh 4C **12**
Dudley Gro. EH6: Newh 4C **12**
Dudley Ter. EH6: Newh 4C **12**
Duff Rd. EH11: Edin 5D **20**
Duff St. EH11: Edin 5D **20**
Duff St. La. EH11: Edin 5D **20**
Dugald Stewart Monument . . .2G **5**
Duke Pl. EH6: Leith 6F **13**
Duke St. EH6: Edin 6F **13**
EH22: Dalk 2C **42**
Duke's Wlk. EH8: Edin 2B **22**
Dumbeg Pl. EH14: Cur 4F **31**
Dumbiedykes Rd.
EH8: Edin 5J **5** (4K **21**)
Dumbryden Dr. EH14: Edin . . .3H **31**
Dumbryden Gdns.
EH14: Edin 3G **31**
Dumbryden Gro. EH14: Edin . . .3G **31**
Dumbryden Ind. Est.
EH14: Edin 3H **31**
Dumbryden Rd. EH14: Edin . . .3H **31**
Dun-Ard Gdn. EH9: Edin 1H **33**
Dunbar's Cl. EH8: Edin 3H **5**
Dunbar St. EH3: Edin 6B **4** (5F **21**)
Duncan Gdns. EH33: Tran 1G **27**
Duncans Gait EH14: Edin 2J **31**
Duncan St. EH9: Edin 7J **21**
Dundas Av. EH30: S Q'fry 2H **7**
Dundas Cres. EH22: Dalk 4A **42**
Dundas Gdns. EH23: Gore 5D **48**
Dundas Gro. EH22: Dalk 3A **42**
Dundas Pk. EH19: Bonn 6J **41**
Dundas Pl. EH29: Kltn 1B **16**

Dundas Rd.—Eskdaill Ct.

Dundas Rd. EH22: Dalk . . . 3A **42**
Dundas St. EH3: Edin . . . 1C **4** (1G **21**)
EH19: Bonn . . . 6J **41**
Dundee St. EH11: Edin . . . 6D **20**
Dundee Ter. EH11: Edin . . . 6D **20**
Dundonald St. EH3: Edin . . . 1G **21**
Dundrennan Cotts.
EH16: Edin . . . 2C **34**
Dunedin St. EH7: Edin . . . 7C **12**
Dunlaw Wynd EH16: Edin . . . 6B **34**
Dunlop's Ct. EH1: Edin . . . 5D **4**
Dunlop Ter. EH26: Pen . . . 2E **50**
Dunollie Ct. EH12: Edin . . . 4D **18**
Dunrobin Pl. EH3: Edin . . . 7A **12**
Dunsmuir Ct. EH12: Edin . . . 5E **18**
Dunsyre Ho. EH11: Edin . . . 3E **30**
Dunvegan Ct. EH4: Cram . . . 6J **9**
Durar Dr. EH4: Edin . . . 3E **18**
DURHAM . . . **4F 23**
Durham Av. EH15: Edin, Port . . . 4F **23**
Durham Bank EH19: Bonn . . . 7J **41**
Durham Dr. EH15: Edin . . . 5G **23**
Durham Gdns. Nth.
EH15: Edin . . . 4G **23**
Durham Gdns. Sth.
EH15: Edin . . . 5G **23**
Durham Gro. EH15: Edin . . . 4G **23**
EH19: Bonn . . . 7J **41**
Durham Pl. EH19: Bonn . . . 7H **41**
Durham Pl. E. EH15: Edin . . . 4G **23**
Durham Pl. La.
EH15: Edin, Port . . . 4G **23**
Durham Pl. W. EH15: Edin . . . 4F **23**
Durham Rd. EH15: Edin . . . 4G **23**
Durham Rd. Sth. EH15: Port . . . 5G **23**
Durham Sq. EH15: Edin . . . 4F **23**
Durham Ter.
EH15: Port, Edin . . . 4F **23**
Durie's Pk. EH33: Elph . . . 6F **27**
Durward Gro. EH16: Edin . . . 2B **34**
Dury Way EH21: Wall . . . 3J **25**
Dyke's Rd. EH26: Pen . . . 7C **44**

E

Earl Grey St.
EH3: Edin . . . 6B **4** (4F **21**)
Earl Haig Gdns. EH5: Edin . . . 5A **12**
Earlston Pl. EH7: Edin . . . 2A **22**
E. Adam St.
EH8: Edin . . . 5G **5** (4J **21**)
E. Barnton Av. EH4: Edin . . . 7B **10**
E. Barnton Gdns. EH4: Edin . . . 7B **10**
E. Brighton Cres.
EH15: Port . . . 3G **23**
E. Broughton Pl.
EH1: Edin . . . 1F **5** (1H **21**)
E. Caiystane Pl. EH10: Edin . . . 6E **32**
E. Caiystane Rd. EH10: Edin . . . 6E **32**
E. Camus Pl. EH10: Edin . . . 6E **32**
E. Camus Rd. EH10: Edin . . . 6E **32**
E. Castle Rd. EH10: Edin . . . 6E **20**
East Champanyie EH9: Edin . . . 1J **33**
East Clapperfield
EH16: Edin . . . 3A **34**
E. Claremont St. EH7: Edin . . . 1H **21**
East Comiston EH10: Edin . . . 6E **32**
East Ct. EH4: Edin . . . 2A **20**
EH16: Edin . . . 1F **35**
EAST CRAIGS . . . **4E 18**
E. Craigs Rigg EH12: Edin . . . 4C **18**
E. Craigs Wynd EH12: Edin . . . 4C **18**
East Cft. EH28: Rat . . . 2E **28**
E. Cromwell St. EH6: Leith . . . 4E **12**
East Crosscauseway
EH8: Edin . . . 7G **5** (5J **21**)
Easter Belmont Rd.
EH12: Edin . . . 4K **19**
Easter Currie Ct. EH14: Cur . . . 1J **37**
Easter Currie Cres.
H14: Cur . . . 7C **30**
Easter Currie Pl. EH14: Cur . . . 7C **30**
Easter Currie Ter. EH14: Cur . . . 1J **37**
Easter Dalry Dr. EH11: Edin . . . 5D **20**
Easter Dalry Pl. EH11: Edin . . . 4D **20**
Easter Dalry Rigg
EH11: Edin . . . 5D **20**
Easter Dalry Rd. EH11: Edin . . . 4D **20**
Easter Dalry Wynd
EH11: Edin . . . 4D **20**
Easter Drylaw Av. EH4: Edin . . . 7F **11**
Easter Drylaw Bank
EH4: Edin . . . 6F **11**
Easter Drylaw Dr. EH4: Edin . . . 7F **11**
Easter Drylaw Gdns.
EH4: Edin . . . 7F **11**
Easter Drylaw Gro.
EH4: Edin . . . 7F **11**
Easter Drylaw Loan
EH4: Edin . . . 7F **11**
Easter Drylaw Pl. EH4: Edin . . . 6F **11**
Easter Drylaw Vw.
EH4: Edin . . . 6G **11**
Easter Drylaw Way
EH4: Edin . . . 7F **11**
Easter Hailes Ga.
EH13: Edin . . . 4J **31**
EH14: Edin . . . 4K **31**
Easter Haugh EH13: Edin . . . 5C **32**
Easter Hermitage EH6: Edin . . . 7G **13**
Easter Langside Av.
EH22: Dalk . . . 2F **43**
Easter Langside Dr.
EH22: Dalk . . . 2F **43**
Easter Langside Gdns.
EH22: Dalk . . . 2F **43**
Eastern Ind. Est. EH15: Edin . . . 7J **23**
Easter Pk. Dr. EH4: Edin . . . 6B **10**
Easter Pk. Ho. EH4: Edin . . . 6B **10**
Easter Rd. EH6: Edin . . . 2K **21**
EH7: Edin . . . 1K **5** (2K **21**)
Easter Road Stadium . . . **1A 22**
Easter Steil EH10: Edin . . . 3D **32**
Easter Warriston EH7: Edin . . . 6B **12**
E. Farm of Gilmerton
EH17: Edin . . . 6E **34**
E. Fettes Av. EH4: Edin . . . 6J **11**
EASTFIELD . . . **1A 24**
Eastfield EH15: Port . . . 1B **24**
EH26: Pen . . . 1D **50**
Eastfield Dr. EH26: Pen . . . 1D **50**
Eastfield Farm Rd.
EH26: Pen . . . 7D **44**
Eastfield Gdns. EH15: Port . . . 1A **24**
Eastfield Ind. Est.
EH26: Pen . . . 1D **50**
(Eastfield Pk. Rd.)
EH26: Pen . . . 7E **44**
(Yarrow Ct.)
Eastfield Loan EH33: Tran . . . 1H **27**
Eastfield Pk. Rd. EH26: Pen . . . 1D **50**
Eastfield Pl. EH15: Port . . . 1B **24**
Eastfield Rd. EH28: Ing . . . 4G **17**
East Fountainbridge
EH3: Edin . . . 6B **4** (4F **21**)
East Hannahfield EH14: Bal . . . 3C **36**
EAST HERMISTON . . . **3C 30**
E. Hermitage Pl. EH6: Edin . . . 6F **13**
EASTHOUSES . . . **6E 42**
Easthouses Ct. EH22: East . . . 5E **42**
Easthouses Ind. Est.
EH22: East . . . 5F **43**
Easthouses Pl. EH22: East . . . 4F **43**
Easthouses Rd. EH22: East . . . 3E **42**
Easthouses Way EH22: East . . . 4E **42**
E. Kilngate Pl. EH17: Edin . . . 7D **34**
E. Kilngate Rigg EH17: Edin . . . 7D **34**
E. Kilngate Wynd
EH17: Edin . . . 7D **34**
East Lillypot EH5: Edin . . . 5A **12**
East Loan EH32: Pres . . . 5D **14**
E. London St. EH7: Edin . . . 1H **21**
E. Lorimer Pl. EH32: Cock . . . 3G **15**
East Lothian Bowling Club . . . **7F 15**
EAST MAINS OF INGLISTON . . . **5F 17**
E. Market St.
EH1: Edin . . . 3F **5** (3H **21**)
East Mayfield EH9: Edin . . . 7K **21**
E. Montgomery Pl.
EH7: Edin . . . 1K **21**
E. Newington Pl. EH9: Edin . . . 6K **21**
E. Norton Pl. EH7: Edin . . . 1K **5**
East Parkside
EH16: Edin . . . 7K **5** (5K **21**)
E. Pilton Farm Av. EH5: Edin . . . 5H **11**
E. Pilton Farm Cres.
EH5: Edin . . . 5J **11**
E. Pilton Farm Rigg
EH5: Edin . . . 5H **11**
E. Pilton Farm Wynd
EH5: Edin . . . 5J **11**
E. Preston St. EH8: Edin . . . 6J **21**
E. Preston St. La. EH8: Edin . . . 6K **21**
East Princes Street Gdns.
. . . **3E 4 (3G 21)**
East Queensway EH26: Pen . . . 7D **44**
E. Restalrig Ter. EH6: Edin . . . 6G **13**
E. Savile Rd. EH16: Edin . . . 1K **33**
E. Sciennes St. EH9: Edin . . . 6J **21**
East Seaside EH32: Pres . . . 5D **14**
E. Silvermills La. EH3: Edin . . . 1F **21**
E. Suffolk Pk. EH16: Edin . . . 1A **34**
E. Suffolk Rd. EH16: Edin . . . 1A **34**
East Telferton EH7: Edin . . . 2F **23**
East Ter. EH30: S Q'fry . . . 1H **7**
E. Trinity Rd. EH5: Edin . . . 5A **12**
East Way, The EH8: Edin . . . 3E **22**
East Werberside EH4: Edin . . . 6H **11**
E. Werberside Pl. EH4: Edin . . . 6H **11**
Echline EH30: S Q'fry . . . 2E **6**
(not continuous)
Echline Av. EH30: S Q'fry . . . 1E **6**
Echline Dr. EH30: S Q'fry . . . 2E **6**
Echline Gdns. EH30: S Q'fry . . . 1E **6**
Echline Grn. EH30: S Q'fry . . . 1E **6**
Echline Gro. EH30: S Q'fry . . . 1F **7**
Echline Junc. EH30: S Q'fry . . . 2F **7**
Echline Pk. EH30: S Q'fry . . . 2E **6**
Echline Pl. EH30: S Q'fry . . . 2E **6**
Echline Rigg EH30: S Q'fry . . . 1F **7**
Echline Ter. EH30: S Q'fry . . . 2F **7**
Echline Vw. EH30: S Q'fry . . . 2F **7**
Edenhall Bank EH21: Muss . . . 3G **25**
Edenhall Cres. EH21: Muss . . . 3G **25**
EDENHALL HOSPITAL . . . **4G 25**
Edenhall Rd. EH21: Muss . . . 3G **25**
Eden La. EH10: Edin . . . 1F **33**
Eden Ter. *EH10: Edin . . . 1F 33*
(off Eden La.)
Edgefield Ind. Est.
EH20: Loan . . . 4B **40**
Edgefield Pl. EH20: Loan . . . 5C **40**
Edgefield Rd. EH20: Loan . . . 5C **40**
EDGEHEAD . . . **6K 43**
Edina Pl. EH7: Edin . . . 1K **21**
Edina St. EH7: Edin . . . 1K **21**
EDINBURGH . . . **4E 4 (3H 21)**
Edinburgh Academical FC . . . **1E 20**
EDINBURGH AIRPORT . . . **3F 17**
Edinburgh Airport Stop (NET)
(Due to open 2011) . . . **3G 17**
Edinburgh Butterfly & Insect World
. . . **1J 41**
Edinburgh Castle . . . **4C 4 (3G 21)**
Edinburgh City FC . . . **2B 22**
Edinburgh Crematorium
EH7: Edin . . . 6C **12**
Edinburgh Crystal Vis. Cen. . . . **1D 50**
EDINBURGH DENTAL INSTITUTE
. . . **6D 4 (4G 21)**
Edinburgh Dungeon, The . . . **3E 4**
Edinburgh Festival Theatre
. . . **5F 5 (4H 21)**
Edinburgh International
Climbing Arena . . . **1B 28**
Edinburgh International
Conference Cen.
. . . **5A 4 (4F 21)**
Edinburgh Pk. EH12: Edin . . . 6B **18**
(not continuous)
Edinburgh Park Central Stop (NET)
(Due to open 2011) . . . **7B 18**
Edinburgh Park Station (Rail)
. . . **1C 30**
Edinburgh Park Stop (NET)
(Due to open 2011) . . . **1C 30**
Edinburgh Rd. EH4: Cram . . . 6F **9**
EH21: Muss . . . 1B **24**
EH22: Dalk . . . 2C **42**
EH26: Pen, Mil B . . . 1D **50**
EH28: Nbdge . . . 5A **16**
EH30: Cram, S Q'fry . . . 1K **7**
EH30: S Q'fry . . . 1H **7**
EH32: Cock . . . 4E **14**
EH33: Tran . . . 1F **27**
Edinburgh University . . . **7F 5 (5H 21)**
Edinburgh University FC . . . **1C 34**
Edinburgh Waverley Station (Rail)
. . . **3F 5 (3H 21)**
Edinburgh W. Office Pk.
EH12: Edin . . . 6C **18**
Edinburgh Zoo . . . **4H 19**
EDMONSTONE . . . **3F 35**
Edmonstone Av. EH22: Dan . . . 4H **35**
Edmonstone Dr. EH22: Dan . . . 4H **35**
Edmonstone Rd. EH22: Dan . . . 4G **35**
Edmonstones Cl. *EH1: Edin . . . 5E 4*
(off West Bow)
Edmonstone Ter. EH22: Dan . . . 4H **35**
Eglinton Cres. EH12: Edin . . . 4D **20**
Egypt M. EH10: Edin . . . 2G **33**
Eighth St. EH22: Newt . . . 1D **48**
Eildon St. EH3: Edin . . . 7B **12**
Eildon Ter. EH3: Edin . . . 6A **12**
Elbe St. EH6: Leith . . . 5F **13**
Elcho Pl. EH32: Port S . . . 3G **15**
Elcho Ter. EH15: Port . . . 3J **23**
Elder St. EH1: Edin . . . 1F **5** (2H **21**)
EH33: Tran . . . 1G **27**
Elder St. E. EH1: Edin . . . 1F **5** (2H **21**)
ELDINDEAN . . . **5J 41**
Eldindean Pl. EH19: Bonn . . . 5H **41**
Eldindean Rd. EH19: Bonn . . . 5H **41**
Eldindean Ter. EH19: Bonn . . . 5H **41**
Eldin Ind. Est. EH20: Loan . . . 3C **40**
Electra Pl. EH15: Port . . . 2G **23**
Elginhaugh Cotts.
EH22: Dalk . . . 2K **41**
Elgin St. EH7: Edin . . . 1K **21**
Elgin St. Nth. EH7: Edin . . . 1K **21**
Elgin Ter. EH7: Edin . . . 1K **21**
Elizafield EH6: Edin . . . 6D **12**
Ellangowan Ter. EH16: Edin . . . 3C **34**
ELLEN'S GLEN . . . **6C 34**
ELLEN'S GLEN HOUSE . . . **5C 34**
Ellen's Glen Loan
EH17: Edin . . . 5C **34**
(not continuous)
Ellen's Glen Rd. EH17: Edin . . . 6C **34**
Ellersly Rd. EH12: Edin . . . 4K **19**
Elliot Gdns. EH14: Edin . . . 4A **32**
Elliot Pk. EH14: Edin . . . 4A **32**
Elliot Pl. EH14: Edin . . . 4A **32**
Elliot Rd. EH14: Edin . . . 4A **32**
Elliot St. EH7: Edin . . . 1K **21**
Elmfield Bank *EH22: Dalk . . . 2C 42*
(off Elmfield Pk.)
Elmfield Ct. EH22: Dalk . . . 2C **42**
Elmfield Pk. EH22: Dalk . . . 2C **42**
Elmfield Rd. EH22: Dalk . . . 2C **42**
Elm Pl. EH6: Edin . . . 6F **13**
EH22: May . . . 7F **43**
Elm Row EH7: Edin . . . 1G **5** (1J **21**)
(not continuous)
EH18: Las . . . 4G **41**
Elmwood Ter. EH6: Edin . . . 6G **13**
ELPHINSTONE . . . **7F 27**
Elphinstone Ct. EH33: Tran . . . 2G **27**
Elphinstone Rd. EH33: Tran . . . 4F **27**
Elphinstone Wlk. EH33: Tran . . . 3F **27**
Eltringham Gdns.
EH14: Edin . . . 7A **20**
Eltringham Gro. EH14: Edin . . . 7A **20**
Eltringham Ter. EH14: Edin . . . 7A **20**
Emily Ct. EH23: Gore . . . 5D **48**
Emily Pl. EH23: Gore . . . 5F **49**
Engine Rd. EH20: Loan . . . 5C **40**
EH23: Gore . . . 5D **48**
Enterprise Cen. EH20: Loan . . . 6K **39**
Esdaile Bank EH9: Edin . . . 7H **21**
Esdaile Pk. EH9: Edin . . . 7H **21**
ESKBANK . . . **3B 42**
Eskbank Ct. EH22: Dalk . . . 3A **42**
Eskbank Ind. Est.
EH22: Dalk . . . 5A **42**
Eskbank Rd. EH19: Bonn . . . 5J **41**
EH22: Bonn . . . 5J **41**
EH22: Dalk . . . 3B **42**
Eskbank Rd. Rdbt.
EH22: Dalk . . . 4A **42**
Eskbank Ter. EH22: Dalk . . . 3B **42**
Eskbank Toll EH22: Dalk . . . 3A **42**
Esk Bri. EH26: Pen . . . 2E **50**
Eskdaill Ct. *EH22: Dalk . . . 2C 42*
(off Eskdaill St.)

66 A-Z Edinburgh

Eskdaill St.—Gayfield Sq.

Eskdaill St. EH22: Dalk ... 2C **42**
Eskdale Ct. EH19: Bonn ... 6G **41**
Eskdale Dr. EH19: Bonn ... 6G **41**
Eskdale M. EH21: Muss ... 2E **24**
Eskdale Ter. EH19: Bonn ... 6G **41**
Eskfield Gro. EH22: Dalk ... 3K **41**
Esk Glades EH22: Dalk ... 2D **42**
ESKGROVE ... **5F 41**
Eskgrove Dr. EH25: Bil ... 7J **39**
ESKHILL ... **2E 50**
Eskhill EH26: Pen ... 2D **50**
Eskmill Rd. EH26: Pen ... 2E **50**
Eskmills Pk. EH21: Muss ... 3D **24**
Eskmill Vs. EH21: Muss ... 3D **24**
Esk Pl. EH22: Dalk ... 2B **42**
Eskside Ct. EH22: Dalk ... 1B **42**
Eskside E. EH21: Muss ... 2E **24**
Eskside W. EH21: Muss ... 3D **24**
Eskvale Ct. EH26: Pen ... 2E **50**
Eskvale Cres. EH26: Pen ... 2E **50**
Eskvale Dr. EH26: Pen ... 1E **50**
Eskvale Vw. EH26: Pen ... 1E **50**
ESKVIEW ... **3D 24**
Eskview Av. EH21: Muss ... 3D **24**
Eskview Cres. EH21: Muss ... 3D **24**
Eskview Gro. EH21: Muss ... 3D **24**
EH22: Dalk ... 2B **42**
Eskview Rd. EH21: Muss ... 3D **24**
EH22: May ... 7F **43**
Eskview Ter. EH21: Muss ... 3D **24**
Eskview Vs. EH22: Dalk ... 3A **42**
Esplanade
EH1: Edin ... 4D **4** (3G **21**)
Esplanade Ter. EH15: Port ... 3K **23**
Esporta Health Club
Edinburgh ... ***5E 20***
(in Fountainpark)
Essendean Pl. EH4: Edin ... 2F **19**
Essendean Ter. EH4: Edin ... 2F **19**
Essex Brae EH4: Cram ... 6H **9**
Essex Pk. EH4: Cram ... 6H **9**
Essex Rd. EH4: Cram ... 6H **9**
Esslemont Rd. EH16: Edin ... 2K **33**
Ethel Ter. EH10: Edin ... 2E **32**
Eton Ter. EH4: Edin ... 2E **20**
Ettrickdale Pl. EH3: Edin ... 7A **12**
Ettrick Gro. EH10: Edin ... 6E **20**
Ettrick Loan EH10: Edin ... 7D **20**
Ettrick Rd. EH10: Edin ... 7D **20**
Evans Gdns. EH19: Bonn ... 5K **41**
Eva Pl. EH9: Edin ... 2J **33**
Evelyn Ter. EH26: Auch ... 5G **45**
Ewerland EH4: Cram ... 6H **9**
Ewing St. EH26: Pen ... 7D **44**
Eyre Cres. EH3: Edin ... 1G **21**
Eyre Pl. EH3: Edin ... 1G **21**
Eyre Pl. La. EH3: Edin ... 1G **21**
Eyre Ter. EH3: Edin ... 1G **21**

F

Fair-a-Far EH4: Cram ... 5J **9**
Fair-a-Far Cotts. EH4: Cram ... 5J **9**
Fair-a-Far Shot EH4: Cram ... 5J **9**
Fairbrae EH11: Edin ... 1H **31**
Fairford Gdns. EH16: Edin ... 3B **34**
Fairhaven Vs. EH22: Dalk ... 3B **42**
Fairmile Av. EH10: Edin ... 6F **33**
FAIRMILEHEAD ... **7F 33**
Fairmilehead EH10: Edin ... 7F **33**
Fairview Rd. EH28: Ing ... 4F **17**
Fairways EH21: Muss ... 5D **24**
Fala Ct. EH16: Edin ... 6B **34**
Falcon Av. EH10: Edin ... 1F **33**
Falcon Ct. EH10: Edin ... 1F **33**
Falcon Gdns. EH10: Edin ... 1F **33**
Falcon Rd. EH10: Edin ... 1F **33**
Falcon Rd. W. EH10: Edin ... 1F **33**
Falkland Gdns. EH12: Edin ... 2G **19**
Farm Av. EH18: Las ... 7F **41**
Farm Rd. EH25: Rosl ... 7K **45**
Farquhar Ter. EH30: S Q'fry ... 1F **7**
Farrer Gro. EH7: Edin ... 2F **23**
Farrer Ter. EH7: Edin ... 2E **22**
Fa'side Av. EH33: Tran ... 3H **27**
Fa'side Av. Ct. EH21: Wall ... 4K **25**
Fa'side Av. Nth. EH21: Wall ... 4K **25**
Fa'side Av. Sth. EH21: Wall ... 4K **25**
Fa'side Bldgs. *EH21: Wall* ... *4K* ***25***
(off Fa'side Av. Nth.)
Fa'side Cres. EH21: Wall ... 4K **25**
EH33: Tran ... 3H **27**
Fa'side Dr. EH21: Wall ... 4K **25**
Fa'side Gdns. EH21: Wall ... 4K **25**
Fa'side Rd. EH33: Tran ... 3H **27**
Fa'side Ter. EH21: Wall ... 4K **25**
Fa'side Vw. EH33: Tran ... 4F **27**
Fauldburn EH12: Edin ... 2D **18**
Fauldburn Pk. EH12: Edin ... 2D **18**
Featherhall Av. EH12: Edin ... 5F **19**
Featherhall Cres. Nth.
EH12: Edin ... 5E **18**
Featherhall Cres. Sth.
EH12: Edin ... 5E **18**
Featherhall Gro. EH12: Edin ... 5F **19**
Featherhall Pl. EH12: Edin ... 5F **19**
Featherhall Rd. EH12: Edin ... 5F **19**
Featherhall Ter. EH12: Edin ... 5F **19**
Ferguson Ct. EH21: Muss ... 5D **24**
Ferguson Dr. EH21: Muss ... 5D **24**
Ferguson Gdns. EH21: Muss ... 5E **24**
Ferguson Grn. EH21: Muss ... 5D **24**
Ferguson Vw. EH21: Muss ... 5D **24**
Ferguson Way EH22: Newt ... 2D **48**
FERNIEHILL ... **5F 35**
Ferniehill Av. EH17: Edin ... 6E **34**
Ferniehill Dr. EH17: Edin ... 6E **34**
Ferniehill Gdns. EH17: Edin ... 5F **35**
Ferniehill Gro. EH17: Edin ... 5F **35**
Ferniehill Pl. EH17: Edin ... 6E **34**
Ferniehill Rd. EH17: Edin ... 6E **34**
Ferniehill Sq. EH17: Edin ... 6E **34**
Ferniehill St. EH17: Edin ... 5E **34**
Ferniehill Ter. EH17: Edin ... 6E **34**
Ferniehill Way EH17: Edin ... 5F **35**
Fernielaw Av. EH13: Edin ... 7J **31**
Fernieside Av. EH17: Edin ... 5E **34**
Fernieside Cres. EH17: Edin ... 5E **34**
Fernieside Dr. EH17: Edin ... 4E **34**
Fernieside Gdns. EH17: Edin ... 5E **34**
Fernieside Gro. EH17: Edin ... 5F **35**
Fernieside Pl. EH17: Edin ... 5E **34**
Ferryburn *EH30: S Q'fry* ... *2H* ***7***
(off Rosebery Av.)
Ferryburn Grn. EH30: S Q'fry ... 2H **7**
Ferryfield EH5: Edin ... 6J **11**
FERRYFIELD HOUSE ... **6H 11**
Ferry Gait Cres. EH4: Edin ... 6D **10**
Ferry Gait Dr. EH4: Edin ... 6D **10**
Ferry Gait Gdns. EH4: Edin ... 6D **10**
Ferry Gait Pl. EH4: Edin ... 6D **10**
Ferry Gait Wlk. EH4: Edin ... 6D **10**
Ferrymuir EH30: S Q'fry ... 3G **7**
Ferrymuir Gait EH30: S Q'fry ... 2G **7**
Ferrymuir La. EH30: S Q'fry ... 2G **7**
Ferrymuir Rd. EH30: S Q'fry ... 2G **7**
Ferry Rd. EH4: Edin ... 7D **10**
EH5: Edin ... 6H **11**
EH6: Edin ... 5A **12**
Ferry Rd. Av. EH4: Edin ... 6F **11**
Ferry Rd. Dr. EH4: Edin ... 5G **11**
Ferry Rd. Gdns. EH4: Edin ... 6F **11**
Ferry Rd. Gro. EH4: Edin ... 6F **11**
Ferry Rd. Pl. EH4: Edin ... 6F **11**
Festival Sq. EH3: Edin ... 5A **4** (4F **21**)
Fetteresk Cotts. EH26: Pen ... 3C **50**
Fettes Av. EH4: Edin ... 1D **20**
Fettes Ri. EH4: Edin ... 6J **11**
Fettes Row EH3: Edin ... 1G **21**
Fidra Ct. EH4: Edin ... 5D **10**
Fifth St. EH22: Newt ... 1C **48**
Figgate Bank EH15: Port ... 2H **23**
Figgate La. EH15: Port ... 2H **23**
Figgate St. EH15: Port ... 2G **23**
Fillyside Av. EH7: Edin ... 1E **22**
Fillyside Rd. EH7: Edin ... 7K **13**
Fillyside Ter. EH7: Edin ... 7K **13**
Filmhouse Cinema ... **5A 4 (4F 21)**
Findhorn Pl. EH9: Edin ... 6J **21**
Findlay Av. EH7: Edin ... 7H **13**
Findlay Cotts. EH7: Edin ... 7H **13**
Findlay Gdns. EH7: Edin ... 7H **13**
Findlay Gro. EH7: Edin ... 7H **13**
Findlay Medway EH7: Edin ... 7H **13**
Fingal Pl. EH9: Edin ... 6H **21**
Fingzies Pl. EH6: Edin ... 6G **13**
Finlaggan Ct. EH12: Edin ... 3C **18**
Finlay Pl. EH22: May ... 7H **43**
Firrhill Cres. EH13: Edin ... 4B **32**
Firrhill Dr. EH13: Edin ... 5C **32**
Firrhill Loan EH13: Edin ... 5C **32**
Firrhill Pk. EH13: Edin ... 5D **32**
First Gait EH14: Cur ... 4A **30**
First St. EH22: Newt ... 2D **48**
Firth Cres. EH26: Auch ... 5H **45**
Firth Rd. EH25: Rosl ... 7K **45**
EH26: Auch ... 5H **45**
Fir Vw. *EH20: Loan* ... *6K* ***39***
(off Nivensknowe Pk.)
Fishergate Rd. EH32: Port S ... 3J **15**
FISHERROW ... **2D 24**
Fisherrow Ind. Est.
EH21: Muss ... 2C **24**
Fishers Rd. EH32: Port S ... 3H **15**
Fishers Wynd EH21: Muss ... 2D **24**
Fishmarket Sq. EH6: Newh ... 4C **12**
Fishwives' C'way. EH7: Edin ... 2E **22**
EH15: Port ... 2G **23**
Fitness First
Edinburgh ... **1D 4**
Flassches Yd. EH12: Edin ... 7E **18**
Fleets Gro. EH33: Tran ... 4H **27**
Fleets Ind. Est. EH33: Tran ... 5G **27**
Fleets Rd. EH33: Tran ... 3G **27**
Fleets Vw. EH33: Tran ... 4H **27**
Flesh Mkt. EH1: Edin ... 4F **5**
Fletcher Gro. EH26: Pen ... 6D **44**
Floral Clock ... **3D 4**
Foot of the Walk Stop (NET)
(Due to open 2011) ... **6F 13**
Forbes Rd. EH10: Edin ... 7F **21**
Forbes St. EH8: Edin ... 7H **5** (5J **21**)
Ford's Rd. EH11: Edin ... 7K **19**
Forester's Vw. EH33: Tran ... 2H **27**
Forkenford EH16: Edin ... 6D **22**
Forres St. EH3: Edin ... 2A **4** (2F **21**)
Forrester Pk. Av. EH12: Edin ... 7F **19**
Forrester Pk. Dr. EH12: Edin ... 7F **19**
Forrester Pk. Gdns.
EH12: Edin ... 7F **19**
Forrester Pk. Grn.
EH12: Edin ... 7G **19**
Forrester Pk. Gro.
EH12: Edin ... 7F **19**
Forrester Pk. Loan
EH12: Edin ... 7F **19**
Forrester Rd. EH12: Edin ... 4F **19**
Forrest Hill EH1: Edin ... 6E **4** (4H **21**)
Forrest Rd. EH1: Edin ... 6E **4** (4H **21**)
Forteviot Ho. EH17: Edin ... 4D **34**
Forth Bridge ... **1J 7**
Forth Ct. EH32: Port S ... 3J **15**
Forth Gdns. EH32: Port S ... 3J **15**
Forth Gro. EH32: Port S ... 3J **15**
Forth Ind. Est. EH5: Edin ... 2H **11**
Fort Ho. EH6: Newh ... 4D **12**
Forth Pk. EH30: Dalm ... 2J **7**
Forth Pl. EH30: S Q'fry ... 1E **6**
Forth Rd. Bri., The
EH30: S Q'fry ... 1F **7**
Forth St. EH1: Edin ... 1F **5** (2H **21**)
Forth Ter. EH30: Dalm ... 2J **7**
Forth Vw. Av. EH14: Cur ... 1H **37**
Forthview Av. EH21: Wall ... 3J **25**
Forthview Ct. EH33: Tran ... 1H **27**
Forth Vw. Cres. EH14: Cur ... 7B **30**
EH22: Dan ... 4H **35**
Forthview Cres. *EH21: Wall* ... *3J* ***25***
(off Drummohr Av.)
Forthview Dr. EH21: Wall ... 3J **25**
Forth Vw. Loan EH22: Dalk ... 3F **43**
Forth Vw. Pl. EH22: Dalk ... 3F **43**
Forth Vw. Rd. EH14: Cur ... 1H **37**
Forthview Rd. EH4: Edin ... 1A **20**
Forthview Ter. EH4: Edin ... 1K **19**
EH21: Wall ... 3K **25**
Forthview Wlk. EH33: Tran ... 1H **27**
Forth Wynd EH32: Port S ... 3J **15**
Fort Kinnaird EH15: Edin ... 7J **23**
Fort Retail Pk. EH15: Edin ... 7H **23**
Foulis Cres. EH14: J Grn ... 6F **31**
Foundry La. EH20: Loan ... 5C **40**
(not continuous)
FOUNTAINBRIDGE ... **6A 4 (5F 21)**
Fountainbridge
EH3: Edin ... 7A **4** (5E **20**)
Fountainbridge Sq.
EH3: Edin ... 7A **4** (5F **21**)
Fountain Cl. EH1: Edin ... 4G **5**
Fountainhall Rd. EH9: Edin ... 1J **33**
Fountainpark ... **5D 20**
Fountain Pl. EH20: Loan ... 5B **40**
Fourth Gait EH14: Cur ... 5A **30**
Fourth St. EH22: Newt ... 1C **48**
(not continuous)
Fowler Cres. EH20: Loan ... 5D **40**
Fowler's Ct. EH32: Pres ... 5E **14**
Fowler Sq. *EH20: Loan* ... *5D* ***40***
(off Fowler Cres.)
Fowler St. EH33: Tran ... 1G **27**
Fowler Ter. EH11: Edin ... 6D **20**
Fox Covert Av. EH12: Edin ... 2G **19**
Fox Covert Gro. EH12: Edin ... 2G **19**
Fox Spring Cres. EH10: Edin ... 5E **32**
Fox Spring Ri. EH10: Edin ... 5E **32**
Fox St. EH6: Leith ... 5G **13**
Fraser Av. EH5: Edin ... 5K **11**
Fraser Cres. EH5: Edin ... 5K **11**
Fraser Gdns. EH5: Edin ... 5K **11**
Fraser Gro. EH5: Edin ... 5K **11**
Fraser La. EH26: Mil B ... 4F **45**
Frederick St.
EH2: Edin ... 2C **4** (2G **21**)
Freelands Cotts. EH28: Rat ... 1F **29**
Freelands Rd. EH28: Rat ... 1D **28**
Friarton Gdns. EH26: Pen ... 2A **50**
Frogston Av. EH10: Edin ... 7F **33**
Frogston Gdns. EH10: Edin ... 7F **33**
Frogston Gro. EH10: Edin ... 7G **33**
Frogston Rd. E. EH16: Edin ... 1J **39**
EH17: Edin ... 1J **39**
Frogston Rd. W. EH10: Edin ... 7F **33**
Frogston Ter. EH10: Edin ... 7G **33**
Fruitmarket Gallery ... **3F 5**
Furcheons Pk. EH8: Edin ... 3E **22**

G

Gabriel's Rd. EH2: Edin ... 2F **5**
EH3: Edin ... 1F **21**
Gala Bingo
Edinburgh, Moray Pk. ... **1A 22**
Edinburgh, West Granton Rd.
... **3H 11**
Wester Hailes ... **4F 31**
Galachlawshot EH10: Edin ... 6G **33**
Galachlawside EH10: Edin ... 7G **33**
Galadale EH22: Newt ... 7C **42**
(not continuous)
Galadale Cres. EH22: Newt ... 7C **42**
Galadale Dr. EH22: Newt ... 7C **42**
Gallolee, The EH13: Edin ... 6B **32**
Galloway's Entry
EH8: Edin ... 3J **5** (3K **21**)
Galt Av. EH21: Muss ... 2H **25**
Galt Cres. EH21: Muss ... 3J **25**
Galt Dr. EH21: Muss ... 2J **25**
Galt Rd. EH21: Muss ... 3J **25**
Galt Ter. EH21: Muss ... 3J **25**
Gamekeepers Loan EH4: Cram ... 5J **9**
Gamekeeper's Pk. EH4: Cram ... 5J **9**
Gamekeeper's Rd. EH4: Cram ... 6J **9**
Gardener's Cl. EH32: Cock ... 3G **15**
Gardener's Wlk. EH26: Pen ... 1A **50**
Garden Ter. EH4: Edin ... 6B **10**
Gardiner Cres. EH32: Pres ... 6F **15**
Gardiner Gro. EH4: Edin ... 1K **19**
Gardiner Pl. EH22: Newt ... 7C **42**
Gardiner Rd. EH4: Edin ... 1K **19**
EH32: Pres ... 6E **14**
Gardiner's Pl. EH33: Tran ... 1G **27**
Gardiner Ter. EH4: Edin ... 2K **19**
EH32: Pres ... 7E **14**
Gardner's Cres.
EH3: Edin ... 6A **4** (4F **21**)
Garscube Ter. EH12: Edin ... 3B **20**
Garvald Ct. EH16: Edin ... 6B **34**
Gateside Rd. EH29: Kltn ... 2A **16**
GAYFIELD ... **1F 5 (1H 21)**
Gayfield Cl. EH1: Edin ... 1J **21**
Gayfield Pl. EH7: Edin ... 1J **21**
Gayfield Pl. La. EH1: Edin ... 1J **21**
Gayfield Sq.
EH1: Edin ... 1G **5** (1J **21**)

A-Z Edinburgh 67

Gayfield St. EH1: Edin 1J 21
Gayfield St. La. *EH1: Edin* . . .1H 21
   (off Gayfield St.)
Gaynor Av. EH20: Loan 5A 40
Geddes Entry EH1: Edin 4F 5
Gentiles Entry
   EH8: Edin 4J 5 (3K 21)
George IV Bri.
   EH1: Edin 4E 4 (3H 21)
George Av. EH20: Loan 5B 40
George Cres. EH20: Loan 5C 40
George Dr. EH20: Loan 5B 40
George Pl. EH15: Port 2G 23
George Sq. EH8: Edin . . .7F 5 (5H 21)
George Sq. La.
   EH8: Edin 7E 4 (5H 21)
George St. EH2: Edin . . .3B 4 (3F 21)
George Ter. EH20: Loan 5B 40
George Wlk. EH33: Tran 3G 27
George Way EH33: Tran 2G 27
Georgian House 3A 4
Gibbs Entry EH8: Edin 6G 5
Gibraltar Ct. EH22: Dalk 2D 42
Gibraltar Gdns. EH22: Dalk . . .2C 42
Gibraltar Rd. EH22: Dalk 2C 42
Gibraltar Ter. EH22: Dalk 2D 42
Gibson Dr. EH22: Dalk 2E 42
Gibson St. EH7: Edin 6D 12
Gibson Ter. EH11: Edin 5E 20
Gifford Pk. EH8: Edin . . .7G 5 (5J 21)
Gilberstoun EH15: Edin 5J 23
Gilberstoun Brig EH15: Edin . .6K 23
Gilberstoun Loan
   EH15: Edin 6K 23
Gilberstoun Pl. EH15: Edin . . .6K 23
Gilberstoun Wynd
   EH15: Edin 6K 23
Giles St. EH6: Leith 5E 12
Gillespie Cres. EH10: Edin 5F 21
Gillespie Pl.
   EH3: Edin 7B 4 (5F 21)
Gillespie Rd. EH13: Edin 6H 31
Gillespie St.
   EH3: Edin 7A 4 (5F 21)
Gillsland Gro. EH10: Edin 7D 20
Gillsland Pk. EH10: Edin 7D 20
Gillsland Rd. EH10: Edin 7D 20
GILMERTON 6E 34
Gilmerton Dykes Av.
   EH17: Edin 7C 34
Gilmerton Dykes Cres.
   EH17: Edin 6C 34
Gilmerton Dykes Dr.
   EH17: Edin 6D 34
Gilmerton Dykes Gdns.
   EH17: Edin 6C 34
Gilmerton Dykes Gro.
   EH17: Edin 6C 34
Gilmerton Dykes Loan
   EH17: Edin 7D 34
Gilmerton Dykes Pl.
   EH17: Edin 7D 34
Gilmerton Dykes Rd.
   EH17: Edin 1D 40
Gilmerton Dykes St.
   EH17: Edin 7C 34
Gilmerton Dykes Ter.
   EH17: Edin 7D 34
Gilmerton Dykes Vw.
   EH17: Edin 7D 34
GILMERTON JUNC. 1G 41
Gilmerton Pl. EH17: Edin 7D 34
Gilmerton Rd. EH16: Edin 2A 34
   EH17: Edin 2A 34
   EH18: Las 7F 35
   EH22: Dalk 2K 41
Gilmerton Sta. Rd.
   EH17: Edin 2E 40
Gilmore Pk. EH3: Edin 5E 20
Gilmore Pl. EH3: Edin . . .7A 4 (6E 20)
Gilmore Pl. La.
   EH3: Edin 7A 4 (5F 21)
Gilmour Rd. EH16: Edin 1K 33
Gilmour's Cl. EH1: Edin 5D 4
Gilmour's Entry
   EH8: Edin 6H 5 (4J 21)
Gilmour St. EH8: Edin . . .6H 5 (4J 21)
Girdle Wlk. EH32: Pres 6C 14
Gladstone Pl. EH6: Edin 6G 13

Gladstone's Land 4E 4
Gladstone Ter. EH9: Edin 6J 21
Glanville Pl. EH3: Edin 1A 4
Glasgow Rd. EH12: Edin 6H 17
   EH28: Ing, Nbdge, Rat S
   .5B 16
Glaskhill Ter. EH26: Pen 1C 50
Glebe, The EH4: Cram 4J 9
   EH29: Kltn 1A 16
   EH30: Dalm 3K 7
Glebe Gdns. EH12: Edin 5G 19
   EH32: Pres 6D 14
Glebe Gro. EH12: Edin 5F 19
Glebe Pl. EH18: Las 4F 41
Glebe Rd. EH12: Edin 5F 19
Glebe St. EH22: Dalk 2C 42
Glebe Ter. EH12: Edin 5F 19
Glenallan Dr. EH16: Edin 2B 34
Glenallan Loan EH16: Edin . . .2B 34
Glenalmond Ct. *EH11: Edin* . . .2F 31
   (off Sighthill Bank)
GLENBROOK 5A 36
Glenbrook EH14: Bal 5A 36
Glenbrook Rd. EH14: Bal 5A 36
Glencairn Cres. EH12: Edin . . .4D 20
Glencoe Path EH32: Pres 5E 14
Glencorse Rd. EH26: Edin 7J 11
Glencorse Pk. EH26: Mil B 6G 45
Glencross Gdns. EH26: Pen . . .2A 50
Glendevon Av. EH12: Edin 5K 19
Glendevon Gdns. EH12: Edin . .5J 19
Glendevon Gro. EH12: Edin . . .5K 19
Glendevon Pk. EH12: Edin 5K 19
Glendevon Pl. EH12: Edin 5K 19
Glendevon Rd. EH12: Edin 6K 19
Glendevon Ter. EH12: Edin 5K 19
Glendinning Cres.
   EH16: Edin 4A 34
Glendinning Dr. EH29: Kltn . . .7E 6
Glendinning Pl. EH29: Kltn . . .7E 6
Glendinning Rd. EH29: Kltn . . .7E 6
Glendinning Way EH29: Kltn . .1A 16
Glenesk Cres. EH22: Dalk 3B 42
Glenfinlas St.
   EH3: Edin 3A 4 (3F 21)
Glengarry Ter. EH32: Pres 5E 14
Glengyle Ter.
   EH3: Edin 7B 4 (5F 21)
Glenisla Gdns. EH9: Edin 1H 33
Glenisla Gdns. La.
   EH9: Edin 1H 33
Glenlea Cotts. EH11: Edin 7A 20
Glenlee Av. EH8: Edin 3C 22
Glenlee Gdns. EH8: Edin 3C 22
Glenlockhart Bank
   EH14: Edin 3B 32
Glenlockhart Rd. EH10: Edin . .3B 32
   EH14: Edin 3B 32
Glenlockhart Valley
   EH14: Edin 2B 32
Glennie Gdns. EH33: Tran 2H 27
Glenogle Ho. EH3: Edin 1F 21
Glenogle Pl. EH3: Edin 1F 21
Glenogle Rd. EH3: Edin 1F 21
Glenogle Swimming Cen. 1F 21
Glenogle Ter. EH3: Edin 7A 12
Glenorchy Ter. EH9: Edin 7K 21
Glenpark EH14: Bal 4B 36
Glen Pl. EH26: Pen 1C 50
Glen St. EH3: Edin 6C 4 (5G 21)
Glenure Loan EH4: Edin 2F 19
Glenvarloch Cres.
   EH16: Edin 3B 34
Glen Vw. EH26: Pen 1C 50
Glen Vw. Ct. EH23: Gore 6E 48
Glen Vw. Cres. EH23: Gore . . .6E 48
Glen Vw. Pl. EH23: Gore 7E 48
Glen Vw. Rd. EH23: Gore 6E 48
Glen Vw. Wlk. EH23: Gore 7F 49
GLIMERTON DYKES 7D 34
Gloucester La.
   EH3: Edin 1A 4 (2F 21)
Gloucester Pl.
   EH3: Edin 1A 4 (2F 21)
Gloucester Sq.
   EH3: Edin 1A 4 (2F 21)
Gloucester St.
   EH3: Edin 1A 4 (2F 21)
Goff Av. EH7: Edin 1F 23

GOGAR 6K 17
Gogarbank EH12: Edin 2K 29
Gogar Bri. Rd. EH12: Edin A . .4G 17
Gogarburn Stop (NET)
   (Due to open 2011) 6K 17
GOGAR JUNC. 5A 18
Gogarloch Bank EH12: Edin . . .6D 18
Gogarloch Haugh
   EH12: Edin 6D 18
Gogarloch Muir EH12: Edin . . .6D 18
Gogarloch Rd. EH12: Edin 6C 18
Gogarloch Syke EH12: Edin . . .6C 18
Gogar Mains Farm Rd.
   EH12: Edin 4J 17
Gogar Pk. Curling Rink 6A 18
Gogar Sta. Rd. EH12: Edin 6K 17
   EH14: Cur 2B 30
Gogarstone Rd. EH12: Ing 6H 17
GOLDENACRE 6A 12
Goldenacre 6A 12
Goldenacre Ter. EH3: Edin 6A 12
Golf Course Rd. EH19: Bonn . .5H 41
Golf Dr. EH32: Port S 3J 15
Goodtrees Gdns. EH17: Edin . .4D 34
GOOSE GREEN 1F 25
Goose Grn. Av. EH21: Muss . . .1F 25
Goose Grn. Bri. EH21: Muss . .1E 24
Goose Grn. Ct. EH21: Muss . . .1F 25
Goose Grn. Cres.
   EH21: Muss 1F 25
Goose Grn. Pl. EH21: Muss . . .1F 25
Goose Grn. Rd. EH21: Muss . . .1F 25
Gordon Av. EH19: Bonn 7F 41
Gordon Ct. EH6: Edin 6F 13
Gordon Loan EH12: Edin 4G 19
Gordon Rd. EH12: Edin 4G 19
Gordon St. EH6: Edin 6E 12
   EH22: East 6E 42
Gordon Ter. EH16: Edin 2A 34
Gore Av. EH23: Gore 6E 48
GOREBRIDGE 7F 49
Gorebridge Leisure Cen. 6E 48
GORGIE 7C 20
Gorgie Pk. Rd. EH11: Edin 6B 20
Gorgie Rd. EH11: Edin 7B 20
   EH11: Edin 1J 31
Gorton Av. EH18: Las 3D 46
Gorton Loan EH24: Rose 4D 46
Gorton Pl. EH24: Rose 4D 46
Gorton Rd. EH24: Rose 4D 46
Gorton Wlk. EH24: Rose 4D 46
Gosford Pl. EH6: Edin 5C 12
Gosford Rd. EH32: Port S 3G 15
Gosford Wlk. *EH32: Port S* . . .3G 15
   (off Gosford Rd.)
Goshen Farm Steading
   EH21: Muss 1K 25
Gospel Wynd EH18: Las 4G 41
Gote La. EH30: S Q'fry 1H 7
Gowanhill Farm Rd.
   EH14: Cur 7H 29
Gowkley Moss Rdbt.
   EH26: Mil B 3H 45
Gowkshill Farm Cotts.
   EH23: Gore 3D 48
Gracefield Ct. EH21: Muss 2D 24
GRACEMOUNT 6B 34
Gracemount Av. EH16: Edin . . .5B 34
Gracemount Bus. Pav.
   EH16: Edin 7C 34
Gracemount Dr. EH16: Edin . . .6B 34
Gracemount Leisure Cen. 7B 34
Gracemount Pl. EH16: Edin . . .6B 34
Gracemount Rd. EH16: Edin . . .7A 34
Gracemount Sq. EH16: Edin . . .5B 34
Graham's Rd. EH26: Mil B 5F 45
Graham St. EH6: Edin 5D 12
Granby Rd. EH16: Edin 1K 33
Grandfield EH6: Newh 5B 12
Grandville EH6: Newh 4B 12
GRANGE, THE EH9: Edin 6J 21
Grange Ct. EH9: Edin 6J 21
   (off Causewayside)
Grange Cres. EH9: Edin 7H 21
Grange Cres. E. EH32: Pres . . .6D 14
Grange Cres. W. EH32: Pres . . .6D 14
Grange Cricket Ground 1E 20
Grange Gro. EH32: Pres 6D 14
Grange Loan EH9: Edin 7G 21

Grange Loan Gdns.
   EH9: Edin 7H 21
Grange Rd. EH9: Edin 6H 21
   EH32: Pres 6D 14
Grange Ter. EH9: Edin 1H 33
Grannies Pk. Ind. Est.
   EH22: Dalk 1C 42
Grannus M. EH21: Muss 3F 25
Grant Av. EH13: Edin 6J 31
GRANTON 4H 11
Granton Cres. EH5: Edin 4H 11
Granton Gdns. EH5: Edin 4J 11
Granton Gro. EH5: Edin 4J 11
Granton Mains Av. EH4: Edin . .4F 11
Granton Mains Bank
   EH4: Edin 4F 11
Granton Mains Brae
   EH4: Edin 5F 11
Granton Mains Ct.
   EH4: Edin 5G 11
Granton Mains E. EH4: Edin . . .4G 11
Granton Mains Gait
   EH4: Edin 4F 11
Granton Mains Va.
   EH4: Edin 4F 11
Granton Mains Wynd
   EH4: Edin 4F 11
Granton Medway EH5: Edin . . .4H 11
Granton Mill Cres. EH4: Edin . .4F 11
Granton Mill Dr. EH4: Edin 4F 11
Granton Mill March
   EH4: Edin 5E 10
Granton Mill Pk. EH4: Edin . . .5E 10
Granton Mill Pl. EH4: Edin 4E 10
Granton Mill Rd. EH4: Edin . . .4E 10
Granton Mill W. EH4: Edin 5E 10
Granton Pk. Av. EH5: Edin 3H 11
Granton Pier EH5: Edin 3J 11
Granton Pl. EH5: Edin 4J 11
Granton Rd. EH5: Edin 4J 11
Granton Sq. EH5: Edin 3J 11
Granton Ter. EH5: Edin 4J 11
Granton Vw. EH5: Edin 4J 11
Grant Rd. EH32: Pres 5E 14
Grantully Pl. EH9: Edin 7K 21
Granville Ter. EH10: Edin 6E 20
Grassmarket
   EH1: Edin 5D 4 (4G 21)
Gray's Ct. EH8: Edin . . .6G 5 (4J 21)
Graysknowe *EH14: Edin* 2K 31
   (off Inglis Grn. Rd.)
Grays Loan EH10: Edin 7D 20
Gt. Cannon Bank EH15: Port . . .2G 23
Gt. Carleton Pl. EH16: Edin . . .1G 35
Gt. Carleton Sq. EH16: Edin . . .1G 35
Great Junc. St. EH6: Edin 5E 12
Gt. King St.
   EH3: Edin 1C 4 (2G 21)
Gt. Michael Cl. *EH6: Newh* 3C 12
   (off Lindsay Rd.)
Gt. Michael Ri. EH6: Newh 4C 12
Gt. Michael Sq. *EH6: Newh* . . .3C 12
   (off Newhaven Main St.)
Gt. Stuart St.
   EH3: Edin 3A 4 (3E 20)
   (not continuous)
Green, The EH4: Edin 6C 10
   EH14: Bal 5F 37
   EH20: Loan 4C 40
Greenacre EH14: Edin 4F 31
GREENBANK 4D 32
Greenbank Av. EH10: Edin 3E 32
Greenbank Cres. EH10: Edin . .5D 32
Greenbank Dr. EH10: Edin 4C 32
Greenbank Gdns.
   EH10: Edin 4D 32
Greenbank Gro. EH10: Edin . . .4D 32
Greenbank La. EH10: Edin 3D 32
Greenbank Loan EH10: Edin . . .4D 32
Greenbank Pk. EH10: Edin 4D 32
Greenbank Pl. EH10: Edin 3E 32
Greenbank Ri. EH10: Edin 5D 32
Greenbank Row EH10: Edin . . .4D 32
Greenbank Ter. EH10: Edin 3E 32
Greendale Pk. EH4: Edin 6D 10
GREENDYKES 1F 35
Greendykes Av. EH16: Edin . . .1F 35
Greendykes Dr. EH16: Edin . . .1F 35

Greendykes Gdns.
EH16: Edin 1F 35
Greendykes Ho. EH16: Edin 1F 35
Greendykes Loan
EH16: Edin 1F 35
Greendykes Rd. EH16: Edin 1E 34
Greendykes Ter. EH16: Edin . . .1F 35
GREENEND 4C 34
Greenend Dr. EH17: Edin 4C 34
Greenend Gdns.
EH17: Edin 4C 34
Greenend Gro. EH17: Edin 4C 34
Greenfield Cres. EH14: Bal . . .5E 36
Greenfield Pk. EH21: Muss . . .5D 24
Greenfield Rd. EH14: Bal 5E 36
Greenhall Cres. EH23: Gore . .5E 48
Greenhall Rd. EH23: Gore 5E 48
GREENHILL 7F 21
Greenhill Ct. EH9: Edin 6F 21
Greenhill Gdns. EH10: Edin . . .6F 21
Greenhill Pk. EH10: Edin 7F 21
EH26: Pen 2B 50
Greenhill Ter. EH10: Edin 6F 21
Green La. EH18: Las 5F 41
Greenlaw Gro. EH26: Mil B . . .5E 44
Greenlaw Hedge EH13: Edin . .4C 32
GREENLAW MAINS 6E 44
Greenlaw Rig EH13: Edin 4C 32
Greenmantle Loan
EH16: Edin 3B 34
Greenpark EH17: Edin 4C 34
Greens Health & Fitness
Edinburgh 1K 31
GREENSIDE 1G 5 (2J 21)
Greenside End EH1: Edin 1G 5
Greenside La.
EH1: Edin 1G 5 (2J 21)
Greenside Pl. EH1: Edin 1G 5
EH24: Rose 4D 46
Greenside Row
EH1: Edin 2G 5 (2J 21)
Green St. EH7: Edin 1H 21
Greenway, The EH14: Edin . . .3G 31
(Hailesland Gro.)
EH14: Edin 4F 31
(Murrayburn Pl.)
Greyfriars EH1: Edin 5E 4
Greyfriars Bobby 5E 4
Greyfriars EH1: Edin 5E 4
Greyfriars Tolbooth & Highland Kirk
. . . . .5E 4
Grey School Cnr. EH32: Pres . .6D 14
Grierson Av. EH5: Edin 4K 11
Grierson Cres. EH5: Edin 4K 11
Grierson Gdns. EH5: Edin 4K 11
Grierson Rd. EH5: Edin 4J 11
Grierson Sq. EH5: Edin 4K 11
Grierson Vs. EH5: Edin 4K 11
Grieve Ct. EH26: Pen 7D 44
Grigor Av. EH4: Edin 7G 11
Grigor Dr. EH4: Edin 7G 11
Grigor Gdns. EH4: Edin 7G 11
Grigor Ter. EH4: Edin 7G 11
Grindlay St.
EH3: Edin 5B 4 (4F 21)
Grindlay St. Ct.
EH3: Edin 6B 4 (4F 21)
Groathill Av. EH4: Edin 1A 20
Groathill Gdns. E. EH4: Edin . .1A 20
Groathill Gdns. W.
EH4: Edin 1A 20
Groathill Loan EH4: Edin 7F 11
Groathill Rd. Nth. EH4: Edin . .6F 11
Groathill Rd. Sth. EH4: Edin . .5F 11
Grosvenor Cres. EH12: Edin . . .4D 20
Grosvenor Gdns. EH12: Edin . .4D 20
Grosvenor St. EH12: Edin 4E 20
Grove, The EH21: Muss 3G 25
Grove End EH18: Las 5H 41
Grove Pl. EH14: J Grn 6F 31
Grove St. EH3: Edin 7A 4 (4E 20)
EH21: Muss 3F 25
Grove Ter. EH3: Edin 4E 20
Grundieswell Rd.
EH17: Edin 6E 34
Guardianswood EH12: Edin . . .4A 20
Guardwell Cres. EH17: Edin . . .5C 34
Guardwell Glen EH17: Edin . . .5D 34

Gullan's Cl.
EH8: Edin 4G 5 (3J 21)
(not continuous)
Gunnet Ct. EH4: Edin 5D 10
Guthrie St. EH1: Edin . .5F 5 (4H 21)
GYLE, THE 5C 18
Gyle Av. EH12: Edin 6B 18
Gyle Centre Stop (NET)
(Due to open 2011) 6B 18
Gylemuir Rd. EH12: Edin 5E 18
Gyle Pk. Gdns. EH12: Edin . . .5C 18
Gyle Rdbt. EH12: Edin 6B 18
Gyle Shop. Cen.
EH12: Edin 5B 18

H

Haddington Pl. EH7: Edin 1J 21
Haddington Rd. EH21: Muss . . .2J 25
EH33: Tran 2J 27
Haddon's Ct. EH8: Edin 6G 5
Hailes App. EH13: Edin 5J 31
Hailes Av. EH13: Edin 4J 31
Hailes Cres. EH13: Edin 5J 31
Hailes Gdns. EH13: Edin 5H 31
Hailes Gro. EH13: Edin 5J 31
Hailesland Gdns.
EH14: Edin 3G 31
(not continuous)
Hailesland Gro. EH14: Edin . . .3G 31
Hailesland Pk. EH14: Edin 3G 31
Hailesland Pl. EH14: Edin 3G 31
Hailesland Rd. EH14: Edin 3F 31
Hailes Pk. EH13: Edin 5H 31
Hailes St. EH3: Edin 7B 4 (5F 21)
Hailes Ter. EH13: Edin 5J 31
Hainburn Pk. EH10: Edin 7D 32
Hallcroft Cl. EH28: Rat 2C 28
Hallcroft Cres. EH28: Rat 2C 28
Hallcroft Gdns. EH28: Rat 2C 28
Hallcroft Grn. EH28: Rat 2C 28
Hallcroft Neuk EH28: Rat 2C 28
Hallcroft Pk. EH28: Rat 2C 28
Hallcroft Ri. EH28: Rat 2C 28
Hallhead Rd. EH16: Edin 2K 33
Hall Ter. EH12: Edin 5F 19
(off Corstorphine High St.)
Hallyards Cotts. EH29: Kltn . . .3B 16
Hallyards Rd. EH28: Ing 5D 16
EH29: Kltn 3B 16
Halmyre St. EH6: Edin 7E 12
Hamburgh Pl. EH6: Newh 4D 12
Hamilton Cres. EH22: Newt . . .7D 42
Hamilton Dr. EH15: Port 4F 23
Hamilton Dr. W. EH15: Port . . .4F 23
Hamilton Folly M.
EH8: Edin 7H 5 (5J 21)
Hamilton Gdns. EH15: Port 4F 23
Hamilton Gro. EH15: Port 4F 23
Hamilton Pk. EH15: Port 3F 23
Hamilton Pl.
EH3: Edin 1A 4 (1F 21)
Hamilton's Cl. EH30: S Q'fry . . .1G 7
Hamilton Ter. EH15: Port 3G 23
Hammermen's Entry
EH8: Edin 4H 5 (3J 21)
Hampton Pl. EH12: Edin 4C 20
Hampton Ter. EH12: Edin 4C 20
Hanover St.
EH2: Edin 2D 4 (2G 21)
Harbour Pl. EH32: Port S 3H 15
Harbour La. EH30: S Q'fry 1G 7
(off High St.)
Harbour Pl. EH15: Port 2G 23
Harbour Rd. EH15: Port 2G 23
EH21: Muss 2C 24
Harbour Vw. EH21: Muss 2D 24
HARDENGREEN 5A 42
Hardengreen Bus. Pk.
EH22: Dalk 4A 42
Hardengreen Ind. Est.
EH22: Dalk 4A 42
Hardengreen La. EH22: Dalk . .4A 42
Hardengreen Rdbt.
EH22: Dalk 6A 42
Harden Pl. EH11: Edin 6D 20

Hardwell Cl.
EH8: Edin 6H 5 (5J 21)
Harelaw EH22: Dalk 4K 35
Harelaw Rd. EH13: Edin 6J 31
Hares Cl. EH32: Cock 3G 15
Harewood Cres. EH16: Edin . . .7E 22
Harewood Dr. EH16: Edin 7E 22
Harewood Rd. EH16: Edin 7E 22
Harkenburn Gdns.
EH26: Pen 1A 50
Harkness Cres. EH33: Tran . . .2H 27
Harlaw Bank EH14: Bal 4E 36
Harlaw Gait EH14: Bal 4F 37
Harlaw Gro. EH26: Pen 2B 50
Harlaw Hill EH32: Pres 5D 14
Harlawhill Gdns. EH32: Pres . .5E 14
Harlaw March EH14: Bal 5F 37
Harlaw Rd. EH14: Bal, Cur 4K 36
Harmony Ct. EH19: Bonn 6K 41
Harmony Cres. EH19: Bonn . . .6K 41
(not continuous)
Harmony St. EH19: Bonn 6K 41
Harmony Wlk. EH19: Bonn 6K 41
Harnes Ct. EH20: Loan 6C 40
Harper's Brae EH26: Pen 7F 45
Harrismith Pl. EH7: Edin 1A 22
Harrison Gdns. EH11: Edin 7C 20
Harrison La. EH11: Edin 6D 20
Harrison Pl. EH11: Edin 7C 20
Harrison Rd. EH11: Edin 6D 20
Hartington Gdns. EH10: Edin . .6E 20
Hartington Pl. EH10: Edin 6E 20
Hart St. EH1: Edin 1F 5 (1H 21)
Hart St. La. EH1: Edin 1F 5
Harvest Dr. EH28: Nbdge 6B 16
Harvesters Way EH14: Edin . . .4F 31
Harvest Rd.
EH28: Nbdge, Rat S 6A 16
Harvest Wynd EH28: Rat S 6C 16
Harvieston Vs. EH23: Gore 7F 49
Hastie's Cl. EH1: Edin 5F 5
Hatton Pl. EH9: Edin 6H 21
Hatton Sports Club 6C 28
Haugh Pk. EH14: Edin 2J 31
Haugh St. EH4: Edin . .1A 4 (1F 21)
Hawes Brae EH30: S Q'fry 1J 7
Hawk Cres. EH22: Dalk 2G 43
Hawkhead Cres. EH16: Edin . . .4A 34
Hawkhead Gro. EH16: Edin 4A 34
Hawkhill EH7: Edin 7G 13
Hawkhill Av. EH7: Edin 7F 13
Hawkhill Cl. EH7: Edin 7F 13
Hawkhill Ct. EH7: Edin 7G 13
Hawkins Ter. EH26: Pen 6F 45
Hawmuirside EH14: Edin 3K 31
Hawthorn Bank EH30: S Q'fry . .1G 7
Hawthornbank EH32: Cock 3F 15
Hawthornbank La. EH4: Edin . .3E 20
Hawthornbank Pl.
EH6: Newh 4C 12
Hawthornbank Ter.
EH6: Newh 4D 12
Hawthorn Bldgs. EH4: Edin 3E 20
(off Hawthornbank La.)
Hawthorn Cres. EH22: May 5F 43
Hawthornden Av.
EH19: Bonn 7G 41
Hawthornden Gdns.
EH19: Bonn 6G 41
Hawthornden Pl. EH7: Edin 7D 12
Hawthorn Gdns. EH20: Loan . . .4B 40
Hawthorn Pl. EH17: Edin 6E 34
Hawthorn Ter. EH4: Edin 3D 20
EH32: Cock 4F 15
Hawthornvale EH6: Newh 4C 12
Hay Av. EH16: Edin 7F 23
Hay Dr. EH16: Edin 6G 23
Hayfield EH12: Edin 3C 18
Hay Gdns. EH16: Edin 6F 23
Haymarket EH12: Edin 4E 20
Haymarket Station (Rail)
(Due to open 2011) 4D 20
Haymarket Ter. EH12: Edin 4D 20
Haymarket Yards
EH12: Edin 4D 20
Hay Pl. EH16: Edin 7F 23
Hay Rd. EH16: Edin 7F 23

Hays Community Bus. Cen.
EH16: Edin 7F 23
Hay Ter. EH16: Edin 7F 23
Hazelbank Ter. EH11: Edin 7C 20
Hazeldean Ter. EH16: Edin 2B 34
Hazel Dr. EH19: Bonn 7H 41
Hazel La. EH20: Loan 6J 39
Hazelwood Gro. EH16: Edin . . .2C 34
Headrigg Row EH16: Edin 3B 34
Headrig Rd. EH30: S Q'fry 1C 6
Heart of Midlothian FC 5C 20
Hedge Row EH20: Loan 6J 39
Hedges, The EH33: Tran 3G 27
Helen's Wlk. EH6: Newh 4D 12
(off Portland St.)
Henderland Rd. EH12: Edin 4B 20
Henderson Gdns. EH6: Leith . . .5E 12
EH33: Tran 2H 27
Henderson Pl. La.
EH3: Edin 1G 21
Henderson Row EH3: Edin 1F 21
Henderson St. EH6: Leith 5E 12
Henderson Ter. EH11: Edin 6D 20
Henry Pl. EH8: Edin 5K 21
Henry Ross Pl. EH30: S Q'fry . . .1G 7
Henry St. EH8: Edin 5K 21
Hepburn Dr. EH22: Dalk 3E 42
Hercus Loan EH21: Muss 2D 24
(not continuous)
Herd Ter. EH20: Loan 6A 40
Heriot Bri. EH1: Edin . .5D 4 (4G 21)
Heriot Cross
EH1: Edin 5D 4 (4G 21)
Heriot Hill Ter. EH7: Edin 7B 12
Heriot Mt. EH1: Edin 6H 5 (4J 21)
Heriot Pl. EH3: Edin 6D 4 (4G 21)
Heriot Row EH3: Edin . . .2B 4 (2F 21)
Heriots Rugby Club 6A 12
Heriot-Watt Research Pk.
EH14: Cur 4B 30
Heriot-Watt University
Riccarton Campus 5A 30
Hermand Cres. EH11: Edin 7C 20
Hermand St. EH11: Edin 7B 20
Hermand Ter. EH11: Edin 7B 20
HERMISTON 3B 30
Hermiston (Park & Ride) 3C 30
Hermiston Ct. EH11: Edin 2F 31
(off Sighthill Bank)
HERMISTON GAIT INTERCHANGE
. . . . .1C 30
Hermiston Ga. Retail Pk.
EH11: Edin 2C 30
Hermiston Ho. Rd.
EH12: Edin 2K 29
EH14: Cur 2K 29
Hermiston Wlk. EH14: Cur 4B 30
Hermitage Dr. EH10: Edin 3F 33
Hermitage Gdns. EH10: Edin . .3F 33
Hermitage House Vis. Cen. 3F 33
Hermitage Pk. EH6: Edin 7F 13
Hermitage Pk. Gro.
EH6: Edin 7G 13
Hermitage Pk. Lea
EH6: Edin 7G 13
Hermitage Pk. Sth.
EH6: Edin 7G 13
Hermitage Ter. EH6: Edin 6F 13
Hermitage Ter. EH10: Edin 2F 33
Hermits Cft. EH8: Edin 7J 5
Heron Pl. EH5: Edin 3J 11
Hesperus Crossway
EH5: Edin 3J 11
Heugh, The EH33: Tran 1G 27
(not continuous)
Hibernian FC 1A 22
Higginson Loan EH22: May 1G 49
High Buckstone EH10: Edin . . .6G 33
Highlea Circ. EH14: Bal 6D 36
Highlea Gro. EH14: Bal 5D 36
High Pk. Ri. EH26: Pen 3D 50
High Riggs EH3: Edin . . .6B 4 (4F 21)
High School Wynd EH1: Edin . . .4G 5
High School Yards
EH1: Edin 5G 5 (4J 21)
High St. EH1: Edin 4E 4 (3H 21)
EH18: Las 4G 41
EH19: Bonn 5H 41

High St. EH20: Loan 6C **40**
(not continuous)
EH21: Muss 2E **24**
EH22: Dalk 2C **42**
EH26: Pen 3D **50**
EH29: Kltn 2B **16**
EH30: S Q'fry 1G **7**
EH32: Cock 3F **15**
EH32: Pres 6C **14**
EH33: Tran 2H **27**
High Way, The EH8: Edin 3E **22**
Hillcoat Loan EH15: Port 2G **23**
Hillcoat Pl. EH15: Port 2G **23**
Hill Ct. EH30: S Q'fry 1G **7**
Hillend EH10: Edin 3G **39**
Hillend Pl. *EH8: Edin* 2C **22**
(off London Rd.)
Hill Head EH19: Bonn 5H **41**
Hillhead Ct. EH19: Bonn 5H **41**
Hillhouse Rd. EH4: Edin 7C **10**
Hillpark Av. EH4: Edin 7C **10**
Hillpark Brae EH4: Edin 1H **19**
Hillpark Ct. EH4: Edin 7C **10**
Hillpark Cres. EH4: Edin 1H **19**
Hillpark Dr. EH4: Edin 7C **10**
Hillpark Gdns. EH4: Edin 1H **19**
Hillpark Grn. EH4: Edin 1H **19**
Hillpark Gro. EH4: Edin 1H **19**
Hillpark Loan EH4: Edin 1J **19**
Hillpark Rd. EH4: Edin 1H **19**
Hillpark Ter. EH4: Edin 1H **19**
Hillpark Way EH4: Edin 1J **19**
Hillpark Wood EH4: Edin 1J **19**
Hill Pl. EH8: Edin 6G **5** (4J **21**)
EH22: May 1G **49**
Hillside Cres. . . . .
EH7: Edin 1H **5** (1J **21**)
Hillside Cres. Nth. . . . .
EH23: Gore 6F **49**
Hillside Cres. Sth. . . . .
EH23: Gore 6F **49**
Hillside Rd. EH30: S Q'fry 6E **8**
Hillside St. EH7: Edin . .1J **5** (1K **21**)
Hillside Ter. EH30: S Q'fry 5E **8**
Hill Sq. EH8: Edin 5G **5**
Hill St. EH2: Edin 2B **4** (2F **21**)
Hill St. Nth. La. . . . .
EH2: Edin 2B **4** (2F **21**)
Hill St. Sth. La. . . . .
EH2: Edin 3B **4** (3F **21**)
HILLTOWN 3J **35**
Hilltown Ter. EH22: Dalk 3J **35**
Hillview EH4: Edin 1K **19**
Hillview Cotts. EH28: Rat 2D **28**
Hillview Cres. EH12: Edin 4F **19**
Hillview Dr. EH12: Edin 4E **18**
Hillview Gdns. *EH20: Loan* 6K **39**
(off Nivensknowe Pk.)
Hillview Rd. EH12: Edin 4F **19**
Hillview Ter. EH12: Edin 4F **19**
Hillwood Av. EH28: Rat S 6C **16**
Hillwood Cres. EH28: Rat S 6C **16**
Hillwood Gdns. . . . .
EH28: Rat S 5C **16**
Hillwood Pl. EH30: S Q'fry 1G **7**
Hillwood Ri. EH28: Rat S 6C **16**
Hillwood Rd. EH28: Rat S 6C **16**
Hillwood Ter. EH28: Rat S 6C **16**
HMP Edinburgh EH11: Edin . . .1J **31**
Hogarth Av. EH23: Gore 4D **48**
Hoggan Vw. EH20: Loan 6C **40**
Holly Bank EH22: May 6G **43**
Hollybank Ter. EH11: Edin 7C **20**
Holly Ter. EH19: Bonn 7H **41**
Holly Wlk. EH20: Loan 6J **39**
Holmes Place Health Club . . .
Edinburgh 1G **5**
(off Greenside Pl.)
Holyrood Abbey (remains) . . . .
. . . . .3K **5** (3K **21**)
Holyrood Bus. Cen. . . . .
EH16: Edin 7D **22**
Holyrood Ct. . . . .
EH8: Edin 4J **5** (3K **21**)
Holyrood Gait . . . .
EH8: Edin 4J **5** (3K **21**)
Holyrood Pk. 6J **5** (4A **22**)
Holyrood Pk. Rd. . . . .
EH16: Edin 7K **5** (6K **21**)

Holyrood Rd. . . . .
EH8: Edin 4H **5** (3J **21**)
Home St. EH3: Edin 7B **4** (5F **21**)
Hopefield Pk. EH19: Bonn 7G **41**
Hopefield Pl. EH19: Bonn 7G **41**
Hopefield Ter. EH6: Newh 4D **12**
EH19: Bonn 7G **41**
Hope La. EH15: Port 4H **23**
Hope La. Nth. EH15: Port 3H **23**
Hope Pk. Cres. EH8: Edin 5J **21**
Hope Pk. Sq. . . . .
EH8: Edin 7G **5** (5J **21**)
Hope Pk. Ter. EH8: Edin 5J **21**
Hope Pl. EH21: Muss 1H **25**
EH33: Tran 1G **27**
EH8: Edin 3A **4** (3F **21**)
EH30: S Q'fry 2G **7**
Hope St. La. . . . .
EH2: Edin 4A **4** (3F **21**)
Hope Ter. EH9: Edin 7G **21**
Hopetoun Cres. EH7: Edin . . .1J **21**
Hopetoun Rd. EH30: S Q'fry . . .1F **7**
Hopetoun St. EH7: Edin 1J **21**
Horne Ter. EH11: Edin 5E **20**
Horsburgh Bank EH14: Bal . . .2E **36**
Horsburgh Gdns. EH14: Bal . . .2E **36**
Horsburgh Gro. EH14: Bal 2E **36**
Horse Wynd . . . .
EH8: Edin 3K **5** (3K **21**)
Hoseason Gdns. EH4: Edin 2F **19**
Hosie Rigg EH15: Edin 6H **23**
House o'Hill Av. EH4: Edin 7D **10**
House o'Hill Brae EH4: Edin . . .7D **10**
House o'Hill Cres. . . . .
H4: Edin 7D **10**
House o'Hill Gdns. . . . .
EH4: Edin 7E **10**
House o'Hill Grn. EH4: Edin . . .7D **10**
House o'Hill Gro. EH4: Edin . . .7D **10**
House o'Hill Pl. EH4: Edin 7D **10**
House o'Hill Rd. EH4: Edin 7D **10**
House o'Hill Row EH4: Edin . . .7E **10**
House o'Hill Ter. EH4: Edin . . .1K **19**
Howard Pl. EH3: Edin 7B **12**
EH3: Edin 7B **12**
Howden Hall Cotts. . . . .
EH16: Edin 6A **34**
Howden Hall Ct. EH16: Edin . . .6K **33**
Howden Hall Cres. . . . .
EH16: Edin 7K **33**
Howden Hall Dr. EH16: Edin . . .6K **33**
Howden Hall Gdns. . . . .
EH16: Edin 6A **34**
Howden Hall Loan . . . .
EH16: Edin 6K **33**
Howden Hall Pk. EH16: Edin . . .6K **33**
Howden Hall Rd. EH16: Edin . . .6A **34**
Howden Hall Way . . . .
EH16: Edin 7A **34**
Howden St. EH8: Edin . .6G **5** (5J **21**)
Howe Pk. EH10: Edin 7D **32**
Howe St. EH3: Edin . .1C **4** (2G **21**)
Hub, The . . . .
Edinburgh 4E **4**
Hughes Cres. EH22: May 7H **43**
Hugh Miller Pl. EH3: Edin 1F **21**
Hugh Russell Pl. . . . .
EH30: S Q'fry 2G **7**
Huly Hill Rd. EH28: Nbdge 6A **16**
Humbie Rd. EH29: Kltn 1A **16**
Hungerage Sq. EH33: Tran 3H **27**
Hunt Cl. EH22: Dalk 1C **42**
Hunter Av. EH20: Loan 5D **40**
Hunter Ct. EH20: Loan 5D **40**
HUNTERFIELD 5E **48**
Hunterfield Ct. EH23: Gore 6E **48**
Hunterfield Pk. EH23: Gore 5E **48**
Hunterfield Rd. EH23: Gore 5E **48**
Hunterfield Ter. EH23: Gore . . .5D **48**
Hunter's Cl. EH1: Edin 5D **4**
Hunter's Hill EH26: Pen 1A **50**
Hunter Sq. EH1: Edin . .4F **5** (3H **21**)
EH23: Gore 7F **49**
Hunter Ter. EH19: Bonn 6H **41**
EH20: Loan 5D **40**
Huntingdon Pl. EH7: Edin 1J **21**
Huntly St. EH3: Edin 7B **12**
Hursted Av. EH22: East 6F **43**
Hutchison Av. EH14: Edin 1A **32**

Hutchison Cotts. EH14: Edin . . .1A **32**
Hutchison Crossway . . . .
EH14: Edin 7A **20**
(not continuous)
Hutchison Gdns. . . . .
EH14: Edin 1A **32**
Hutchison Gro. EH14: Edin 1B **32**
Hutchison Ho. EH14: Edin 7B **20**
Hutchison Loan EH14: Edin . . .1A **32**
Hutchison Medway . . . .
EH14: Edin 1A **32**
Hutchison Pk. EH14: Edin 7A **20**
Hutchison Pl. EH14: Edin 1A **32**
Hutchison Rd. EH14: Edin 1A **32**
Hutchison Ter. EH14: Edin 1A **32**
Hutchison Vw. EH14: Edin 7A **20**
Hyndford's Cl. EH1: Edin 4G **5**
Hyvot Av. EH17: Edin 6D **34**
Hyvot Bank Av. EH17: Edin . . .6E **34**
Hyvot Ct. EH17: Edin 7D **34**
Hyvot Gdns. EH17: Edin 6D **34**
Hyvot Grn. EH17: Edin 7D **34**
Hyvot Gro. EH17: Edin 7D **34**
Hyvot Loan EH17: Edin 6D **34**
Hyvot Mill Dr. EH17: Edin 6D **34**
Hyvot Pk. EH17: Edin 7D **34**
HYVOTS BANK 6D **34**
Hyvot Ter. EH17: Edin 6D **34**
Hyvot Vw. EH17: Edin 7D **34**

Imex Bus. Cen. EH20: Loan 6A **40**
Imrie Pl. EH26: Pen 2D **50**
INCH 3B **34**
Inchcolm Ct. EH4: Edin 5F **11**
Inchcolm Ter. EH30: S Q'fry . . .2G **7**
Inch Garvie Ct. EH4: Edin 6F **11**
Inchgarvie Pk. EH30: S Q'fry . . .1F **7**
Inchkeith Av. EH30: S Q'fry . . .2H **7**
Inchkeith Ct. EH7: Edin 7D **12**
Inchkeith Gro. EH33: Tran 1H **27**
Inchmickery Ct. EH4: Edin 5D **10**
Inch Vw. EH32: Pres 6C **14**
Inchview Cres. EH21: Wall 3A **26**
Inchview Nth. EH32: Pres 6B **14**
Inchview Rd. EH21: Wall 3K **25**
Inchview Ter. EH7: Edin 2F **23**
India Bldgs. EH1: Edin 5E **4**
India Pl. EH3: Edin 1A **4** (2F **21**)
India St. EH3: Edin 1B **4** (2F **21**)
Industrial Rd. EH6: Edin 6G **13**
Industry Homes EH6: Newh 5D **12**
Industry La. EH6: Newh 5D **12**
Infirmary St. . . . .
EH1: Edin 5G **5** (4J **21**)
Inglewood Pl. EH16: Edin 8B **34**
Inglis Av. EH32: Port S 3G **15**
Inglis Ct. EH1: Edin 5D **4**
Inglis Farm EH32: Cock 4G **15**
Inglis Grn. Gait EH14: Edin . . .2K **31**
Inglis Grn. Rigg EH14: Edin . . .2K **31**
Inglis Grn. Rd. EH14: Edin 2K **31**
Ingliston (Park & Ride) 6G **17**
Ingliston Cotts. EH28: Ing 4E **16**
Ingliston Park & Ride Stop (NET) . .
(Due to open 2011) 5G **17**
Ingliston Rd. EH28: Ing 4E **16**
Inkerman Ct. EH26: Pen 1C **50**
Inveralmond Dr. EH4: Cram 5H **9**
Inveralmond Gdns. . . . .
EH4: Cram 5H **9**
Inveralmond Gro. EH4: Cram . . .5H **9**
Inveravon Rd. EH20: Loan 4B **40**
Inveravon Ter. EH21: Muss 3E **24**
INVERESK 4F **25**
Inveresk Brae EH21: Muss 3F **25**
Inveresk Est., The . . . .
EH21: Muss 4E **24**
Inveresk Ga. EH21: Muss 3F **25**
Inveresk Ind. Est. . . . .
EH21: Muss 3E **24**
Inveresk Lodge Garden 4F **25**
Inveresk Mills Ind. Pk. . . . . . .
EH21: Muss 4D **24**
Inveresk Rd. EH21: Muss 3E **24**
Inveresk Village . . . .
EH21: Muss 3E **24**

Inveresk Village Rd. . . . .
EH21: Muss 3F **25**
INVERLEITH 7J **11**
Inverleith 6K **11**
Inverleith Av. EH3: Edin 6A **12**
Inverleith Av. Sth. EH3: Edin . . .6A **12**
Inverleith Gdns. EH3: Edin 6K **11**
Inverleith Gro. EH3: Edin 7J **11**
Inverleith House 7K **11**
Inverleith Pl. EH3: Edin 7J **11**
Inverleith Pl. La. EH3: Edin 6A **12**
Inverleith Row EH3: Edin 6A **12**
Inverleith Ter. EH3: Edin 7A **12**
Inverleith Ter. La. EH3: Edin . . .7A **12**
Iona St. EH6: Edin 7E **12**
Iona St. La. EH6: Edin 7E **12**
Ironmills Rd. EH22: Dalk 2B **42**
Ivanhoe Cres. EH16: Edin 3B **34**
Ivy Ter. EH11: Edin 6C **20**

J

Jack Kane Cen., The 7G **23**
Jackson's Cl. EH1: Edin 4F **5**
Jackson's Entry EH8: Edin 3J **5**
Jackson St. EH26: Pen 2C **50**
Jacobite Way EH32: Pres 6F **15**
Jacobs Way EH23: Gore 6E **48**
Jamaica M. EH3: Edin 1B **4**
Jamaica St. . . . .
EH3: Edin 1B **4** (2F **21**)
(not continuous)
Jamaica St. Nth. La. . . . .
EH3: Edin 1B **4** (2F **21**)
Jamaica St. Sth. La. . . . .
EH3: Edin 1B **4** (2F **21**)
James' Ct. EH1: Edin 4E **4**
James Craig Wlk. EH1: Edin 2F **5**
James Lean Av. EH22: Dalk . . .2D **42**
James Leary Way . . . .
EH19: Bonn 5J **41**
Jameson Pl. EH6: Edin 7E **12**
James St. EH15: Port 3J **23**
EH21: Muss 2F **25**
James St. La. EH15: Port 3J **23**
Janefield EH17: Edin 1A **40**
Jane St. EH6: Edin 6E **12**
Jane Ter. EH7: Edin 2A **22**
Jarnac Ct. *EH22: Dalk* 2C **42**
(off High St.)
Jawbone Wlk. . . . .
EH3: Edin 7E **4** (5H **21**)
Jean Armour Av. EH16: Edin . . .3A **34**
Jean Armour Dr. EH22: Dalk . . .3F **43**
Jeanette Stewart Dr. . . . .
EH22: Newt 2B **48**
Jeffrey Av. EH4: Edin 2K **19**
Jeffrey St. EH1: Edin 3F **5** (3J **21**)
Jenks Loan EH22: Newt 1C **48**
Jessfield Ter. EH6: Newh 4C **12**
Jewel, The EH15: Edin 6H **23**
Jim Bush Dr. EH32: Pres 7C **14**
JOCKS LODGE 2D **22**
Jocks Lodge EH8: Edin 2C **22**
John Bernard Way . . . .
EH23: Gore 7E **48**
John Cres. EH33: Tran 2G **27**
John Humble St. EH22: May . . .1G **49**
John Kerr Ct. EH17: Edin 6D **20**
John Knox House 3G **5** (3J **21**)
John Knox Pl. EH26: Pen 2D **50**
John Mason Ct. EH30: S Q'fry . . .2H **7**
Johnnie Cope's Rd. . . . .
EH32: Pres 7E **14**
EH33: Tran 1E **26**
Johnny Moat Pl. EH32: Pres 6D **14**
Johnsburn Grn. EH14: Bal 4D **36**
Johnsburn Haugh EH14: Bal . . .4D **36**
Johnsburn Pk. EH14: Bal 5D **36**
Johnsburn Rd. EH14: Bal 4D **36**
John's La. EH6: Leith 5F **13**
John's Pl. EH6: Leith 5F **13**
Johnston Pl. EH26: Pen 6D **44**
Johnston Ter. . . . .
EH1: Edin 5C **4** (4G **21**)
EH32: Port S 3H **15**
John St. EH15: Port 3J **23**
EH26: Pen 1C **50**

John St. La. EH15: Port 3J 23
  EH26: Pen 2C 50
John St. La. E. EH15: Port 3J 23
John St. La. W. EH15: Port 3J 23
JOPPA 4J 23
Joppa Gdns. EH15: Port 4J 23
Joppa Gro. EH15: Port 4J 23
Joppa Pans EH15: Port 1A 24
Joppa Pk. EH15: Port 3J 23
Joppa Rd. EH15: Port 4J 23
Joppa Sta. Ter. EH15: Port 4J 23
Joppa Ter. EH15: Port 4J 23
Jordan La. EH10: Edin 1F 33
Jubilee Cres. EH23: Gore 5E 48
Jubilee Rd. EH12: Edin A 3F 17
Junction Pl. EH6: Leith 6E 12
Juner Pl. EH23: Gore 5E 48
Juniper Av. EH14: J Grn 7E 30
Juniper Gdns. EH14: J Grn 6E 30
JUNIPER GREEN 6F 31
Juniper Gro. EH14: J Grn 6E 30
Juniper La. EH14: J Grn 6F 31
Juniperlee EH14: J Grn 6F 31
Juniper Pk. Rd.
  EH14: J Grn 6F 31
Juniper Pl. EH14: J Grn 7E 30
Juniper Ter. EH14: J Grn 6E 30

K

KAIMES 7A 34
Kaimes Ct. EH12: Edin 5H 19
Kaimes Rd. EH12: Edin 4G 19
Kaimes Vw. EH22: Dan 5H 35
Katesmill Rd. EH14: Edin 4J 31
Kay Gdns. EH32: Cock 3G 15
Kedslie Pl. EH16: Edin 5K 33
Kedslie Rd. EH16: Edin 5K 33
Keir St. EH3: Edin 6D 4 (4G 21)
Keith Cres. EH4: Edin 2K 19
Keith Ho. EH17: Edin 7C 18
Keith Row EH4: Edin 2A 20
Keith Ter. EH4: Edin 2K 19
Kekewich Av. EH7: Edin 1F 23
Kemp Pl. EH3: Edin 1F 21
Kempston Pl. EH30: S Q'fry . . .2H 7
Kenilworth Dr. EH16: Edin 4A 34
Kenmure Av. EH8: Edin 3C 22
Kennedy Cres. EH33: Tran 1H 27
Kennington Av. EH20: Loan 6B 40
Kennington Ter. EH20: Loan . . .5B 40
Kenp's End EH33: Tran 4G 27
Keppock Cres. EH32: Pres 5F 15
Kerr Av. EH22: Dalk 3A 42
Kerr-McNeill Service Rd.
  EH33: Tran 3G 27
    (off King's Rd.)
Kerr Rd. EH33: Tran 2G 27
Kerr St. EH3: Edin 1A 4 (1F 21)
Kerr's Wynd EH21: Muss 2F 25
Kerr Way EH33: Tran 2G 27
Kevock Rd. EH18: Las 5F 41
Kevock Va. Pk. EH18: Las 5G 41
Kew Ter. EH12: Edin 4C 20
Kilchurn Ct. EH12: Edin 4C 18
    (off Craigievar Wynd)
Kilgraston Ct. EH9: Edin 7G 21
Kilgraston Rd. EH9: Edin 7H 21
Kilmaurs Rd. EH16: Edin 7A 22
Kilmaurs Ter. EH16: Edin 7A 22
Kilncroftside EH14: Edin 2K 31
Kilngate Brae EH17: Edin 7D 34
Kilwinning Pl. EH21: Muss 2E 24
Kilwinning St. EH21: Muss 2F 25
Kilwinning Ter. EH21: Muss . . .2F 25
Kimmerghame Dr.
  EH4: Edin 6H 11
Kimmerghame Ho.
  EH4: Edin 7H 11
Kimmerghame Loan
  EH4: Edin 6H 11
Kimmerghame Path
  EH4: Edin 6H 11
Kimmerghame Pl.
  EH4: Edin 6H 11
Kimmerghame Row
  EH4: Edin 6H 11

Kimmerghame Ter.
  EH4: Edin 6H 11
Kimmerghame Vw.
  EH4: Edin 7H 11
Kincaid's Ct. EH1: Edin 5F 5
Kinellan Gdns. EH12: Edin 4A 20
Kinellan Rd. EH12: Edin 3A 20
King Edward VII Memorial 3K 5
King Edward's Way
  EH29: Kltn 2A 16
Kinghorn Pl. EH6: Edin 5C 12
King Malcolm Cl.
  EH10: Edin 7H 33
Kingsburgh Cres. EH5: Edin . .3H 11
Kingsburgh Rd. EH12: Edin . . .4A 20
Kings Cramond EH4: Cram 6J 9
Kings Ga. Junc. EH22: Dalk . . .1A 42
Kings Haugh EH16: Edin 7C 22
KINGSKNOWE 3J 31
Kingsknowe Av. EH14: Edin . . .4J 31
Kingsknowe Ct. EH14: Edin . . .3H 31
Kingsknowe Cres.
  EH14: Edin 3J 31
Kingsknowe Dr. EH14: Edin . . .3J 31
Kingsknowe Gdns.
  EH14: Edin 4J 31
Kingsknowe Gro. EH14: Edin . .4J 31
Kingsknowe Pk. EH14: Edin . . .4J 31
Kingsknowe Pl. EH14: Edin . . .3H 31
Kingsknowe Rd. Nth.
  EH14: Edin 2J 31
Kingsknowe Rd. Sth.
  EH14: Edin 3J 31
Kingsknowe Station (Rail) . . .3J 31
Kingsknowe Ter. EH14: Edin . . .3J 31
Kingslaw Ct. EH33: Tran 3H 27
King's Mdw. EH16: Edin 7B 22
King's Pl. EH15: Port 1G 23
King's Rd. EH15: Port 2G 23
King's Stables La.
  EH1: Edin 5C 4 (4G 21)
King's Stables Rd.
  EH1: Edin 4B 4 (3F 21)
King's Ter. EH15: Port 1G 23
King's Theatre
  Edinburgh 7C 4 (5F 21)
Kingston Av. EH16: Edin 3C 34
King St. EH6: Leith 5E 12
Kinleith Ind. Est. EH14: Cur . . .1K 37
Kinnear Ri. EH3: Edin 6K 11
Kinnear Rd. EH3: Edin 6J 11
Kippielaw Dr. EH22: East 3E 42
Kippielaw Gdns. EH22: East . . .4E 42
Kippielaw Medway
  EH22: East 4E 42
Kippielaw Pk. EH22: May 5F 43
Kippielaw Rd. EH22: East 4E 42
Kippielaw Steading
  EH22: Dalk 4E 42
Kippielaw Wlk. EH22: East 3E 42
Kirk Brae EH16: Edin 3A 34
  EH26: Mil B 4F 45
Kirk Cramond EH4: Cram 4J 9
Kirkgate EH6: Leith 5E 12
  EH14: Cur 1K 37
  EH16: Edin 5A 34
Kirkgate Ho. EH6: Leith 5F 13
KIRKHILL 1E 50
Kirkhill Ct. EH23: Gore 7E 48
Kirkhill Dr. EH16: Edin 7A 22
Kirkhill Gdns. EH16: Edin 6A 22
  EH26: Pen 2D 50
Kirkhill Rd. EH16: Edin 6A 22
  EH26: Pen 2D 50
  EH23: Gore 5C 48
Kirkhill Way EH26: Pen 2D 50
Kirklands EH12: Edin 7F 19
  EH26: Pen 2C 50
Kirklands Pk. Cres.
  EH29: Kltn 7E 6
    (off Kirklands Pk. St.)
Kirklands Pk. Gdns.
  EH29: Kltn 1A 16
Kirklands Pk. Gro. EH29: Kltn . .7E 6
Kirklands Pk. Rigg
  EH29: Kltn 1A 16

Kirklands Pk. St.
  EH29: Kltn . . . . . .7E 6 & 1A 16
KIRKLISTON 1A 16
Kirkliston Leisure Cen. 7E 6
Kirkliston Rd. EH28: Nbdge . . .4A 16
  EH30: S Q'fry 1G 7
Kirk Loan EH12: Edin 5G 19
Kirk Pk. EH16: Edin 4A 34
Kirk St. EH6: Edin 6E 12
  EH32: Pres 6D 14
Kirkstyle Gdns. EH29: Kltn 2B 16
Kirkton Bank EH26: Pen 2B 50
Kirk Vw. EH26: Pen 3D 50
    (off Bridge St.)
Kirk Wynd EH32: Pres 5D 14
Kisimul Ct. EH12: Edin 4C 18
Kittle Yards EH9: Edin 7J 21
Klondyke St. EH21: Edin 4A 24
Knightslaw Pl. EH26: Pen 2B 50
Knockill Braehead
  EH16: Edin 4J 31
Knowetop Pl. EH25: Rosl 3K 45
Komarom Ct. EH22: Dalk 2C 42
    (off Buccleuch St.)
Komarom Pl. EH22: Dalk 2F 43
Kyle Pl. EH7: Edin 1K 5 (2K 21)

L

Laburnum Arch Ct.
  EH32: Pres 6D 14
Laburnum Av.
  EH32: Port S 3H 15
Laburnum Rd. EH22: May 7G 43
Lade, The EH14: Bal 5F 37
Ladehead EH6: Edin 6C 12
Ladiebridge EH12: Edin 6F 19
    (off Ladywell Av.)
Ladiemeadow EH12: Edin 6G 19
Lady Brae EH23: Gore 7F 49
Lady Brae Pl. EH23: Gore 6F 49
Ladycroft EH14: Bal 3E 36
    (not continuous)
Lady Emily Way EH23: Gore . . .6E 48
Lady Lawson St.
  EH3: Edin 5C 4 (4G 21)
Lady Menzies Pl.
  EH7: Edin 1K 5 (2A 22)
Lady Nairne Cres. EH8: Edin . .4D 22
Lady Nairne Gro. EH8: Edin . . .4D 22
Lady Nairne Loan EH8: Edin . . .4D 22
Lady Nairne Pl. EH8: Edin 4D 22
Lady Rd. EH16: Edin 1A 34
Lady Rd. Pl. EH22: Newt 7D 42
Ladysmith Rd. EH9: Edin 2J 33
Lady Stairs Cl. EH1: Edin 4E 4
Lady Victoria Bus. Cen.
  EH22: Newt 3C 48
Ladywell EH21: Muss 2E 24
Ladywell Av. EH12: Edin 5F 19
Ladywell Ct. EH12: Edin 5F 19
Ladywell Gdns. EH12: Edin . . .5F 19
Ladywell Ho. EH12: Edin 5E 18
Ladywell Rd. EH12: Edin 5E 18
Ladywell Way EH21: Muss 2E 24
Ladywood Leisure Cen. 7E 44
Lady Wynd EH1: Edin 5C 4
Laichfield EH14: Edin 1K 31
Laichpark Loan EH14: Edin . . .1K 31
    (off Laichpark Rd.)
Laichpark Pl. EH14: Edin 1K 31
Laichpark Rd. EH14: Edin 1K 31
Laildlaw Gdns. EH33: Tran 3G 27
Laing Ter. EH15: Port 3J 23
  EH26: Pen 7D 44
Laird Ter. EH19: Bonn 7J 41
Lamb Ct. EH19: Bonn 6H 41
Lamb's Cl. EH8: Edin 7H 5
Lambs Cres. EH6: Newh 3B 12
Lamb's Pend EH26: Pen 3D 50
Lammermoor Gdns.
  EH33: Tran 2F 27
Lammermoor Ter.
  EH16: Edin 3C 34
  EH33: Tran 2F 27
Lammerview EH33: Tran 3G 27
Lampacre Rd. EH12: Edin 6G 19

Lanark Rd. EH13: Edin 5H 31
  EH14: Edin 5H 31
  EH14: J Grn 7F 31
Lanark Rd. W.
  EH14: Bal, Cur 4A 36
  EH14: Cur 2F 37
Lane, The EH21: Whit 7G 25
Langlaw Rd. EH22: May 5F 43
Lang Loan EH20: Loan 3B 40
Lang Loan Rd. EH17: Edin 2B 40
Langton Rd. EH9: Edin 1J 33
Laning Mills EH7: Edin 1C 22
Lansbury Ct. EH22: Dalk 2C 42
Lansdowne Cres.
  EH12: Edin 4D 20
Lapicide Pl. EH6: Newh 5D 12
Larbourfield EH11: Edin 3F 31
Larch Cres. EH22: May 7H 43
Larchfield EH14: Bal 3E 36
Larchfield Neuk EH14: Bal 3E 36
Largo Pl. EH6: Edin 5D 12
Larkfield Dr. EH22: Dalk 4K 41
Larkfield Rd. EH22: Dalk 3A 42
Laserquest
  Edinburgh 4D 20
    (off Dalry Rd.)
LASSWADE 4F 41
Lasswade Bank EH17: Edin . . .7C 34
Lasswade Gro. EH17: Edin . . .7C 34
LASSWADE JUNC. 2E 40
Lasswade Rd. EH16: Edin 5B 34
  EH17: Edin, Las 7C 34
    (not continuous)
  EH18: Las 4F 41
  EH20: Loan 3K 40
  EH22: Dalk 3K 41
Latch Pk. EH13: Edin 5B 32
Lauder Ct. EH3: Edin 6G 21
Lauderdale St. EH9: Edin 6G 21
Lauder Loan EH9: Edin 7H 21
Lauder Rd. EH9: Edin 6H 21
  EH22: Dalk 3D 42
Laundry Cotts. EH23: Gore . . .5D 48
Laurel Bank EH22: Dalk 3E 42
Laurelbank Pl. EH22: May 7G 43
    (not continuous)
Laurel Ter. EH11: Edin 6C 20
Laurie St. EH6: Leith 6F 13
LAURISTON 7C 4 (4G 21)
Lauriston Castle 5B 10
Lauriston Farm Rd.
  EH4: Edin 6B 10
Lauriston Gdns.
  EH3: Edin 6C 4 (4G 21)
Lauriston Pk.
  EH3: Edin 6C 4 (5G 21)
Lauriston Pl.
  EH3: Edin 6C 4 (4G 21)
Lauriston St.
  EH3: Edin 6C 4 (4G 21)
Lauriston Ter.
  EH3: Edin 6D 4 (4G 21)
Laverockbank Av. EH5: Edin . .4B 12
Laverockbank Cres.
  EH5: Edin 4B 12
Laverockbank Gdns.
  EH5: Edin 4B 12
Laverockbank Gro.
  EH5: Edin 4B 12
Laverockbank Rd. EH5: Edin . .4B 12
Laverockbank Ter. EH5: Edin . .4B 12
Laverockdale Cres.
  EH13: Edin 6K 31
Laverockdale Loan
  EH13: Edin 7K 31
Laverockdale Pk.
  EH13: Edin 7K 31
Laverock Dr. EH26: Pen 7B 44
Lawers Sq. EH26: Pen 7E 44
Lawfield Cotts. EH22: Dalk 5H 43
Lawfield Rd. EH22: May 6F 43
Lawhead Pl. EH26: Pen 7B 44
Lawhouse Toll EH15: Edin 7J 23
Lawnmarket
  EH1: Edin 4E 4 (3H 21)
Law Pl. EH15: Port 2G 23
Lawrie Dr. EH26: Pen 7C 44
Lawrie Ter. EH20: Loan 6B 40
Lawson Cres. EH30: S Q'fry . . .2H 7

Lawson Way EH33: Tran 3G 27
Leadervale Rd. EH16: Edin 4K 33
Leadervale Ter. EH16: Edin 4K 33
Leamington La. EH10: Edin ...6E 20
Leamington Pl. EH10: Edin ...5F 21
Leamington Rd.
  EH3: Edin 7A 4 (5E 20)
Leamington Ter.
  EH10: Edin 5F 21
Learmonth Av. EH4: Edin 1D 20
Learmonth Ct. EH4: Edin 2D 20
Learmonth Cres. EH4: Edin ...2D 20
Learmonth Gdns. EH4: Edin ...2D 20
Learmonth Gdns. La.
  EH4: Edin 2D 20
Learmonth Gdns. M.
  EH4: Edin 1E 20
Learmonth Gro. EH4: Edin 1D 20
Learmonth Pk. EH4: Edin 1D 20
Learmonth Pl. EH4: Edin 1D 20
Learmonth Ter. EH4: Edin 2D 20
Learmonth Ter. La.
  EH4: Edin 2D 20
Learmonth Vw. EH4: Edin 2E 20
Ledi Ter. EH26: Pen 7E 44
Lee Cres. EH15: Port 3H 23
Leighton Cres. EH22: East ...6E 42
LEITH 5F 13
LEITH DOCKS 3D 12
Leith Gallery, The 5F 13
  (off Shore Pl.)
Leith St. EH1: Edin 2F 5 (2H 21)
Leith Theatre 4D 12
Leith Victoria Swimming Cen.
  ....6E 12
Leith Wlk. EH1: Edin ...1G 5 (2J 21)
  EH6: Edin 1J 21
  EH6: Edin 1G 5 (1J 21)
Leith Waterworld 6E 12
Lennel Av. EH12: Edin 3A 20
LENNIE 1J 17
Lennie Cotts. EH12: Edin ...3K 17
Lennox Row EH5: Edin 4A 12
Lennox St. EH4: Edin 2E 20
Lennox St. La. EH4: Edin ...2E 20
Lennymuir EH12: Edin A 2H 17
Leopold Pl. EH7: Edin 1G 5
Leslie Pl. EH4: Edin 1A 4 (1F 21)
Leven Cl. EH3: Edin 7B 4 (5F 21)
LEVENHALL 2J 25
Leven St. EH3: Edin 7B 4 (5F 21)
Leven Ter. EH3: Edin ...7C 4 (5G 21)
Lewis Ter. EH11: Edin 4E 20
Lewisvale Av. EH21: Muss ...3G 25
Lewisvale Ct. EH21: Muss ...3G 25
Leyden Pk. EH19: Bonn 5H 41
Leyden Pl. EH19: Bonn 6H 41
LIBERTON 6A 34
Liberton Brae EH16: Edin ...3A 34
Liberton Dr. EH16: Edin 4K 33
Liberton Gdns. EH16: Edin ..6A 34
LIBERTON HOSPITAL 6B 34
Liberton Pl. EH16: Edin 5A 34
Liberton Rd. EH16: Edin ...3A 34
Liberton Twr. La.
  ....4K 33
Liddesdale Pl. EH3: Edin ...7A 12
Lidgate Shot EH28: Rat 2D 28
Lilac Av. EH22: May 7H 43
Lily Hill Ter. EH8: Edin 2C 22
Lily Ter. EH11: Edin 7C 20
Limefield EH17: Edin 7E 34
Lime Gro. EH22: May 7G 43
Lime Pl. EH19: Bonn 7H 41
Limes, The EH10: Edin 7E 20
Linburn Pk. EH27: Wilk 7A 28
Linburn Rd. EH27: Wilk 7B 28
Lindean Pl. EH6: Edin 6G 13
Lindean Ter. EH27: Wilk 6A 28
Linden Pl. EH20: Loan 5D 40
Lindores Dr. EH24: Rose ...5C 46
Lindsay Cir. EH24: Rose ...5C 46
Lindsay Pl. EH6: Newh 4D 12
Lindsay Rd. EH6: Newh 3C 12
Lindsay Row EH24: Rose ...5D 46
Lindsay St. EH6: Newh 4D 12
Linear Pk. EH14: Edin 1B 32
Lingerwood Cotts.
  EH22: Newt 2C 48

Lingerwood Farm Cotts.
  EH22: Newt 2D 48
Lingerwood Rd.
  EH22: Newt 2C 48
Lingerwood Wlk.
  EH22: Newt 2D 48
Linkfield Ct. EH21: Muss ...2G 25
Linkfield Rd. EH21: Muss ...2F 25
Links Av. EH21: Muss 1D 24
Links Ct. EH32: Port S 3H 15
Links Gdns. EH6: Leith 5G 13
Links Gdns. La. EH6: Leith .5G 13
Links La. EH6: Leith 5F 13
Links Pl. EH6: Leith 5F 13
  EH32: Port S 3J 15
Links Rd. EH32: Port S 3H 15
Links St. EH21: Muss 2E 24
Links Vw. EH21: Muss 1D 24
  EH32: Port S 3J 15
Linksview Ho. EH6: Leith ...5F 13
Links Wlk. EH32: Port S 3J 15
Linn Mill EH30: S Q'fry 1D 6
Linty La. EH26: Pen 1B 50
Lismore Av. EH8: Edin 2C 22
Lismore Cres. EH8: Edin ...2C 22
Lister Sq. EH3: Edin ...7D 4 (5G 21)
Liston Dr. EH29: Kltn 1A 16
Liston Pl. EH29: Kltn 1A 16
Liston Rd. EH29: Kltn 2A 16
Little Acre EH22: East 5F 43
Lit. France Cres. EH16: Edin ..3D 34
Lit. France Ho. EH17: Edin ...4D 34
Lit. France Mills EH16: Edin ..3D 34
Littlejohn Av. EH10: Edin ...4C 32
Littlejohn Wynd EH10: Edin ..4D 32
Lit. King St.
  EH1: Edin 1F 5 (2H 21)
Little Rd. EH16: Edin 5A 34
Livesey Ter. EH26: Pen 6E 44
Livingstone Pl. EH9: Edin ...6H 21
Lixmount Av. EH5: Edin 4B 12
Lixmount Gdns. EH5: Edin ..4B 12
Loan, The EH20: Loan 6A 40
  EH21: Muss, Wall 2K 25
  EH30: S Q'fry 1G 7
Loanburn Av. EH26: Pen ...2C 50
Loanburn Av. EH26: Pen ...2C 50
LOANHEAD 5C 40
LOANHEAD HOSPITAL 5D 40
Loanhead Leisure Cen. 5B 40
Loanhead Rd. EH20: Loan ..3A 40
Loaning Cres. EH7: Edin ...1D 22
Loaning Rd. EH7: Edin 1C 22
Loch Cen. 3H 27
LOCHEND
  EH7 ....1B 22
  EH28 ....5B 16
Lochend EH28: Rat S 5B 16
Lochend Av. EH7: Edin 7G 13
Lochend Castle Barns
  EH7: Edin 1B 22
Lochend Cl.
  EH8: Edin 3H 5 (3J 21)
Lochend Cres. EH7: Edin ...1C 22
Lochend Dr. EH7: Edin 1B 22
Lochend Gdns. EH7: Edin ...1B 22
Lochend Gro. EH7: Edin 1C 22
Lochend Ho. EH7: Edin 1C 22
Lochend Ind. Est.
  EH28: Nbdge 5B 16
Lochend Pk. EH7: Edin 1B 22
Lochend Pk. Vw. EH7: Edin ..1A 22
Lochend Quad. EH7: Edin ...1C 22
Lochend Rd. EH6: Edin 6F 13
  EH7: Edin 6F 13
  EH28: Rat S 4A 16
  EH29: Kltn, Rat S 3A 16
Lochend Rd. Nth.
  EH21: Muss 2D 24
Lochend Rd. Sth. EH7: Edin ..7G 13
  EH21: Muss 2D 24
Lochend Sq. EH7: Edin 1B 22
Lochrin Bldgs.
  EH3: Edin 7B 4 (5F 21)
Lochrin Pl. EH3: Edin ...7B 4 (5F 21)
Lochrin Ter. EH3: Edin 7B 4

Loch Rd. EH4: Edin 1J 19
  EH30: S Q'fry 1G 7
  EH33: Tran 2H 27
Lochside Av. EH12: Edin ...6B 18
Lochside Ct. EH12: Edin 7C 18
Lochside Cres. EH12: Edin ..6B 18
Lochside Pl. EH12: Edin 7C 18
Lochside Vw. EH12: Edin ...6B 18
Lochside Way EH12: Edin ...7C 18
Loch Sq. EH33: Tran 2H 27
Lochview Ct.
  EH8: Edin 4J 5 (3K 21)
Lockerby Cotts. EH16: Edin ..6C 34
Lockerby Cres. EH16: Edin ..6C 34
Lockerby Gro. EH16: Edin ...6C 34
Lockharton Av. EH14: Edin ..2B 32
Lockharton Cres. EH14: Edin ..2C 32
Lockharton Gdns.
  EH14: Edin 1C 32
Lockhart Ter. EH25: Rosl ...3K 45
Lodeneia Pk. EH22: Dalk 1F 43
Loganlea Av. EH7: Edin 1D 22
Loganlea Dr. EH7: Edin 2C 22
Loganlea Gdns. EH7: Edin ..1C 22
Loganlea Loan EH7: Edin ...2D 22
Loganlea Pl. EH7: Edin 2D 22
Loganlea Rd. EH7: Edin 1D 22
Loganlea Ter. EH7: Edin 1D 22
Logan St. EH3: Edin 1G 21
Logie Grn. Gdns. EH7: Edin ..7B 12
Logie Grn. Loan EH7: Edin ..7B 12
Logie Grn. Rd. EH7: Edin ...7B 12
Logie Mill EH7: Edin 7B 12
Lomond Rd. EH5: Edin 4A 12
Lomond Va. EH26: Pen 7E 44
Lomond Wlk. EH20: Loan ...4A 40
London Rd. EH7: Edin ...1G 5 (2J 21)
  EH8: Edin 2C 22
  EH22: Dalk 2C 42
London St. EH3: Edin 1H 21
Long Craig Rigg EH5: Edin ..3F 11
Longcraig Rd. EH30: S Q'fry ..1J 7
Long Craigs EH32: Port S ...3J 15
Long Crook EH30: S Q'fry ...2F 7
Long Dalmahoy Rd.
  EH14: Cur 7K 29
  EH27: Kntn 1A 36
Longdykes Rd. EH32: Pres ..5F 15
Longformacus Rd.
  EH16: Edin 5A 34
LONGSTONE 2J 31
Longstone Av. EH14: Edin ..2J 31
Longstone Cotts. EH14: Edin ..2J 31
Longstone Cres. EH14: Edin ..1J 31
Longstone Gdns. EH14: Edin ..1H 31
Longstone Gro. EH14: Edin ..1J 31
Longstone Pk. EH14: Edin ..1H 31
Longstone Rd. EH14: Edin ..1H 31
Longstone St. EH14: Edin ...2J 31
Longstone Ter. EH14: Edin ..1H 31
Longstone Vw. EH14: Edin ..1H 31
Lonsdale Ter.
  EH3: Edin 7C 4 (5G 21)
Lord Russell Pl. EH9: Edin ...6J 21
  (off Sciennes Pl.)
Loretto Ct. EH21: Muss 4D 24
Lorimer Vw. EH14: J Grn ...6G 31
Lorne Gro. EH20: Loan 4A 40
Lorne Ho. EH3: Edin 3E 20
Lorne Pl. EH6: Edin 7E 12
Lorne Sq. EH6: Edin 7E 12
Lorne St. EH6: Edin 7E 12
Lothian Bank EH22: Dalk ...4B 42
LOTHIANBRIDGE 7C 42
LOTHIANBURN 2G 39
LOTHIANBURN JUNC. 1F 39
Lothian Dr. EH22: East 5K 42
Lothian Rd. EH1: Edin 4A 4 (3F 21)
  EH3: Edin 4A 4 (3F 21)
  EH22: Dalk 2C 42
Lothian St. EH1: Edin ...6F 5 (4H 21)
  EH19: Bonn 6H 41
  EH22: Dalk 2C 42
  EH24: Rose 4D 46
Lothian Ter. EH22: Newt ...2D 48
Lothian Thistle FC 7K 19
Louisa Sq. EH24: Rose 4D 46
Lovedale Av. EH14: Bal 4D 36
Lovedale Cres. EH14: Bal ...4D 36

Lovedale Gdns. EH14: Bal ...4E 36
Lovedale Gro. EH14: Bal 4D 36
Lovedale Rd. EH14: Bal 4E 36
Lover's La. EH30: S Q'fry 2H 7
  (not continuous)
Lover's Loan EH9: Edin 6H 21
Lower Broomieknowe
  EH18: Las 5G 41
Lwr. Gilmore Bank EH3: Edin ..7A 4
Lwr. Gilmore Pl.
  EH3: Edin 7A 4 (5F 21)
Lwr. Granton Rd. EH5: Edin ..3J 11
Lower Joppa EH15: Port 3J 23
Lwr. London Rd. EH7: Edin ..2A 22
Lwr. Valleyfield Vw.
  EH26: Pen 3D 50
Lowrie Av. EH26: Pen 2A 50
Lowrie's Den Rd. EH26: Pen ..2A 50
Lufra Bank EH5: Edin 4K 11
Lugton Brae EH22: Dalk 1B 42
Lumsden Ct. EH28: Rat 2D 28
Lussielaw Rd. EH9: Edin ...2J 33
Lutton Pl. EH8: Edin 5J 21
Lygon Rd. EH16: Edin 2K 33
Lyndene Sq. EH20: Loan ...4K 39
Lynedoch Pl. EH3: Edin 3E 20
Lynedoch Pl. La. EH3: Edin ..3E 20
Lyne St. EH7: Edin ...1K 5 (2A 22)
Lyne Ter. EH26: Pen 7E 44
Lyon's Cl. EH1: Edin 4F 5

M

Macbeth Moir Rd.
  EH21: Muss 2J 25
McCathie Dr. EH22: Newt ...7D 42
Maccormick Ter. EH26: Pen ..6D 44
McDiarmid Gro. EH22: Newt ..2D 48
McDonald Pl. EH7: Edin 7C 12
McDonald Rd. EH7: Edin ...7C 12
McDonald St. EH7: Edin 7D 12
Macdowall Rd. EH9: Edin ...1J 33
Macfarlane Ct. EH33: Elph ..7F 27
McGahey Ct. EH22: Newt ...2D 48
McGregor Pend EH32: Pres ..5F 15
McKelvie Pde. EH5: Edin ...3A 12
Mackenzie Pl.
  EH3: Edin 1A 4 (2E 20)
Mackies Way EH32: Pres 6C 14
  (off Inch Vw.)
McKinlay Ter. EH20: Loan ...6A 40
McKinnon Dr. EH22: May 2G 49
McLachlan Gdns. EH32: Pres ..5F 15
McLaren Rd. EH9: Edin 7A 22
McLaren Ter. EH11: Edin ...4E 20
McLean Pl. EH18: Las 7E 40
  EH23: Gore 5F 49
McLean Wlk. EH22: Newt ...2D 48
McLeod Cres. EH32: Pres ...6D 14
McLeod St. EH11: Edin 5C 20
McNeill Av. EH20: Loan 5B 40
McNeill Path EH33: Tran 2G 27
McNeill Pl. EH20: Loan 5B 40
McNeill St. EH11: Edin 5E 20
McNeill Ter. EH20: Loan 6A 40
McNeill Way EH33: Tran 3G 27
McPhail Sq. EH33: Tran 2H 27
McQuade St. EH19: Bonn ...5K 41
Mactaggart Loan
  EH22: Newt 2D 48
Madeira Pl. EH6: Newh 5D 12
Madeira St. EH6: Newh 4D 12
Maesterton Pl. EH22: Newt ..2D 48
Magdala Cres. EH12: Edin ..4D 20
Magdala M. EH12: Edin 4D 20
Magdalen Chapel 5E 4
MAGDALENE 5H 23
Magdalene Av. EH15: Port ..5H 23
Magdalene Cotts.
  EH21: Port 1B 24
Magdalene Ct. EH15: Port ..6H 23
Magdalene Dr. EH15: Port ..5G 23
Magdalene Gdns.
  EH15: Port 5H 23
Magdalene Loan EH15: Port ..5H 23
Magdalene Medway
  EH15: Port 5H 23

Magdalene Pl. EH15: Port 5H 23
Magpe Gdns. EH22: Dalk 3F 43
Maidencraig Ct. EH4: Edin ...1A 20
Maidencraig Cres.
  EH4: Edin 1A 20
Maidencraig Gro.
  EH4: Edin 1A 20
Maid of the Forth (Boat Trips)
  ....1J 7
Main Point EH3: Edin 6C 4
Mains Gdns. EH33: Tran 1H 27
Mains of Craigmillar
  EH16: Edin 2D 34
Main St. EH4: Edin 7C 10
  EH14: Bal 3E 36
  EH20: Loan 6K 39
  EH22: Newt 7C 42
  EH23: Gore 7E 48
  EH25: Rosl 3A 46
  EH28: Rat 2D 28
  EH29: Kltn 1A 16
  EH30: Dalm 3K 7
  EH33: Elph 7F 27
  EH52: Winch 7A 6
Maitland Av. EH21: Muss 2C 24
Maitland Hog La.
  EH29: Kltn 2A 16
Maitland Pk. Rd.
  EH21: Muss 2C 24
Maitland Rd. EH29: Kltn 1A 16
Maitland St. EH21: Muss 2C 24
Malbet Pk. EH16: Edin 5B 34
Malbet Wynd EH16: Edin 5B 34
Malcolm Ho. EH4: Edin 6J 11
Mall Av. EH21: Muss 2E 24
Malleny Av. EH14: Bal 4E 36
Malleny Garden 3F 37
Malleny Millgate EH14: Bal ..6F 37
MALLENY MILLS 5F 37
Malleny Pk. 3F 37
Malta Grn. EH4: Edin 1F 21
Malta Ter. EH4: Edin 1F 21
Manderston Ct. EH6: Edin ...6F 13
Manderston St. EH6: Edin ...6E 12
Mannering Pl. EH16: Edin ...4B 34
Manor Pl. EH3: Edin 3E 20
Manse La. EH21: Muss 2F 25
  EH32: Port S 3G 15
Manse Rd. EH12: Edin 5F 19
  EH25: Rosl 3A 46
  EH29: Kltn 2A 16
Manse St. EH12: Edin 5F 19
Mansfield Av. EH21: Muss ...3E 24
  EH22: Newt 7D 42
Mansfield Ct. EH21: Muss ...3F 25
Mansfield Pl. EH3: Edin 1H 21
  EH21: Muss 3E 24
  EH22: Newt 7D 42
Mansfield Rd. EH14: Bal 4E 36
  EH21: Muss 2E 24
  EH22: Newt 7D 42
Mansionhouse Rd.
  EH9: Edin 6H 21
Marchbank Dr. EH14: Bal 5E 36
Marchbank Gdns. EH14: Bal ..5E 36
Marchbank Gro. EH14: Bal ...5E 36
Marchbank Pl. EH14: Bal 5E 36
Marchbank Way EH14: Bal ...4E 36
Marchburn Dr. EH26: Pen ...2A 50
Marchfield Gro. EH4: Edin ...7D 10
Marchfield Pk. EH4: Edin 7C 10
Marchfield Pk. La.
  EH4: Edin 7C 10
Marchfield Ter. EH4: Edin ...1J 19
March Gait EH4: Edin 1H 19
March Gro. EH4: Edin 1H 19
Marchhall Cres. EH16: Edin ..6A 22
Marchhall Pl. EH16: Edin 6K 21
Marchhall Rd. EH16: Edin ...6A 22
MARCHMONT 6H 21
Marchmont Cres. EH9: Edin ..6H 21
  (not continuous)
Marchmont Rd. EH9: Edin ...6G 21
Marchmont St. EH9: Edin ...6G 21
March Pines EH4: Edin 1H 19
March Rd. EH4: Edin 1H 19
Marchwood Ct. EH33: Elph ..7F 27
Marco's Leisure Cen.
  ....7A 4 (4E 20)

Mardale Cres. EH10: Edin 7E 20
Margaret Rose Av.
  EH10: Edin 7G 33
Margaret Rose Cres.
  EH10: Edin 7G 33
Margaret Rose Dr.
  EH10: Edin 7G 33
Margaret Rose Loan
  EH10: Edin 7G 33
Margaret Rose Wlk.
  EH10: Edin 7G 33
Margaret Rose Way
  EH10: Edin 7G 33
MARIE CURIE CENTRE, FAIRMILE
  ....7H 33
Marine Dr. EH4: Edin 4A 10
Marine Esplanade
  EH6: Edin, Leith 4H 13
Marionville Av. EH7: Edin ...1B 22
Marionville Cres. EH7: Edin ..1C 22
Marionville Dr. EH7: Edin 1C 22
Marionville Gro. EH7: Edin ...1C 22
Marionville Medway
  EH7: Edin 1C 22
Marionville Pk. EH7: Edin ...1B 22
Marionville Rd. EH7: Edin ...2B 22
Marischal Pl. EH4: Edin 2A 20
Maritime La. EH6: Leith 5F 13
Maritime St. EH6: Leith 5F 13
Market Loan EH33: Tran 1G 27
Market Pl. EH22: Dalk 2C 42
Market St. EH1: Edin ...4E 4 (3H 21)
  EH21: Muss 2D 24
Market Vw. EH33: Tran 1G 27
Market Way EH33: Tran 1G 27
Marlborough St. EH15: Port ..3H 23
Marmion Av. EH25: Rosl 2K 45
Marmion Cres. EH16: Edin ...2B 34
Marmion Rd. EH29: Kltn 2A 16
Marshall Pl. EH4: Edin 7C 10
Marshall Rd. EH29: Kltn 2A 16
Marshall's Ct.
  EH1: Edin 1G 5 (2J 21)
Marshall St.
  EH1: Edin 6F 5 (4H 21)
  EH32: Cock 3F 15
Martello Ct. EH4: Edin 5D 10
Martin Gro. EH19: Bonn 5K 41
Martin Pl. EH22: Dalk 3A 42
Maryburn Rd. EH22: East 5E 42
Maryfield EH7: Edin ...1K 5 (1K 21)
  EH15: Port 7H 23
Maryfield Pl.
  EH7: Edin 1K 5 (1A 22)
  EH19: Bonn 6J 41
Mary's Pl. EH4: Edin 1E 20
  (off Raeburn Pl.)
Mary Tree Ho. EH17: Edin ...4D 34
Masefield Way EH12: Edin A ...2H 17
Mason Pl. EH18: Las 7F 41
Matthews Dr. EH22: Newt 1B 48
Maulsford Av. EH22: Dan 5H 35
Maurice Pl. EH9: Edin 2H 33
MAURICEWOOD 7D 44
Mauricewood Av. EH26: Pen ..7D 44
Mauricewood Bank
  EH26: Pen 7D 44
Mauricewood Gro.
  EH26: Pen 7D 44
Mauricewood Pk. EH26: Pen ..7D 44
Mauricewood Ri. EH26: Pen ..7D 44
Mauricewood Rd.
  EH26: Pen 5C 44
Mavisbank EH20: Loan 6C 40
Mavisbank Pl. EH18: Las 7E 40
Maxton Ct. EH22: Dalk 2C 42
Maxwell St. EH10: Edin 1E 32
Maybank Vs. EH12: Edin 4F 19
Mayburn Av. EH20: Loan 5B 40
Mayburn Bank EH20: Loan ...5B 40
Mayburn Cl. EH20: Loan 5B 40
Mayburn Ct. EH20: Loan 5B 40
Mayburn Cres. EH20: Loan ...5B 40
Mayburn Dr. EH20: Loan 5B 40
Mayburn Gdns. EH20: Loan ..5B 40
Mayburn Gro. EH20: Loan ...5B 40
Mayburn Hill EH20: Loan 5B 40
Mayburn Loan EH20: Loan ...4B 40
Mayburn Ter. EH20: Loan 4B 40
Mayburn Va. EH20: Loan 5A 40

Mayburn Wlk. EH20: Loan ...5B 40
Maybury Dr. EH12: Edin 3C 18
MAYBURY JUNC. 5C 18
Maybury Rd. EH4: Edin 5C 18
  EH12: Edin 5C 18
May Ct. EH4: Edin 5D 10
MAYFIELD
  EH9 ....7K 21
  EH22 ....6F 43
Mayfield Av. EH21: Muss 5D 24
Mayfield Ct. EH20: Loan 6C 40
Mayfield Cres. EH20: Loan ...6C 40
  EH21: Muss 4C 24
Mayfield Gdns. EH9: Edin ...7K 21
Mayfield Gdns. La.
  EH9: Edin 7K 21
Mayfield Ind. Est.
  EH22: May 1E 48
  EH22: Newt 7E 42
Mayfield Leisure Cen. 6F 43
Mayfield Pk. EH21: Muss 5D 24
Mayfield Pl. EH12: Edin 5F 19
  EH21: Muss 5D 24
  EH22: May 7F 43
Mayfield Rd. EH9: Edin 7K 21
  EH22: East 5F 43
Mayfield Ter. EH9: Edin 7K 21
MAYSHADE 5K 41
Mayshade Rd. EH20: Loan ...4B 40
Mayville Bank EH21: Muss ...2J 25
Mayville Gdns. EH5: Edin 4B 12
Mayville Gdns. E.
  EH5: Edin 4B 12
McDonald Road Stop (NET)
  (Due to open 2011) 1J 21
MEADOWBANK 2C 22
Meadowbank EH8: Edin 2B 22
Meadowbank Av. EH8: Edin ..2B 22
Meadowbank Cres.
  EH8: Edin 2B 22
Meadowbank Pl. EH8: Edin ..2B 22
Meadowbank Shop. Pk.
  EH7: Edin 1A 22
Meadowbank Sports Cen. ...2B 22
Meadowbank Stadium 2B 22
Meadowbank Ter. EH8: Edin ..2B 22
MEADOWFIELD 4D 22
Meadowfield Av. EH8: Edin ..4D 22
Meadowfield Ct. EH8: Edin ...4D 22
Meadowfield Dr. EH8: Edin ...4D 22
Meadowfield Gdns.
  EH8: Edin 5D 22
Meadowfield Rd.
  EH12: Edin 3A 18
Meadowfield Ter. EH8: Edin ..5D 22
Meadowhouse Ct.
  EH12: Edin 5G 19
Meadowhouse Rd.
  EH12: Edin 5G 19
Meadow La.
  EH8: Edin 7F 5 (5H 21)
MEADOWMILL 6G 15
Meadowmill Loan
  EH33: Tran 1H 27
Meadowmill Sports Cen. 7F 15
Meadow Pl. EH9: Edin 5G 21
  EH25: Bil 7J 39
Meadow Pl. La. EH9: Edin ...6H 21
  (off Roseneath Ter.)
Meadow Pl. Rd.
  EH12: Edin 5E 18
Meadow Rd. EH14: Cur 5B 30
Meadowside EH33: Tran 3J 27
Meadowspot EH10: Edin 2C 32
Mearenside EH12: Edin 3C 18
Medwin Ho. EH11: Edin 3E 30
Meetinghouse Dr.
  EH33: Tran 2G 27
Megabowl
  Edinburgh 5E 20
Meggat Pl. EH26: Pen 7E 44
Meggetgate EH14: Edin 1A 32
Meggetland 1B 32
Meggetland Sq. EH14: Edin ..1B 32
Meggetland Ter. EH14: Edin ..1C 32
Meggetland Vw. EH14: Edin ..1B 32
Meggetland Wynd
  EH14: Edin 1B 32
Melgund Ter. EH7: Edin 1H 21

Melville Cres. EH3: Edin 3E 20
Melville Dr.
  EH9: Edin 7C 4 (5G 21)
Melville Dykes Rd.
  EH18: Las 4H 41
  EH22: Dalk 4H 41
Melville Ga. EH22: Dalk 2K 41
Melville Ga. Rd. EH22: Dalk ..2K 41
Melville Grange Cotts.
  EH18: Las 1H 41
Melville Monument ...2E 4 (2H 21)
Melville Pl. EH3: Edin 3A 4
Melville Rd. EH22: Dalk 3A 42
Melville St.
  EH3: Edin 4A 4 (3E 20)
Melville St. La. EH3: Edin ...3E 20
  EH15: Port 3H 23
Melville Ter. EH9: Edin 6H 21
  EH22: Dalk 4A 42
Melville Vw. EH18: Las 5G 41
Mentone Av. EH15: Port 2H 23
Mentone Gdns. EH9: Edin ...7K 21
Mentone Ter. EH9: Edin 1K 33
Mercat Cross 4F 5
Merchant St. EH1: Edin 5E 4
MERCHISTON 7D 20
Merchiston Av. EH10: Edin ..6E 20
Merchiston Bank Av.
  EH10: Edin 7E 20
Merchiston Bank Gdns.
  EH10: Edin 7E 20
Merchiston Cres. EH10: Edin ..7E 20
Merchiston Gdns.
  EH10: Edin 1D 32
Merchiston Gro. EH11: Edin ..7C 20
Merchiston M. EH10: Edin ...6E 20
Merchiston Pk. EH10: Edin ...6E 20
Merchiston Pl. EH10: Edin ...6E 20
Merlyon Way EH26: Pen 7B 44
Mertoun Pl. EH11: Edin 6D 20
Methven Ter. EH18: Las 7F 41
Meuse La. EH2: Edin ...3E 4 (3H 21)
Middleby St. EH9: Edin 7K 21
Middlefield EH7: Edin 7D 12
Middleknowe EH14: Edin 4E 30
Middle Mdw. Wlk.
  EH3: Edin 7E 4 (5H 21)
Middlepark EH14: Edin 4E 30
Middleshot EH14: Edin 4E 30
Middleshot Sq. EH32: Pres ...4F 15
Midfield Ho. EH18: Las 1E 46
Mid Gillsland Rd.
  EH10: Edin 7D 20
Mid Gogarloch Syke
  EH12: Edin 6C 18
Mid Liberton EH16: Edin 2A 34
Midlothian Indoor Bowling Club
  ....2B 42
Midlothian Ski Cen. 3E 38
Midmar Av. EH10: Edin 2G 33
Midmar Dr. EH10: Edin 2G 33
Midmar Gdns. EH10: Edin ...2F 33
Mid New Cultins EH11: Edin ..2C 30
Mid Rd. EH32: Pres 7D 14
Mid Rd. Ind. Est. EH32: Pres ..7D 14
Mid Steil EH10: Edin 3C 32
Mid Ter. EH30: S Q'fry 1H 7
MILESTONE HOUSE (HOSPICE)
  ....4B 32
Millar Cres. EH10: Edin 1E 32
Millar Pl. EH10: Edin 1E 32
Millar Pl. La. EH10: Edin 1E 32
Millar Rd. EH33: Tran 3G 27
Millbank EH14: Bal 4E 36
Millbank Gro. EH23: Gore ...7E 48
Millbrae Wynd EH14: Edin ...2K 31
  (off Inglis Grn. Rd.)
Miller Ct. EH33: Tran 3F 27
Millerfield Pl. EH9: Edin 6H 21
Millerhill Rd. EH22: Dalk 2H 35
Miller Row EH4: Edin 3E 20
Millhill EH21: Muss 2F 25
Millhill Cotts. EH22: Newt ...6C 42
Millhill La. EH21: Muss 2F 25
Millhill Wynd EH21: Muss ...2F 25
Mill La. EH6: Leith 5E 12
Millstone Brow Cotts.
  EH23: Gore 7G 49
Mill Wynd EH32: Pres 5D 14

Milnacre EH6: Edin 5C **12**
Milne's Ct. EH1: Edin 4D **4**
Milrig Cotts. EH29: Kltn 3A **16**
MILTON BRIDGE 4F **45**
Milton Cres. EH15: Port 5G **23**
Milton Dr. EH15: Port 4K **23**
Milton Gdns. Nth.
 EH15: Port 5G **23**
Milton Gdns. Sth.
 EH15: Port 5G **23**
Milton Gro. EH15: Port 1A **24**
Milton Link EH15: Port 5J **23**
Milton Rd. EH15: Port 5G **23**
Milton Rd. E. EH15: Port 5J **23**
Milton Rd. W. EH15: Port 5E **22**
Milton St. EH8: Edin 2A **22**
Milton Ter. EH15: Port 1A **24**
Miner's Ter. EH21: Wall 3K **25**
Miners Wlk. EH22: Dalk 1F **43**
Minstrel Ct. EH25: Rosl 3A **46**
Mint Casino 4F **13**
Minto St. EH9: Edin 6K **21**
Mitchell St. EH6: Leith 5F **13**
 EH22: Dalk 2B **42**
Mitchell Way EH33: Tran 1H **27**
Moat Dr. EH14: Edin 7B **20**
Moat Ho. EH21: Edin 7B **20**
Moat Pl. EH14: Edin 7B **20**
Moat St. EH14: Edin 7B **20**
Moat Ter. EH14: Edin 7B **20**
Moat Vw. EH25: Rosl 3K **45**
Moffat Av. EH19: Bonn 7H **41**
Moffat Ter. EH33: Tran 4G **27**
Moira Pk. EH7: Edin 2E **22**
Moira Ter. EH7: Edin 2E **22**
 (not continuous)
Moira Ter. La. EH7: Edin 2E **22**
Moir Av. EH21: Muss 2J **25**
Moir Cres. EH21: Muss 2J **25**
Moir Dr. EH21: Muss 2J **25**
Moir Pl. EH21: Muss 2J **25**
Moir Ter. EH21: Muss 2J **25**
Moncrieffe Ho. EH17: Edin 4D **34**
Moncrieff Ter. EH9: Edin 6J **21**
Monkbarns Gdns.
 EH16: Edin 4B **34**
Monksrig Rd. EH26: Pen 2A **50**
MONKSWOOD 2D **48**
Monkswood Rd. EH22: Newt . . .2D **48**
MONKTONHALL 5D **24**
Monktonhall Pl.
 EH21: Muss 5D **24**
Monktonhall Ter.
 EH21: Muss 4D **24**
Monkwood Ct. EH9: Edin 7H **21**
Monmouth Ter. EH3: Edin 5A **12**
Montague St.
 EH8: Edin 7H **5** (5J **21**)
Montagu Ter. EH3: Edin 6A **12**
Montgomery St.
 EH7: Edin 1K **5** (1J **21**)
Montgomery St. La.
 EH7: Edin 1G **5** (1J **21**)
Montpelier EH10: Edin 6E **20**
Montpelier Pk. EH10: Edin 6E **20**
Montpelier Ter. EH10: Edin 6E **20**
Montrose Ter.
 EH7: Edin 1K **5** (2K **21**)
Moorfield Cotts. EH22: Dalk . . .4J **35**
Moorfoot Ct. EH19: Bonn 6H **41**
Moorfoot Pl. EH19: Bonn 7H **41**
 EH26: Pen 1C **50**
Moorfoot Vw. EH19: Bonn 7H **41**
 EH23: Gore 7E **48**
 EH25: Bil 1J **45**
Moray Pk. EH7: Edin 1A **22**
Moray Pk. Ter. EH7: Edin 1A **22**
Moray Pl. EH3: Edin 2A **4** (2F **21**)
MOREDUN 5E **34**
Moredun Dell EH17: Edin 5E **34**
Moredun Dykes Rd.
 EH17: Edin 7D **34**
Moredun Ho. EH4: Edin 7J **11**
 EH17: Edin 4D **34**
Moredun Pk. Ct. EH17: Edin . . .5D **34**
Moredun Pk. Dr.
 EH17: Edin 5D **34**
Moredun Pk. Gdns.
 EH17: Edin 4D **34**

Moredun Pk. Grn.
 EH17: Edin 5E **34**
Moredun Pk. Gro.
 EH17: Edin 5E **34**
Moredun Pk. Loan
 EH17: Edin 5D **34**
Moredun Pk. Rd.
 EH17: Edin 5D **34**
Moredun Pk. St. EH17: Edin . . .5D **34**
Moredun Pk. Vw. EH17: Edin . . .5E **34**
Moredun Pk. Wlk.
 EH17: Edin 5E **34**
Moredun Pk. Way
 EH17: Edin 5D **34**
Moredunvale Bank
 EH17: Edin 4D **34**
Moredunvale Grn.
 EH17: Edin 4D **34**
Moredunvale Gro.
 EH17: Edin 4D **34**
Moredunvale Loan
 EH17: Edin 4D **34**
Moredunvale Pk.
 EH17: Edin 4D **34**
Moredunvale Pl.
 EH17: Edin 4D **34**
Moredunvale Rd.
 EH17: Edin 4C **34**
Moredunvale Vw.
 EH17: Edin 4D **34**
Moredunvale Way
 EH17: Edin 4D **34**
Morham Gait EH10: Edin 4C **32**
Morham Gdns. EH10: Edin . . .4C **32**
Morham Lea EH10: Edin 4C **32**
Morham Pk. EH10: Edin 4C **32**
Morison Gdns. EH30: S Q'fry . .1G **7**
MORNINGSIDE 2D **32**
Morningside Dr. EH10: Edin . . .2D **32**
Morningside Dr. EH10: Edin . . .2D **32**
Morningside Gdns.
 EH10: Edin 2D **32**
Morningside Gro.
 EH10: Edin 2D **32**
Morningside Pk. EH10: Edin . . .1E **32**
Morningside Pl. EH10: Edin . . .1E **32**
Morningside Rd. EH10: Edin . . .7E **20**
Morningside Ter. EH10: Edin . . .1E **32**
Morrison Av. EH33: Tran 3J **27**
Morrison Cir. EH3: Edin 4E **20**
 (off Morrison Cres.)
Morrison Cres. EH3: Edin 4E **20**
Morrison Link EH3: Edin 4E **20**
Morrison's Cl. EH1: Edin 4G **5**
Morrison's Haven
 EH32: Pres 7A **14**
Morrison St.
 EH3: Edin 6A **4** (4E **20**)
Morris Rd. EH22: Newt 7E **42**
MORTONHALL 6G **33**
Mortonhall Cvn. Pk.
 EH16: Edin 6J **33**
Mortonhall Crematorium
 EH16: Edin 7K **33**
Mortonhall Ga. EH16: Edin 7H **33**
Mortonhall Pk. Av.
 EH17: Edin 7K **33**
Mortonhall Pk. Bank
 EH17: Edin 7A **34**
Mortonhall Pk. Cres.
 EH17: Edin 7A **34**
Mortonhall Pk. Dr.
 EH17: Edin 7A **34**
Mortonhall Pk. Gdns.
 EH17: Edin 7K **33**
Mortonhall Pk. Grn.
 EH17: Edin 7A **34**
Mortonhall Pk. Gro.
 EH17: Edin 7K **33**
Mortonhall Pk. Loan
 EH17: Edin 7K **33**
Mortonhall Pk. Pl.
 EH17: Edin 7A **34**
Mortonhall Pk. Ter.
 EH17: Edin 7A **34**
Mortonhall Pk. Vw.
 EH17: Edin 7K **33**
Mortonhall Pk. Way
 EH17: Edin 7K **33**

Mortonhall Rd. EH9: Edin 1H **33**
Morton Mains Cotts.
 EH10: Edin 1G **39**
Morton St. EH15: Port 4J **23**
Morvenside EH14: Edin 4E **30**
Morvenside Cl. EH14: Edin 4E **30**
Morven St. EH4: Edin 2E **18**
Mossend Cotts. EH23: Gore . . .6G **49**
Mossgiel Wlk. EH16: Edin 3A **34**
Moston Ter. EH9: Edin 7K **21**
Moubray Gro. EH30: S Q'fry . . .2H **7**
Mound, The
 EH1: Edin 3D **4** (3G **21**)
 EH2: Edin 3D **4** (3G **21**)
Mound Pl. EH1: Edin 4D **4** (3G **21**)
Mt. Alvernia EH16: Edin 5B **34**
MOUNTCASTLE 3F **23**
Mountcastle Bank EH8: Edin . . .3F **23**
Mountcastle Cres. EH8: Edin . . .3E **22**
Mountcastle Dr. Nth.
 EH8: Edin 3E **22**
 EH15: Port 3E **22**
Mountcastle Dr. Sth.
 EH15: Edin, Port 4F **23**
Mountcastle Gdns.
 EH8: Edin 3E **22**
Mountcastle Grn. EH8: Edin . . .2E **22**
Mountcastle Gro. EH8: Edin . . .3E **22**
Mountcastle Loan EH8: Edin . . .3E **22**
Mountcastle Pk. EH8: Edin 3E **22**
Mountcastle Pl. EH8: Edin 2E **22**
Mountcastle Ter. EH8: Edin 3E **22**
Mt. Grange EH9: Edin 7G **21**
Mounthooly Loan
 EH10: Edin 7G **33**
Mountjoy Ct. EH21: Muss 1E **24**
Mountjoy Ter. EH21: Muss 1E **24**
Mt. Lodge Pl. EH15: Port 3H **23**
Mt. Vernon Rd. EH16: Edin 4B **34**
Mucklets Av. EH21: Muss 4C **24**
Mucklets Ct. EH21: Muss 4C **24**
Mucklets Cres. EH21: Muss 4C **24**
Mucklets Dr. EH21: Muss 4C **24**
Mucklets Pl. EH21: Muss 4C **24**
Muirdale Ter. EH4: Edin 1K **19**
Muirend Av. EH14: J Grn 5G **31**
Muirfield Gdns. EH20: Loan . . .6C **40**
Muir Hall EH4: Edin 3E **20**
Muirhead Pl. EH26: Pen 6D **44**
MUIRHOUSE 5D **10**
Muirhouse Av. EH4: Edin 6E **10**
Muirhouse Av. Nth.
 EH4: Edin 5E **10**
Muirhouse Bank EH4: Edin 6E **10**
Muirhouse Cl. EH4: Edin 6D **10**
Muirhouse Ct. EH4: Edin 5D **10**
Muirhouse Cres. EH4: Edin 6D **10**
Muirhouse Dr. EH4: Edin 5D **10**
Muirhouse Gdns. EH4: Edin . . .5D **10**
Muirhouse Grn. EH4: Edin 6D **10**
Muirhouse Gro. EH4: Edin 5D **10**
Muirhouse Loan EH4: Edin 5E **10**
Muirhouse Medway
 EH4: Edin 6D **10**
Muirhouse Pk. EH4: Edin 6D **10**
Muirhouse Parkway
 EH4: Edin 5D **10**
Muirhouse Pl. E. EH4: Edin 6E **10**
Muirhouse Pl. W. EH4: Edin . . .6E **10**
Muirhouse Ter. EH4: Edin 6D **10**
Muirhouse Vw. EH4: Edin 5D **10**
Muirhouse Way EH4: Edin 6E **10**
Muirpark EH22: Dalk 4A **42**
Muirpark Ct. EH33: Tran 3J **27**
Muirpark Dr. EH33: Tran 3J **27**
Muirpark Gdns. EH33: Tran 3J **27**
Muirpark Gro. EH33: Tran 3J **27**
Muirpark Pl. EH33: Tran 3J **27**
Muirpark Rd. EH33: Tran 3J **27**
Muirpark Ter. EH33: Tran 3J **27**
Muirpark Wynd EH33: Tran 3J **27**
Muirside EH10: Edin 7C **32**
Muirside Dr. EH33: Tran 3G **27**
Muir Wood Cres. EH14: Cur . . .7D **30**
Muir Wood Dr. EH14: Cur 7D **30**
Muir Wood Gro. EH14: Cur 7D **30**
Muir Wood Pl. EH14: Cur 7C **30**
Muir Wood Rd. EH14: Cur 7C **30**
Mulberry Pl. EH6: Edin 5C **12**

Multrees Wlk. EH1: Edin 2E **4**
Munro Dr. EH13: Edin 7J **31**
Munro Pl. EH3: Edin 7B **12**
Murano Pl. EH7: Edin 1K **21**
Murderdean Rd. EH22: Newt . . .7B **42**
Murdoch Ter. EH11: Edin 5E **20**
Murieston Cres. EH11: Edin 5C **20**
Murieston Cres. La.
 EH11: Edin 5C **20**
Murieston La. EH11: Edin 5C **20**
Murieston Pl. EH11: Edin 5C **20**
Murieston Rd. EH11: Edin 5C **20**
Murieston Ter. EH11: Edin 5C **20**
Murrayburn App. EH14: Edin . . .3F **31**
Murrayburn Dr. EH14: Edin 3E **30**
Murrayburn Gdns.
 EH14: Edin 3F **31**
Murrayburn Ga. EH14: Edin 4F **31**
Murrayburn Grn. EH14: Edin . . .3G **31**
Murrayburn Gro. EH14: Edin . . .3G **31**
Murrayburn Pk. EH14: Edin 3F **31**
Murrayburn Pl. EH14: Edin 3F **31**
Murrayburn Rd. EH14: Edin 3F **31**
Murray Cotts. EH12: Edin 5E **18**
MURRAYFIELD 4A **20**
Murrayfield Av. EH12: Edin 4B **20**
Murrayfield Dr. EH12: Edin 4A **20**
Murrayfield Gdns.
 EH12: Edin 4B **20**
Murrayfield Ice Rink 5A **20**
Murrayfield Pl. EH12: Edin 4B **20**
Murrayfield Rd. EH12: Edin 3A **20**
MURRAYFIELD SPIRE HOSPITAL
 . . . . .4J **19**
Murrayfield Stadium 5A **20**
Murrayfield Stadium Stop (NET)
 (Due to open 2011) 5B **20**
Murrayfield Wanderers FC 5A **20**
Murray Pl. EH12: Edin 5G **19**
Murrays, The EH17: Edin 1C **40**
Murrays Brae, The
 EH17: Edin 1C **40**
Mus. of Edinburgh, The
 . . . . .3H **5** (3J **21**)
Mus. of Fire 6C **4** (4G **21**)
Mus. on the Mound (HBOS) . . .4E **4**
MUSSELBURGH 2E **24**
Musselburgh By-Pass
 EH15: Edin 6J **23**
 EH21: Muss, Wall 6E **24**
 EH33: Tran 6E **24**
Musselburgh Mus. 2E **24**
Musselburgh Race Course 1G **25**
Musselburgh Rd. EH15: Port . . .4K **23**
 EH22: Dalk 1C **42**
MUSSELBURGH SERVICE AREA
 . . . . .6D **24**
Musselburgh Sports Cen. 3F **25**
Musselburgh Station (Rail) . . .4C **24**
Myre Dale EH19: Bonn 7J **41**
MYRESIDE 1D **32**
Myreside 1C **32**
Myreside EH19: Bonn 1K **47**
Myreside Ct. EH10: Edin 1D **32**
Myreside Rd. EH10: Edin 1D **32**
Myreside Vw. EH14: Edin 1C **32**
Myrtle Cres. EH25: Bil 7J **39**
Myrtle Gro. EH22: May 6F **43**
Myrtle Ter. EH11: Edin 6C **20**

N

Namur Rd. EH26: Pen 6D **44**
Nantwich Dr. EH7: Edin 7K **13**
Napier Loan EH10: Edin 7D **20**
Napier Rd. EH10: Edin 7D **20**
Napier University
 Craiglockhart Campus 2C **32**
 Craiglockhart Campus 3B **32**
 Marchmont Campus 6H **21**
 Merchiston Campus 7E **20**
 Morningside Campus 7F **21**
 Sighthill Campus 2C **32**
National Gallery 4D **4** (3G **21**)
National Library of Scotland
 George IV Bri. 4E **4** (4H **21**)
 Salisbury Pl. 6J **21**
National Monument . . .2H **5** (2J **21**)

National Mus. of Scotland
.... .5F 5 (4H 21)
National War Mus. 4C 4 (3G 21)
Neidpath Ct. EH12: Edin 4C 18
Nellfield EH16: Edin 4B 34
Nelson Monument 2H 5
Nelson Pl. EH3: Edin ..1D 4 (1G 21)
Nelson St. EH3: Edin ..1D 4 (2G 21)
Ness Pl. EH33: Tran 4G 27
Nether Bakehouse EH8: Edin ..4J 5
Netherbank EH16: Edin 6K 33
Netherbank Vw. EH16: Edin ..6K 33
Netherbow Arts Cen. . . .4G 5 (3J 21)
Netherby Rd. EH5: Edin 5K 11
Nether Craigour EH17: Edin ..3D 34
Nether Craigwell EH8: Edin 3J 5
Nether Currie Cres.
    EH14: Cur 7D 30
Nether Currie Pl. EH14: Cur ..7D 30
Nether Currie Rd.
    EH14: Cur 7D 30
NETHER LIBERTON 2A 34
Nether Liberton Ct.
    EH16: Edin 2A 34
Nether Liberton La.
    EH16: Edin 2A 34
Nethershot Rd. EH32: Pres 5E 14
Nevis Gdns. EH26: Pen 1E 50
New Arthur Pl.
    EH8: Edin 5H 5 (4J 21)
NEWBATTLE 5B 42
Newbattle Abbey Cres.
    EH22: Dalk 5B 42
Newbattle Gdns. EH22: Dalk ..4C 42
Newbattle Pool 1C 48
Newbattle Rd.
    EH22: Dalk, Newt 3B 42
Newbattle Ter. EH10: Edin ...7F 21
New Belfield EH8: Edin 4E 22
New Bells Ct. EH6: Leith ...5F 13
NEWBIGGING 3G 7
Newbigging EH21: Muss 2F 25
        (not continuous)
NEWBRIDGE 5A 16
Newbridge Ind. Est.
    EH28: Nbdge 6A 16
NEWBRIDGE JUNC. 5A 16
Newbridge Rd. EH28: Nbdge ...5A 16
Newbridge Sth.
    EH28: Nbdge 7A 16
New Broompark EH5: Edin ...3H 11
New Broughton
    EH3: Edin 1E 4 (1H 21)
Newbyres Av. EH23: Gore 5E 48
Newbyres Castle (remains of)
    ....7E 48
        (off Main St.)
Newbyres Cres. EH23: Gore ...6E 48
Newbyres Gdns. EH23: Gore ...6E 48
NEWCRAIGHALL 6K 23
Newcraighall Bus. Pk.
    EH15: Edin 7H 23
        (off Blackchapel)
Newcraighall Dr. EH21: Edin ..7K 23
Newcraighall Junc.
    EH15: Edin 7J 23
Newcraighall Rd.
    EH15: Edin 7H 23
    EH21: Edin 7H 23
Newcraighall Station (Rail) ..7K 23
New Cut Rigg EH6: Newh 5C 12
NEWHAILES 2B 24
Newhailes 2B 24
Newhailes Av. EH21: Muss ...2C 24
Newhailes Bus. Pk.
    EH21: Muss 2C 24
Newhailes Cres.
    EH21: Muss 2B 24
Newhailes Ind. Est.
    EH21: Muss 3B 24
Newhailes Rd. EH21: Muss ...3B 24
Newhalls Rd. EH30: S Q'fry ...1J 7
NEWHAVEN 4C 12
Newhaven Heritage Mus. ...3C 12
Newhaven Main St.
    EH6: Newh 4B 12
Newhaven Pl. EH6: Newh 3C 12
Newhaven Rd.
    EH6: Edin, Newh 4C 12

Newhaven Stop (NET)
    (Due to open 2011) 3C 12
New Hunterfield
    EH23: Gore 3C 48
NEWINGTON 5K 21
Newington Rd. EH9: Edin 6J 21
New John's Pl.
    EH8: Edin 7H 5 (5J 21)
Newkirkgate EH6: Leith 6E 12
        (off Kirkgate)
Newkirkgate Shop. Cen.
    EH6: Leith 5E 12
        (off Kirkgate)
New Lairdship Pl.
    EH11: Edin 1F 31
New Lairdship Yards
    EH11: Edin 1F 31
NEWLANDRIG 4K 49
Newlands Pk. EH9: Edin 7K 21
New La. EH6: Newh 4C 12
New Liston Rd. EH29: Kltn ...3A 16
Newmains Farm La.
    EH29: Kltn 1A 16
Newmains Rd. EH29: Kltn ...1A 16
New Mkt. Rd. EH14: Edin ...1A 32
New Mart Gdns. EH14: Edin ..1K 31
New Mart Pl. EH14: Edin ...1K 31
New Mart Rd. EH14: Edin ...1K 31
New Mart Sq. EH14: Edin ...1K 31
New Meadowspott
    EH22: Dalk 3B 42
Newmills Av. EH14: Bal 1F 37
Newmills Ct. EH14: Bal 2F 37
Newmills Cres. EH14: Bal ...2F 37
Newmills Gro. EH14: Bal ...2F 37
Newmills Rd. EH14: Bal 2F 37
    EH14: Bal, Cur 1E 36
    EH22: Dalk 2C 42
Newmills Ter. EH22: Dalk ...2D 42
New Orchardfield EH6: Leith ..6E 12
NEW PENTLAND 5A 40
New Row EH33: Tran 2G 27
New Skinner's Cl. EH1: Edin ..4G 5
News Steps, The EH1: Edin ...4E 4
New Star Bank EH22: Newt ...1C 48
New St. EH8: Edin ..3G 5 (3J 21)
    EH21: Muss 2C 24
    EH32: Cock 3G 15
    EH32: Pres 6D 14
    EH33: Tran 1G 27
New Swanston EH10: Edin ...7C 32
Newtoft St. EH17: Edin 7D 34
NEWTON 2A 6
New Chu. Rd. EH22: Dan ...5H 35
NEWTONGRANGE 1D 48
Newtongrange Pl.
    EH22: Newt 1D 48
NEWTONLOAN 3D 48
Newtonloan Ct. EH23: Gore ...4K 48
Newton St. EH11: Edin 6C 20
    EH22: East 5E 42
NEWTON VILLAGE 4K 35
Newton Village EH22: Dalk ..4K 35
New Tower Pl. EH15: Port 2H 23
NEW TOWN 1C 4 (2G 21)
Next Generation Club
    Edinburgh 3C 12
Nichollfield EH6: Newh 4C 12
Nicolson Sq.
    EH8: Edin 6G 5 (4J 21)
Nicolson St.
    EH8: Edin 5G 5 (4J 21)
NIDDRIE 7G 23
Niddrie Cotts. EH15: Edin ...7J 23
Niddrie Farm Gro.
    EH16: Edin 7E 22
Niddrie Ho. Av. EH16: Edin ..1F 35
Niddrie Ho. Dr. EH16: Edin ..7G 23
Niddrie Ho. Gdns.
    EH16: Edin 1F 35
Niddrie Ho. Gro. EH16: Edin ..1F 35
Niddrie Ho. Pk. EH16: Edin ..1F 35
Niddrie Ho. Sq. EH16: Edin ..1F 35
NIDDRIE MAINS 6F 23
Niddrie Mains Ct.
    EH16: Edin 7F 23
Niddrie Mains Dr.
    EH16: Edin 7E 22
        (not continuous)

Niddrie Mains Rd.
    EH15: Edin 7D 22
    EH16: Edin 7D 22
Niddrie Mains Ter.
    EH16: Edin 7E 22
        (not continuous)
NIDDRIE MARISCHAL 1G 35
Niddrie Marischal Cres.
    EH16: Edin 7F 23
Niddrie Marischal Dr.
    EH16: Edin 1F 35
Niddrie Marischal Gdns.
    EH16: Edin 7F 23
Niddrie Marischal Grn.
    EH16: Edin 1F 35
Niddrie Marischal Gro.
    EH16: Edin 7G 23
Niddrie Marischal Loan
    EH16: Edin 7F 23
Niddrie Marischal Pl.
    EH16: Edin 1F 35
Niddrie Marischal Rd.
    EH16: Edin 7G 23
Niddrie Marischal St.
    EH16: Edin 7F 23
NIDDRIE MILL 7G 23
Niddrie Mill Av.
    EH16: Edin 7G 23
Niddrie Mill Cres.
    EH16: Edin 7G 23
Niddrie Mill Dr. EH15: Edin ..7G 23
Niddrie Mill Gro.
    EH16: Edin 7G 23
Niddrie Mill Pl. EH15: Edin ..7G 23
Niddrie Mill Ter. EH16: Edin ..7G 23
Niddry St. EH1: Edin 4F 5 (3J 21)
Niddry St. Sth.
    EH1: Edin 5G 5 (4J 21)
Nigel Loan EH16: Edin 4B 34
Nightingale Way
    EH3: Edin 7D 4 (5G 21)
Nile Gro. EH10: Edin 1F 33
Nimmo Av. EH32: Pres 6E 14
Ninth St. EH22: Newt 7D 42
Nisbet Ct. EH7: Edin 7G 13
NIVEN'S KNOWE 6K 39
Nivensknowe Pk.
    EH20: Loan 6J 39
Niven's Knowe Rd.
    EH20: Loan 6K 39
Nobel Pl. EH25: Rosl 3K 45
Noble Pl. EH6: Leith 6G 13
Nth. Bank Rd. EH32: Pres ...6C 14
Nth. Bank St.
    EH1: Edin 4E 4 (3H 21)
North Bri. EH1: Edin ..3F 5 (3H 21)
North Bri. Arc. EH1: Edin 4F 5
Nth. Bughtlin Bank
    EH12: Edin 2D 18
Nth. Bughtlin Brae
    EH12: Edin 2D 18
North Bughtlinfield
    EH12: Edin 2C 18
Nth. Bughtlin Ga.
    EH12: Edin 2D 18
Nth. Bughtlin Neuk
    EH12: Edin 2D 18
Nth. Bughtlin Pl. EH12: Edin ..2D 18
North Bughtlinrig
    EH12: Edin 2C 18
Nth. Bughtlin Rd.
    EH12: Edin 2D 18
North Bughtlinside
    EH12: Edin 2C 18
North Cairntow EH16: Edin ...6D 22
Nth. Castle St.
    EH2: Edin 2B 4 (2F 21)
Nth. Charlotte St.
    EH2: Edin 2A 4 (3F 21)
Nth. Clyde St. La.
    EH1: Edin 1E 4 (2H 21)
Northcote St. EH11: Edin 5D 20
North Cres. EH32: Pres 6E 14
North E. Circus Pl. EH3: Edin ..1B 4
NORTHFIELD 3D 22
Northfield EH32: Pres 7D 14
    EH33: Tran 2J 27
Northfield Av. EH8: Edin 3D 22
Northfield B'way. EH8: Edin ...2D 22

Northfield Cir. EH8: Edin 3D 22
Northfield Ct. EH32: Pres 7D 14
Northfield Cres. EH8: Edin ...3D 22
Northfield Dr. EH8: Edin 4E 22
Northfield E. EH33: Tran 2J 27
Northfield Farm Av.
    EH8: Edin 4E 22
Northfield Farm Rd.
    EH8: Edin 3E 22
Northfield Gdns. EH8: Edin ..4E 22
    EH32: Pres 7D 14
Northfield Gro. EH8: Edin ...4E 22
Northfield Hgts. EH8: Edin ...7F 22
        (off Northumberland Rd.)
Northfield Pk. EH8: Edin 3E 22
Northfield Pk. Gro.
    EH8: Edin 3E 22
Northfield Rd. EH8: Edin 3D 22
Northfield Sq. EH8: Edin 3D 22
Northfield Ter. EH8: Edin 3D 22
Nth. Fort St. EH6: Newh 4D 12
Nth. Grange Av. EH32: Pres ...7C 14
Nth. Grange Gro.
    EH32: Pres 6D 14
Nth. Grange Rd. EH32: Pres ...6D 14
Nth. Gray's Cl. EH1: Edin 4F 5
North Greens EH15: Edin 6H 23
Nth. Gyle Av. EH12: Edin ...5D 18
Nth. Gyle Dr. EH12: Edin ...4D 18
Nth. Gyle Farm Ct.
    EH12: Edin 5C 18
Nth. Gyle Farm La.
    EH12: Edin 5C 18
Nth. Gyle Gro. EH12: Edin ...4C 18
Nth. Gyle Loan EH12: Edin ...4C 18
Nth. Gyle Pk. EH12: Edin ...4C 18
Nth. Gyle Rd. EH12: Edin ...4D 18
Nth. Gyle Ter. EH12: Edin ...5C 18
Nth. High St. EH21: Muss ...2D 24
North Hillhousefield
    EH6: Newh 4D 12
Nth. Junc. St. EH6: Newh ...4D 12
Northlawn Ct. EH4: Edin 6B 10
Northlawn Ter. EH4: Edin 6B 10
NORTH LEITH 4E 12
Nth. Leith Mill EH6: Leith ...4D 12
Nth. Leith Sands EH6: Leith ..4D 12
Nth. Lorimer Pl. EH32: Cock ..3F 15
North Mdw. Wlk.
    EH3: Edin 7C 4 (5G 21)
    EH8: Edin 7E 4 (5H 21)
North Meggetland
    EH14: Edin 1B 32
Northpark EH6: Newh 5C 12
North Pk. Ter. EH4: Edin 1E 20
Nth. Peffer Pl. EH16: Edin ...7D 22
Nth. Pilrig Hgts. EH6: Edin ...6D 12
Nth. Richmond St.
    EH8: Edin 5G 5 (4J 21)
Nth. St Andrew La.
    EH2: Edin 2E 4 (2H 21)
Nth. St Andrew St.
    EH2: Edin 1E 4 (2H 21)
Nth. St David St.
    EH2: Edin 2D 4 (2H 21)
Nth. Seton Pk. EH32: Port S ...3G 15
North St. EH28: Rat 2D 28
Northumberland Pl.
    EH3: Edin 1D 4 (2G 21)
Northumberland Pl. La.
    EH3: Edin 1D 4
Northumberland St.
    EH3: Edin 1C 4 (2G 21)
Northumberland St. Nth. E. La.
    EH3: Edin 1D 4 (2G 21)
Northumberland St. Nth. W. La.
    EH3: Edin 1C 4 (2G 21)
Northumberland St. Sth. E. La.
    EH3: Edin 1D 4 (2G 21)
Northumberland St. Sth. W. La.
    EH3: Edin 1C 4 (2G 21)
Northview Ct. EH4: Edin 5E 10
North Wlk., The EH10: Edin ...2E 32
North Way, The EH10: Edin ...3D 22
Nth. Werber Pk. EH4: Edin ...7H 11
Nth. Werber Pl. EH4: Edin ...6H 11
Nth. Werber Rd. EH4: Edin ...7H 11
North W. Circus Pl.
    EH3: Edin 1A 4 (2F 21)

North Wynd EH22: Dalk 2C 42
Norton Mains Cotts.
  EH28: Ing 6F 17
NORTON PARK 1K 5 (1A 22)
Norton Pk. EH7: Edin 1A 22
Nursey, The EH18: Las 6F 41

O

Oak Av. EH20: Loan 6K 39
Oak Cres. EH22: May 7G 43
Oakfield Pl. EH8: Edin . . .5H 5 (4J 21)
Oak La. EH12: Edin 2G 19
Oaklea Cotts. EH23: Gore 6G 49
Oak Pl. EH22: May 6G 43
Oakville Ter. EH6: Edin 6G 13
Oak Way EH26: Mil B 5E 44
Observatory Grn. EH9: Edin 2J 33
Observatory Rd. EH9: Edin 2H 33
Ocean Dr. EH6: Leith 4D 12
Ocean Terminal EH6: Leith 3D 12
Ocean Terminal Stop (NET)
  (Due to open 2011) 4E 12
Ocean Way EH6: Leith 4F 13
  (off Constitution Pl.)
Ochil Ct. EH30: S Q'fry 2H 7
Ochiltree Gdns. EH16: Edin 3C 34
Odeon Cinema
  Edinburgh 6B 4 (4F 21)
  Wester Hailes 4F 31
Ogilvie Ter. EH11: Edin 7C 20
Old Assembly Cl. EH1: Edin 4F 5
Old Broughton
  EH3: Edin 1E 4 (1H 21)
Old Burdiehouse Rd.
  EH17: Edin 2A 40
Old Church La. EH15: Edin 5C 22
Old Course Ga. EH21: Muss . . .1F 25
OLD CRAIGHALL 7C 24
OLD CRAIGHALL JUNC. 6D 24
Old Craighall Rd.
  EH21: Muss 7B 24
  EH22: Dalk . . . . .7B 24 & 5K 35
Old Dalkeith Rd. EH16: Edin . . .1B 34
  EH17: Edin 4F 35
  EH22: Dalk 1K 41
  EH22: Dan 5F 35
Old Edinburgh Rd.
  EH22: Dalk 2B 42
Old Farm Av. EH13: Edin 5K 31
Old Farm Ct. EH13: Edin 5K 31
Old Farm Pl. EH13: Edin 6K 31
Old Fishmarket Cl.
  EH1: Edin 4F 5 (3H 21)
Old Kirk Rd. EH12: Edin 4G 19
Old Liston Rd. EH28: Nbdge . . .5A 16
Old Mill La. EH16: Edin 2A 34
Old Newmills Rd. EH14: Bal . . .2F 37
OLD PENTLAND 4J 39
Old Pentland Rd. EH10: Edin . .5H 39
Old Playhouse Cl. EH8: Edin . . .4H 5
Old Star Rd. EH22: Newt 1B 48
Old Tolbooth Wynd
  EH8: Edin 3H 5 (3J 21)
OLD TOWN 5E 4 (4H 21)
Oliphant Gdns. EH21: Wall . . .3K 25
Olivebank Retail Pk.
  EH21: Muss 2C 24
Olive Bank Rd. EH21: Muss . . .2C 24
Omni Cen. EH1: Edin . . .1G 5 (2J 21)
Open Eye Gallery 1D 4
Orchard, The EH21: Muss 3D 24
  (off Stoneyhill Farm Rd.)
  EH33: Tran 1G 27
Orchard Bank EH4: Edin 2C 20
Orchard Brae EH4: Edin 1D 20
Orchard Brae Av. EH4: Edin . . .2C 20
Orchard Brae Gdns.
  EH4: Edin 2C 20
Orchard Brae Gdns. W.
  EH4: Edin 2C 20
Orchard Brae W. EH4: Edin . . .1D 20
Orchard Cres. EH4: Edin 2B 20
  EH32: Pres 6D 14
Orchard Dr. EH4: Edin 2B 20
Orchardfield Av. EH12: Edin . . .5F 19
Orchardfield La. EH6: Edin 7E 12
Orchardfield Ter. EH27: Wilk . .7A 28

Orchard Gro. EH4: Edin 2D 20
Orchardhead Loan
  EH16: Edin 4A 34
Orchardhead Rd. EH16: Edin . . .3A 34
Orchard Pk. EH33: Tran 1G 27
Orchard Pl. EH4: Edin 1C 20
Orchard Rd. EH4: Edin 2C 20
Orchard Rd. Sth. EH4: Edin . . .2B 20
Orchard Ter. EH4: Edin 2C 20
Orchard Toll EH4: Edin 2C 20
Orchard Vw. EH22: Dalk 3A 42
Ormelie Ter. EH15: Port 3J 23
Ormidale Ter. EH12: Edin 4A 20
Ormiston Av. EH33: Tran 2J 27
Ormiston Cres. E.
  EH33: Tran 2J 27
Ormiston Cres. W.
  EH33: Tran 2J 27
Ormiston Pl. EH32: Pres 6C 14
Ormiston Rd. EH33: Tran 2H 27
Ormiston Ter. EH12: Edin 5F 19
Orrock La. EH16: Edin 3A 34
Orrock Pl. EH16: Edin 2A 34
Orwell Pl. EH11: Edin 5D 20
Orwell Ter. EH11: Edin 5D 20
Osborne Ct. EH32: Cock 3G 15
Osborne Ter. EH12: Edin 4D 20
  EH32: Cock, Port S 3G 15
Oswald Ct. EH9: Edin 1H 33
Oswald Rd. EH9: Edin 1H 33
Oswald Ter. EH12: Edin 5F 19
  EH32: Pres 6E 14
Otterburn Pk. EH14: Edin 4K 31
Our Dynamic Earth 4J 5 (3K 21)
Oxcars Ct. EH4: Edin 5D 10
Oxcraig St. EH5: Edin 3J 11
Oxford St. EH8: Edin 5K 21
Oxford Ter. EH4: Edin 2E 20
Oxgangs Av. EH13: Edin 6C 32
Oxgangs Bank EH13: Edin 6D 32
Oxgangs Brae EH13: Edin 6D 32
Oxgangs B'way. EH13: Edin . . .6D 32
  (off Oxgangs Bank)
Oxgangs Cres. EH13: Edin 5D 32
Oxgangs Dr. EH13: Edin 5D 32
  (not continuous)
Oxgangs Farm Av.
  EH13: Edin 6C 32
Oxgangs Farm Dr.
  EH13: Edin 6C 32
Oxgangs Farm Gdns.
  EH13: Edin 6C 32
Oxgangs Farm Gro.
  EH13: Edin 6C 32
Oxgangs Farm Loan
  EH13: Edin 6C 32
Oxgangs Farm Ter.
  EH13: Edin 6C 32
Oxgangs Gdns. EH13: Edin 5C 32
Oxgangs Grn. EH13: Edin 5D 32
Oxgangs Gro. EH13: Edin 5D 32
Oxgangs Hill EH13: Edin 5D 32
Oxgangs Ho. EH13: Edin 5C 32
Oxgangs Loan EH13: Edin 5D 32
Oxgangs Medway
  EH13: Edin 6D 32
Oxgangs Pk. EH13: Edin 6D 32
Oxgangs Path EH13: Edin 6D 32
Oxgangs Path E. EH13: Edin . .6D 32
  (off Oxgangs Brae)
Oxgangs Pl. EH13: Edin 5C 32
Oxgangs Ri. EH13: Edin 5D 32
Oxgangs Rd. EH10: Edin 7D 32
Oxgangs Rd. Nth.
  EH13: Edin 4B 32
  EH14: Edin 4B 32
Oxgangs Row EH13: Edin 6D 32
Oxgangs St. EH13: Edin 6D 32
Oxgangs Ter. EH13: Edin 6C 32
Oxgangs Vw. EH13: Edin 6D 32
Ox Wlk. EH32: Pres 6C 14

P

Paddock, The EH21: Muss 1F 25
Paddockholm, The
  EH12: Edin 5G 19

Paisley Av. EH8: Edin 3D 22
Paisley Cl. EH1: Edin 4G 5
Paisley Cres. EH8: Edin 3C 22
Paisley Dr. EH8: Edin 4D 22
Paisley Gdns. EH8: Edin 3C 22
Paisley Gro. EH8: Edin 4D 22
Paisley Ter. EH8: Edin 3C 22
Palace of Holyroodhouse
  . . . . .3K 5 (3K 21)
Palmer Pl. EH14: Cur 1H 37
Palmer Rd. EH14: Cur 7B 30
Palmerston Pl. EH12: Edin 3D 20
Palmerston Pl. La.
  EH12: Edin 4E 20
Palmerston Rd. EH9: Edin 6H 21
Pandore Wlk. EH32: Pres 6C 14
Pankhurst Loan
  EH22: Dalk 2F 43
Panmure Cl. EH8: Edin 3H 5
Panmure Pl.
  EH3: Edin 7C 4 (5G 21)
Pansey Wlk. EH11: Edin 6A 20
Papermill Wynd EH7: Edin 7D 12
Pape's Cotts. EH12: Edin 4B 20
Paradykes Av. EH20: Loan 5A 40
Park & Ride
  Hermiston 3C 30
  Ingliston 6G 17
  Sheriffhall 6J 35
  Straiton 3A 40
Park Av. EH15: Port 4G 23
  EH20: Loan 6A 40
  EH21: Muss 3G 25
  EH23: Gore 5E 48
  EH25: Bil 7H 39
Park Ct. EH21: Muss 3G 25
Park Cres. EH16: Edin 4B 34
  EH19: Bonn 6H 41
  EH20: Loan 6B 40
  EH22: East 5E 42
Park Dr. EH21: Wall 4J 25
Parker Av. EH7: Edin 2E 22
Parker Rd. EH7: Edin 2E 22
Parker Ter. EH7: Edin 2F 23
Park Gdns. EH16: Edin 4B 34
  EH21: Muss 3F 25
  EH21: Wall 3J 25
Park Gro. EH16: Edin 5B 34
Parkgrove Av. EH4: Edin 1E 18
Parkgrove Bank EH4: Edin 1E 18
Parkgrove Cres. EH4: Edin 1E 18
Parkgrove Dr. EH4: Edin 1D 18
Parkgrove Gdns. EH4: Edin 1E 18
Parkgrove Grn. EH4: Edin 1E 18
Parkgrove Loan EH4: Edin 1E 18
Parkgrove Neuk EH4: Edin 1E 18
Parkgrove Path EH4: Edin 1E 18
Park Gro. Pl. EH21: Muss 3G 25
Parkgrove Pl. EH4: Edin 1E 18
Parkgrove Rd. EH4: Edin 1E 18
Parkgrove Row EH4: Edin 1E 18
Parkgrove St. EH4: Edin 1E 18
Park Gro. Ter. EH21: Muss 3G 25
Parkgrove Ter. EH4: Edin 1E 18
Parkgrove Vw. EH4: Edin 1E 18
PARKHEAD 2G 31
Parkhead Av. EH11: Edin 2G 31
Parkhead Cres. EH11: Edin 2G 31
Parkhead Dr. EH11: Edin 2G 31
Parkhead Gdns.
  EH11: Edin 2G 31
Parkhead Gro. EH11: Edin 2G 31
Parkhead Loan EH11: Edin 2H 31
Parkhead Pk. EH22: East 5E 42
Parkhead Pl. EH11: Edin 2G 31
  EH22: East 5E 42
Parkhead St. EH11: Edin 2G 31
Parkhead Ter. EH11: Edin 2H 31
Parkhead Vw. EH11: Edin 2G 31
Parkhill EH23: Gore 5D 48
Park La. EH15: Port 4G 23
  EH21: Muss 3G 25
Park Pl. EH6: Newh 4B 12
Park Rd. EH6: Newh 4B 12
  EH19: Bonn 6H 41
  EH22: Dalk 3B 42
  EH22: Newt 7D 42
  EH23: Gore 5E 48
  EH32: Port S 3H 15

Parkside EH28: Nbdge 5A 16
Parkside Ct. EH22: Dalk 3B 42
Parkside Pl. EH22: Dalk 2C 42
Parkside St.
  EH8: Edin 7J 5 (5K 21)
Parkside Ter.
  EH16: Edin 7J 5 (5K 21)
Park Ter. EH21: Muss 4A 24
Parkvale Pl. EH6: Edin 6G 13
Park Vw. EH20: Loan 6B 40
  EH21: Edin 7K 23
  EH21: Muss 3G 25
  EH21: Muss 6E 14
Park Vw. E. EH32: Port S 3H 15
Park Vw. W. EH32: Port S 3H 15
Parliament Sq. EH1: Leith 4E 4
Parliament St. EH6: Leith 5E 12
Parrot La. EH23: Gore 6E 48
Parrotshot EH15: Edin 6H 23
Parsonage EH21: Muss 2F 25
PARSONS GREEN 3C 22
Parsons Grn. Ter.
  EH8: Edin 2C 22
Parsonspool EH19: Bonn 1J 47
Path Brae EH29: Kltn 2A 16
Patie's Rd. EH14: Edin 4A 32
Patriothall EH3: Edin 1A 4 (1F 21)
Patriothall Gallery 1A 4 (1F 21)
Pattison St. EH6: Leith 5F 13
Peacock Av. EH19: Bonn 7A 42
Peacock Ct. EH6: Newh 4C 12
Peacock Parkway
  EH19: Bonn 7A 42
Peacock Pl. EH19: Bonn 7K 41
Peacock Rd. EH30: S Q'fry 1D 8
Peacocktail Cl.
  EH15: Edin 7H 23
Pearce Av. EH12: Edin 4E 18
Pearce Gro. EH12: Edin 4E 18
Pearce Rd. EH12: Edin 4E 18
Peatville Gdns. EH14: Edin 3J 31
Peatville Ter. EH14: Edin 3J 31
Peebles Rd. EH26: Pen 4D 50
Peel Pentland Cen.
  EH20: Loan 4A 40
Peel Ter. EH9: Edin 7K 21
Peffer Bank EH16: Edin 7D 22
Peffer Ind. Est. EH16: Edin 6D 22
Peffermill Ct. EH16: Edin 7C 22
Peffermill Ind. Est.
  . . . . .7C 22
Peffermill Rd. EH16: Edin 1B 34
Peffer Pl. EH16: Edin 7D 22
Peffer St. EH16: Edin 7D 23
Peggy's Mill Rd.
  EH4: Cram 6H 9
Pembroke Pl. EH12: Edin 4C 20
Pend, The EH30: S Q'fry 2E 6
Pendreich Av. EH19: Bonn 5J 41
Pendreich Dr. EH19: Bonn 5J 41
Pendreich Gro. EH19: Bonn 4J 41
Pendreich Ter. EH19: Bonn 5J 41
Pendreich Vw. EH19: Bonn 5J 41
PENICUIK 1D 50
Penicuik Rd. EH25: Rosl 3J 45
Pennywell Cotts. EH4: Edin 4E 10
Pennywell Ct. EH4: Edin 5E 10
Pennywell Gdns. EH4: Edin 5D 10
Pennywell Gro. EH4: Edin 5E 10
Pennywell Medway
  EH4: Edin 5E 10
Pennywell M. EH4: Edin 5D 10
Pennywell Pl. EH4: Edin 5E 10
Pennywell Rd. EH4: Edin 5E 10
Pennywell Vs. EH4: Edin 4E 10
Pentland Av. EH13: Edin 6J 31
  EH14: Cur 1H 37
  EH23: Gore 3D 48
  EH26: Pen 1C 50
Pentland Ct. EH25: Bil 7J 39
Pentland Cres. EH10: Edin 5E 32
  EH24: Rose 3D 46
Pentland Dr. EH10: Edin 6D 32
Pentlandfield Bus. Pk.
  EH25: Rosl 7G 39
Pentland Gdns. EH10: Edin 5E 32
Pentland Gro. EH10: Edin 5E 32
Pentland Ind. Est.
  EH20: Loan 6K 39

Pentland Pk. EH20: Loan 5J 39
Pentland Pl. EH14: Cur 1H 37
Pentland Rd. EH10: Edin 3G 39
　　EH13: Edin 5J 31
　　EH19: Bonn 7F 41
　　EH20: Edin, Loan 4J 39
Pentlands Science Pk.
　　EH26: Pen 3G 45
Pentland Ter. EH16: Edin 4E 32
　　　　　　　　　(not continuous)
　　EH26: Pen 1C 50
Pentland Vw. EH10: Edin 6E 32
　　EH14: Cur 1H 37
　　EH22: Dalk 3E 42
Pentland Vw. Cres.
　　EH25: Rosl 3K 45
Pentland Vw. Pl. EH25: Rosl . .3K 45
Pentland Vw. Rd.
　　EH25: Rosl 3K 45
　　EH29: Kltn 2A 16
Pentland Vw. Ter.
　　EH25: Rosl 3K 45
Pentland Vs. EH14: J Grn 7E 30
People's Story, The 3H 5 (3J 21)
Perdrixknowe EH14: Edin 1B 32
Perth's Gro. EH32: Pres 5E 14
Perth St. EH3: Edin 1F 21
Pettigrew's Cl. EH22: Dalk 2C 42
Peveril Ter. EH16: Edin 4A 34
Pheasant Gro. EH22: Dalk 2F 43
Philip Pl. EH26: Pen 7C 44
Picardy Pl.
　　EH1: Edin 1F 5 (2H 21)
PICARDY PLACE RDBT. 1G 5
Picardy Place Stop (NET)
　　(Due to open 2011)
　　. . . . . .1F 5 (2H 21)
Pier Pl. EH6: Newh 3B 12
Piersfield Gro. EH8: Edin 2D 22
Piersfield Pl. EH8: Edin 2D 22
Piersfield Ter. EH8: Edin 2D 22
Piershill La. EH8: Edin 2C 22
Piershill Pl. EH8: Edin 2C 22
　　　　　　　　(off Portobello Rd.)
Piershill Sq. E. EH8: Edin 2D 22
Piershill Sq. W. EH8: Edin 2D 22
Piershill Ter. EH8: Edin 2D 22
Pilmuir Gro. EH14: Bal 3D 36
PILRIG 6D 12
Pilrig Cotts. EH6: Edin 7E 12
Pilrig Gdns. EH6: Edin 7D 12
Pilrig Glebe EH6: Edin 7E 12
Pilrig Hgts. EH6: Edin 7D 12
Pilrig Ho. Cl. EH6: Edin 6D 12
Pilrig Ind. Est. EH6: Edin 6D 12
Pilrig Pl. EH6: Edin 7E 12
Pilrig St. EH6: Edin 6D 12
PILTON 5F 11
Pilton Av. EH5: Edin 5G 11
Pilton Cres. EH5: Edin 5J 11
Pilton Dr. EH5: Edin 5H 11
Pilton Dr. Nth. EH5: Edin 4H 11
Pilton Gdns. EH5: Edin 5H 11
Pilton Loan EH5: Edin 5H 11
Pilton Pl. EH5: Edin 5H 11
Pinegrove Gdns.
　　EH4: Edin 1D 18
Pine Rd. EH26: Mil B 5E 44
Pinewood Pl. EH22: May 7G 43
Pinewood Rd. EH22: May 7G 43
Pinewood Vw. EH22: May 7G 43
Pinkhill EH12: Edin 5H 19
Pinkhill Pk. EH12: Edin 5H 19
Pinkie Av. EH21: Muss 3G 25
PINKIE BRAES 2H 25
Pinkie Dr. EH21: Muss 3G 25
Pinkie Hill Cres.
　　EH21: Muss 3G 25
Pinkie Pl. EH21: Muss 3G 25
Pinkie Rd. EH21: Muss 3F 25
Pinkie Ter. EH21: Muss 3G 25
Pinkie Wlk. EH33: Tran 3G 27
Pipe La. EH15: Port 2G 23
Pipe St. EH15: Port 2G 23
Pirniefield Bank EH6: Edin 6H 13
Pirniefield Gdns. EH6: Edin 6H 13
Pirniefield Gro. EH6: Edin 6H 13

Pirniefield Pl. EH6: Edin 6H 13
Pirniefield Ter. EH6: Edin 6H 13
Pirrie St. EH6: Edin 6E 12
Pitlochry Pl. EH7: Edin 1A 22
Pitsligo Rd. EH10: Edin 7F 21
Pittencrieff Ct. EH21: Muss 2H 25
Pitt St. EH6: Edin 5C 12
Pittville St. EH15: Port 3H 23
Pittville St. La. EH15: Port 3H 23
Place Charente EH22: Dalk 2E 42
Playfair Steps EH1: Edin 4D 4
Playhouse Theatre 1G 5 (2J 21)
Pleasance EH8: Edin 4G 5 (4J 21)
Pleasance Theatre 5H 5 (4J 21)
Plewlandcroft EH30: S Q'fry . . .1G 7
Plewlands Av. EH10: Edin 2D 32
Plewlands Gdns.
　　EH10: Edin 2D 32
Plewlands Pl. EH30: S Q'fry . . .1G 7
Plewlands Ter. EH10: Edin 2D 32
Pleydell Pl. EH16: Edin 4B 34
Plough La. EH33: Tran 2H 27
Poet's Glen EH14: Cur 1K 37
Police Info. Cen. & Exhibition
　　. . . . . .4F 5
　　　　　　　　　　　(off High St.)
Pollard Glebe EH11: Edin 7J 19
Pollock Halls of Residence
　　EH16: Edin 6A 22
Polson Gdns. EH33: Tran 2F 27
POLTON 7E 40
Polton Av. Rd. EH19: Bonn 7F 41
Polton Bank EH18: Las 7D 40
Polton Bank Ter. EH18: Las . . .7E 40
Polton Cotts. EH18: Las 7D 40
Polton Ct. EH19: Bonn 6H 41
Polton Dr. EH18: Las 7F 41
Polton Gdns. EH18: Las 6G 41
Polton Pl. EH19: Bonn 6H 41
Polton Rd. EH18: Las 6G 41
　　　　　　　　　　　(Eskdale Dr.)
　　EH18: Las 6C 40
　　　　　　　　　　　(Traprain Ter.)
Polton Rd. W. EH18: Las 7E 40
Polton St. EH19: Bonn 7H 41
Polton Ter. EH18: Las 6G 41
Polton Va. EH20: Loan 7H 41
Polwarth Cres. EH11: Edin 6E 20
　　EH32: Pres 6E 14
Polwarth Gdns. EH11: Edin 6D 20
Polwarth Pk. EH11: Edin 6D 20
Polwarth Pl. EH11: Edin 6D 20
Polwarth Ter. EH11: Edin 1C 32
　　EH32: Pres 6E 14
Pomathorn Bank
　　EH26: Pen 3D 50
Pomathorn Rd. EH26: Pen 3D 50
Ponton St. EH3: Edin . . .7B 4 (5F 21)
Poplar La. EH6: Leith 5F 13
Poplar Pk. EH32: Port S 4H 15
Poplar Path EH20: Loan 6K 39
　　　　　　　　(off Nivensknowe Pk.)
Poplar St. EH22: May 7G 43
Poplar Ter. EH19: Bonn 7H 41
Port Edgar Marina
　　(Water Sports Cen.) 1F 7
Porterfield Rd. EH4: Edin 7H 11
Porters Pl. EH6: Leith 5E 12
　　　　　　　　　　　(off Giles St.)
Porters Wlk.
　　EH3: Edin 7E 4 (5H 21)
Portfolio Gallery 5E 4
　　　　　　　(off Candlemaker Row)
Portgower Pl. EH4: Edin 1E 20
Port Hamilton
　　EH3: Edin 6A 4 (4F 21)
Portland Gdns. EH6: Leith 4D 12
Portland Pl. EH6: Newh 4D 12
　　　　　　　　　　　(off Lindsay Rd.)
Portland Row EH6: Leith 4D 12
Portland St. EH6: Newh 4D 12
Portland Ter. EH6: Newh 4D 12
PORTOBELLO 3H 23
Portobello High St.
　　EH15: Port 2G 23

Portobello Indoor Bowls &
　　Leisure Club 2G 23
Portobello Rd. EH7: Edin 2C 22
　　EH8: Edin 2C 22
Portobello Swimming Cen. . . .3H 23
Port of Leith Stop (NET)
　　(Due to open 2011) 4F 13
Portsburgh Sq. EH1: Edin 5C 4
PORT SETON 3H 15
Post Rd. EH33: Tran 1F 27
Potterrow EH8: Edin 6F 5 (4H 21)
Potterrow Port EH1: Edin 5F 5
Potter's Path EH33: Tran 2G 27
Pottery, The EH15: Port 2G 23
Povert Rd. EH19: Gore 4B 48
　　EH23: Gore 4B 48
Powderhall Brae EH7: Edin 6C 12
Powderhall Rigg EH7: Edin 6C 12
Powderhall Rd. EH7: Edin 7C 12
Powdermill Brae EH23: Gore . . .7F 49
Powerleague Soccer Cen.
　　Portobello 2G 23
　　Sighthill 1F 31
PRESTON 6E 14
Preston Av. EH32: Pres 6F 15
Preston Ct. EH32: Pres 7D 14
Preston Cres. EH32: Pres 5F 15
Preston Cross Cotts.
　　EH32: Pres 6E 14
PRESTONFIELD 7A 22
Prestonfield Av. EH16: Edin 7A 22
Prestonfield Bank
　　EH16: Edin 7A 22
Prestonfield Cres.
　　EH16: Edin 1A 34
Prestonfield Gdns.
　　EH16: Edin 7A 22
Prestonfield Rd. EH16: Edin 7A 22
Prestonfield Ter. EH16: Edin 7A 22
Prestongrange Industrial
　　Heritage Mus. 7A 14
Prestongrange Rd.
　　EH32: Pres 6B 14
Prestongrange Ter.
　　EH32: Pres 7C 14
Prestonhall Cres.
　　EH24: Rose 4D 46
Prestonhall Rd. EH24: Rose . . .4D 46
Preston Links Shop. Cen.
　　EH32: Pres 5D 14
PRESTONPANS 5C 14
Prestonpans Station (Rail) 7E 14
Preston Rd. EH32: Pres 7D 14
Preston St. EH24: Rose 4D 46
Preston Ter. EH32: Pres 6F 15
Preston Tower 6D 14
Priestfield Av. EH16: Edin 7B 22
Priestfield Cres. EH16: Edin 7B 22
Priestfield Gdns. EH16: Edin 7B 22
Priestfield Gro. EH16: Edin 6A 22
Priestfield Rd. EH16: Edin 7A 22
Priestfield Rd. Nth.
　　EH16: Edin 6A 22
Priesthill St. EH16: Edin 6B 34
Priesthill St. EH16: Edin 6B 34
Primrose Bank Rd.
　　EH5: Edin 4A 12
Primrose Ct. EH22: Dalk 3E 42
Primrose Dr. EH30: S Q'fry 7E 8
Primrose Gdns. EH30: S Q'fry . . .2H 7
Primrose St. EH6: Leith 6F 13
Primrose Ter. EH11: Edin 6C 20
　　EH22: Dalk 3E 42
Prince Regent St.
　　EH6: Newh 4D 12
Princes Ct. EH3: Edin 6B 4
Princes Mall
　　EH1: Edin 3E 4 (3H 21)
PRINCESS ALEXANDRA EYE PAVILION
　　. . . . . .7C 4 (5G 21)
Princes St. EH1: Edin . . .4A 4 (3F 21)
　　EH2: Edin 4A 4 (3F 21)
Princes Street Stop (NET)
　　(Due to open 2011)
　　. . . . . .3C 4 (3G 21)
Printmakers Workshop & Gallery
　　. . . . . .1G 5
Priory Gro. EH30: S Q'fry 2G 7

Private Rd. EH23: Gore 7E 48
Promenade EH15: Port 7K 13
　　EH21: Muss 1D 24
Promenade, The
　　EH32: Port S 3H 15
Promenade Ter. EH15: Port 2G 23
Prospect Bank Cres.
　　EH6: Edin 6G 13
Prospect Bank Gdns.
　　EH6: Edin 7G 13
Prospect Bank Gro.
　　EH6: Edin 6H 13
Prospect Bank Pl. EH6: Edin 6H 13
Prospect Bank Rd.
　　EH6: Edin 6G 13
Prospect Bank Ter.
　　EH6: Edin 6H 13
Provost Haugh EH14: Cur 7E 30
Provost Milne Gro.
　　EH30: S Q'fry 3H 7
Pryde Av. EH19: Bonn 6G 41
Pryde Ter. EH19: Bonn 6G 41
Pypers Wynd EH32: Pres 5D 14

Q

Quadrant, The EH26: Pen 1D 50
Quality St. EH4: Edin 7C 10
Quality St. La. EH4: Edin 7C 10
Quarrybank EH14: Edin 4E 30
Quarrybank Cl. EH14: Edin 3E 30
Quarrybank Ct. EH14: Edin 3E 30
Quarrybank End
　　EH14: Edin 4E 30
Quarry Cl. EH8: Edin 7G 5 (5J 21)
Quarry Cotts. EH15: Edin 7H 23
　　　　　　　　(off Newcraighall Rd.)
Quarryfoot Gdns.
　　EH19: Bonn 6H 41
Quarryfoot Grn. EH19: Bonn . . .6J 41
Quarryfoot Pl. EH19: Bonn 6H 41
QUARRYHEAD 5H 41
Quarry Howe EH14: Bal 4E 36
　　　　　　　　　(off Deanpark Brae)
Quarry Rd. EH23: Gore 5F 49
Quarryview EH14: Edin 4E 30
Quayside Mills EH6: Leith 5E 12
　　　　　　　　　　(off Quayside St.)
Quayside St. EH6: Leith 5E 12
Queen Anne Dr.
　　EH28: Nbdge 6B 16
Queen Anne Pk.
　　EH28: Nbdge 6B 16
Queen Charlotte La.
　　EH6: Leith 5F 13
Queen Charlotte St.
　　EH6: Leith 5F 13
Queen Margaret Cl.
　　EH10: Edin 7H 33
Queen Margaret Dr.
　　EH21: Muss 5B 24
　　EH30: S Q'fry 2H 7
Queen Margaret University . . .5B 24
Queen Margaret University College
　　Corstorphine Campus 3F 19
　　Leith Campus 6F 13
Queen Margaret Way
　　EH21: Muss 7C 24
Queen's Av. EH4: Edin 1K 19
Queen's Av. Sth. EH4: Edin 1A 20
Queen's Bay Cres.
　　EH15: Port 4K 23
Queen's Cres. EH9: Edin 7K 21
Queen's Dr.
　　EH8: Edin 3K 5 (3K 21)
Queensferry Mus. 1H 7
Queensferry Recreation Cen. . . .2J 7
Queensferry Rd.
　　EH4: Cram, Edin 7G 9
　　EH4: Edin 2A 20
　　EH29: Kltn 7F 7
Queensferry St.
　　EH2: Edin 3A 4 (3E 20)
Queensferry St. La.
　　EH2: Edin 4A 4 (3F 21)
Queensferry Ter. EH4: Edin 2C 20
Queen's Gallery, The 3K 5
Queen's Gdns. EH4: Edin 1A 20

Queen's Hall, The 7H 5 (5J 21)
Queen's Pk. Av. EH8: Edin 2B 22
Queen's Pk. Ct. EH8: Edin 3C 22
Queen's Rd. EH4: Edin 1A 20
Queen St. EH2: Edin . . .2B 4 (2F 21)
Queen St. Gdns. E.
   EH3: Edin 1D 4 (2G 21)
Queen St. Gdns. W.
   EH3: Edin 2C 4 (2G 21)
Queen's Wlk. EH16: Edin 7E 22
Queensway EH26: Pen 7C 44
Queensway Leisure Cen. 7C 44
Quilts, The EH6: Edin 5D 12
Quilts Wynd EH6: Edin 5D 12

R

Radical Rd. EH8: Edin . . .5K 5 (4K 21)
Raeburn M. EH4: Edin 1E 20
Raeburn Place 1E 20
Raeburn Pl. EH4: Edin 1E 20
Raeburn St. EH4: Edin 1E 20
Rae's Ct. EH16: Edin 7A 34
Rae's Gdns. EH19: Bonn 6H 41
Ramillies Ct. EH26: Pen 6E 44
Ramsay Cres. EH22: May 1G 49
Ramsay Gdn.
   EH1: Edin 4D 4 (3G 21)
Ramsay La.
   EH1: Edin 4D 4 (3G 21)
Ramsay Pl. EH15: Port 2H 23
   EH26: Pen 1A 50
Ramsay Ter. EH18: Las 7F 41
Ramsay Wlk. EH22: May 1G 49
Randolph Cliff EH3: Edin 3E 20
Randolph Cres.
   EH3: Edin 3A 4 (3E 20)
Randolph La.
   EH3: Edin 3A 4 (3F 21)
Randolph Pl.
   EH3: Edin 3A 4 (3F 21)
Rankeillor St.
   EH8: Edin 7H 5 (5J 21)
Rankin Av. EH9: Edin 2K 33
Rankin Dr. EH9: Edin 2J 33
Rankin Rd. EH9: Edin 1K 33
Rannoch Gro. EH4: Edin 2F 19
Rannoch Pl. EH4: Edin 2F 19
Rannoch Rd. EH4: Edin 2F 19
Rannoch Ter. EH4: Edin 2F 19
Ransome Gdns. EH4: Edin 2F 19
Ratcliffe Ter. EH9: Edin 7J 21
Rathbone Pl. EH15: Port 2G 23
RATHO 2D 28
Ratho Pk. EH28: Rat S 5C 16
Ratho Rd. EH28: Rat 2E 28
RATHO STATION 6C 16
Rattray Cres. EH10: Edin 4C 32
Rattray Dr. EH10: Edin 4C 32
Rattray Gro. EH10: Edin 4C 32
Rattray Loan EH10: Edin 4C 32
Rattray Way EH10: Edin 4D 32
Ravelrig Dr. EH14: Bal 3D 36
Ravelrig Gait EH14: Bal 3D 36
Ravelrig Hill EH14: Bal 3D 36
Ravelrig Pk. EH14: Bal 3D 36
Ravelrig Rd. EH14: Bal 3D 36
   EH14: Bal, Cur 7H 29
Ravelrig Wynd EH14: Bal 3E 36
RAVELSTON 2A 20
Ravelston Ct. EH12: Edin 3B 20
Ravelston Dykes EH4: Edin . . .3A 20
   EH12: Edin 3A 20
Ravelston Dykes La.
   EH4: Edin 3J 19
Ravelston Dykes Rd.
   EH4: Edin 2K 19
Ravelston Gdn. EH4: Edin 3A 20
Ravelston Hgts. EH4: Edin 2A 20
Ravelston Ho. Gro.
   EH4: Edin 2A 20
Ravelston Ho. Loan
   EH4: Edin 2A 20
Ravelston Ho. Pk.
   EH4: Edin 2A 20
Ravelston Ho. Rd.
   EH4: Edin 2A 20
Ravelston Pk. EH4: Edin 3C 20

Ravelston Pl. EH4: Edin 3D 20
Ravelston Ri. EH4: Edin 3A 20
Ravelston Ter. EH4: Edin 2D 20
Ravelsykes Rd. EH26: Pen 2A 50
Ravendean Gdns. EH26: Pen . . .2A 50
Ravenscroft Gdns.
   EH17: Edin 7E 34
Ravenscroft Pl. EH17: Edin 7D 34
Ravenscroft St. EH17: Edin 7E 34
Ravensheugh Cres.
   EH21: Muss 2J 25
Ravensheugh Rd.
   EH21: Muss 2J 25
   EH32: Pres 2J 25
Ravenswood Av. EH16: Edin . . .3B 34
Real Mary King's Close, The . . .4E 4
   (off Warriston's Cl.)
Redbraes Gro. EH7: Edin 6C 12
Redbraes Pl. EH7: Edin 6C 12
Redburn Rd. EH32: Pres 6C 14
Redburn Rd. Nth.
   EH32: Pres 6C 14
Redcroft St. EH22: Dan 4G 35
Redford Av. EH13: Edin 6K 31
Redford Bank EH13: Edin 6A 32
Redford Cres. EH13: Edin 6A 32
Redford Dr. EH13: Edin 6K 31
Redford Gdns. EH13: Edin 6A 32
Redford Gro. EH13: Edin 6B 32
Redford Loan EH13: Edin 6K 31
Redford Neuk EH13: Edin 6B 32
Redford Pl. EH13: Edin 5B 32
Redford Rd. EH13: Edin 5K 31
Redford Ter. EH13: Edin 6A 32
Redford Wlk. EH13: Edin 6A 32
Redgauntlet Ter. EH16: Edin . . .3C 34
REDHALL 3K 31
Redhall Av. EH14: Edin 2J 31
Redhall Bank Rd.
   EH14: Edin 3K 31
Redhall Cres. EH14: Edin 2J 31
Redhall Dr. EH14: Edin 2J 31
Redhall Gdns. EH14: Edin 2J 31
Redhall Gro. EH14: Edin 2J 31
Redhall Ho. Av. EH14: Edin . . .3K 31
Redhall Ho. Dr. EH14: Edin . . .3K 31
Redhall Pl. EH14: Edin 2J 31
Redhall Rd. EH14: Edin 2J 31
Redhall Vw. EH14: Edin 3K 31
Redheugh Loan EH23: Gore . . .4E 48
Redheughs Av. EH12: Edin 7C 18
Redheughs Rigg EH12: Edin . . .6C 18
Redwood Gro. EH22: Newt . . .1C 48
Redwood Wlk. EH22: Newt . . .1C 48
Reed Dr. EH22: Newt 7D 42
Reekie's Ct.
   EH8: Edin 6G 5 (4J 21)
Regent Pl. EH7: Edin 2A 22
Regent Rd. EH1: Edin . . .2G 5 (2J 21)
   EH7: Edin 2G 5 (2J 21)
Regent St. EH15: Port 3H 23
Regent St. La. EH15: Port 3H 23
Regent Ter. EH7: Edin . . .2J 5 (2K 21)
Regent Ter. M.
   EH7: Edin 2J 5 (2K 21)
Regis Ct. EH4: Cram 6J 9
Register Pl.
   EH2: Edin 2E 4 (2H 21)
Reid Concert Hall Mus. of Instruments
   . . . . .6E 4 (4H 21)
Reid's Cl. EH8: Edin . . .3J 5 (3K 21)
Reid's Ct. EH8: Edin . . .3J 5 (3K 21)
Reid Ter. EH3: Edin 1E 20
Relugas Gdns. EH9: Edin 1J 33
Relugas Pl. EH9: Edin 1J 33
Relugas Rd. EH9: Edin 1J 33
Rennie's Isle EH6: Leith 4F 13
Research Av. Nth.
   EH14: Cur 4A 30
Research Av. Sth.
   EH14: Cur 4B 30
RESTALRIG 1C 22
Restalrig Av. EH7: Edin 2C 22
Restalrig Cir. EH7: Edin 7H 13
Restalrig Cres. EH7: Edin 7H 13
Restalrig Dr. EH7: Edin 1C 22
Restalrig Gdns. EH7: Edin 1C 22
Restalrig Ho. EH7: Edin 1C 22

Restalrig Pk. EH7: Edin 7G 13
Restalrig Rd. EH6: Edin 6G 13
   EH7: Edin 6G 13
Restalrig Rd. Sth. EH7: Edin . . .7H 13
Restalrig Ter. EH6: Edin 6F 13
RICCARTON 5B 30
Riccarton Av. EH14: Cur 7B 30
Riccarton Cres. EH14: Cur 7C 30
Riccarton Dr. EH14: Cur 7B 30
Riccarton Gro. EH14: Cur 7C 30
Riccarton Mains Rd.
   EH14: Cur 3B 30
Richard Corsie Leisure Cen.
   . . . . .5K 23
Richmond La.
   EH8: Edin 6G 5 (4J 21)
Richmond Pl.
   EH8: Edin 5G 5 (4J 21)
Richmond Ter. EH11: Edin 4E 20
Riddle's Ct. EH1: Edin 4E 4
Riding Pk. EH4: Cram 6J 9
Riego St. EH3: Edin . . .6B 4 (4F 21)
Riggonhead Ct. EH33: Tran . . .1H 27
Riggonhead Gdns.
   EH33: Tran 1H 27
Rigley Ter. EH32: Pres 7C 14
Rillbank Cres. EH9: Edin 6H 21
Rillbank Ter. EH9: Edin 6H 21
Ringans Way EH32: Pres 6C 14
   (off Inch Vw.)
Ringwood Pl. EH16: Edin 4B 34
Rintoul Pl. EH3: Edin 1F 21
Riselaw Cres. EH10: Edin 5E 32
Riselaw Pl. EH10: Edin 4E 32
Riselaw Rd. EH10: Edin 4E 32
Ritchie Pl. EH11: Edin 6D 20
River Almond Wlk.
   EH4: Cram 6G 9
River Gore Gro. EH23: Gore . . .6E 48
River Gore Rd. EH23: Gore 6E 48
River Gore Vw. EH23: Gore 6E 48
Riversdale Cres.
   EH12: Edin 5A 20
Riversdale Gro. EH12: Edin 4A 20
Riversdale Rd. EH12: Edin 4A 20
Riverside EH4: Cram 4J 9
Riverside Gdns.
   EH21: Muss 3D 24
Riverside Rd. EH30: S Q'fry 6E 8
Roanshead Cres. EH22: East . . .6E 42
Roanshead Rd. EH22: East 5E 42
Robb's Loan EH14: Edin 7A 20
Robb's Loan Gro.
   EH14: Edin 7A 20
Robert Burns Dr. EH16: Edin . . .3A 34
Robert Burns M. EH22: Dalk . . .2F 43
Robert De Quincy Pl.
   EH32: Pres 7D 14
   (off Northfield Ct.)
Robert Smillie Av.
   EH22: May 1G 49
Robert Smith Pl. EH22: Dalk . . .1B 42
Robertson Av. EH11: Edin 6B 20
   EH33: Tran 1H 27
Robertson Bank EH23: Gore . . .7F 49
Robertson Dr. EH33: Tran 1H 27
Robertson Gait EH11: Edin 6B 20
Robertson's Cl.
   EH1: Edin 5G 5 (4J 21)
   EH22: Dalk 2C 42
Robertson's Ct. EH8: Edin 3J 5
Rocheid Pk. EH4: Edin 6J 11
Rocheid Path EH3: Edin 7A 12
Rochester Ter. EH10: Edin 7E 20
Rockville Ter. EH19: Bonn 5H 41
Roddinglaw Bus. Pk.
   EH12: Edin 1H 29
Roddinglaw Rd. EH12: Edin 7H 17
Rodney Pl. EH7: Edin 1G 21
Rodney St. EH7: Edin 1G 21
Roman Pk. EH22: Dalk 3F 43
Roman St. EH22: Dalk 3F 43
Roman Ter. EH22: Dalk 3F 43
Roman Vw. EH22: Dalk 3F 43
Romero Pl. EH16: Edin 6K 21

Rope Wlk. EH32: Pres 6C 14
Rosabelle Rd. EH25: Rosl 3K 45
Rose Av. EH19: Bonn 7K 41
Rosebank Cotts.
   EH3: Edin 6A 4 (4E 20)
Rosebank Gdns. EH5: Edin 5K 11
Rosebank Gro. EH5: Edin 5K 11
Rosebank Rd. EH5: Edin 5K 11
Rosebery Av. EH30: S Q'fry 2H 7
Rosebery Ct. EH30: S Q'fry 2H 7
Rosebery Cres. EH12: Edin 4D 20
   EH23: Gore 7E 48
Rosebery Cres. La.
   EH12: Edin 4D 20
ROSEBURN 4B 20
Roseburn Av. EH12: Edin 4B 20
Roseburn Cliff EH12: Edin 4C 20
Roseburn Cres. EH12: Edin 4B 20
Roseburn Dr. EH12: Edin 4B 20
Roseburn Gdns. EH12: Edin . . .4B 20
Roseburn Maltings
   EH12: Edin 4C 20
Roseburn Pl. EH12: Edin 4B 20
Roseburn St. EH12: Edin 5B 20
Roseburn Ter. EH12: Edin 4B 20
Rose Cotts. EH19: Bonn 7K 41
Rose Ct. EH4: Edin 6B 10
Rosedale Cl. EH24: Rose 6D 46
Rosedale Gro. EH24: Rose 6D 46
Rosedale Neuk
   EH24: Rose 5D 46
Rosefield Av. EH15: Port 3G 23
Rosefield Av. La.
   EH15: Port 3G 23
Rosefield Pl. EH15: Port 3G 23
Rosefield Pl. La. EH15: Port . . .3G 23
Rosefield St. EH15: Port 3G 23
Rose Gdns. EH19: Bonn 7K 41
Rose Gro. EH19: Bonn 7K 41
Rose La. EH30: S Q'fry 1G 7
Rosemount Bldgs.
   EH3: Edin 6A 4 (4E 20)
Rosemount M. EH32: Pres 5D 14
   (off Mill Wynd)
Roseneath Pl. EH9: Edin 6H 21
Roseneath St. EH9: Edin 6H 21
   (off Warrender Pk. Rd.)
Roseneath Ter. EH9: Edin 6H 21
Rose Neuk EH19: Bonn 7K 41
Rose Pk. EH5: Edin 5A 12
   EH19: Bonn 7K 41
Rose Path EH19: Bonn 7K 41
Rose Pl. EH19: Bonn 7K 41
Rose St. EH2: Edin 3B 4 (3F 21)
Rose St. Nth. La.
   EH2: Edin 3B 4 (3F 21)
   (not continuous)
Rose St. Sth. La.
   EH2: Edin 3B 4 (3F 21)
   (not continuous)
Rose Ter. EH19: Bonn 7K 41
Rosevale Pl. EH6: Edin 6G 13
Rosevale Ter. EH6: Edin 6F 13
Roseville Gdns. EH5: Edin 4B 12
Rose Way EH19: Bonn 7K 41
ROSEWELL 4D 46
Rosewell By-Pass
   EH24: Rose 4D 46
Rosewell Rd. EH19: Bonn 2F 47
ROSLIN 3K 45
Roslin Glen Country Pk. 4K 45
Ross Cres. EH33: Tran 3H 27
Ross Gdns. EH9: Edin 1J 33
Rossgien Ct. EH25: Rosl 3A 46
Rosshill Ter. EH30: Dalm 2J 7
Rossie Pl. EH7: Edin . . .1K 5 (1K 21)
Rosslyn Chapel 3A 46
Rosslyn Cres. EH6: Edin 7D 12
ROSSLYNLEE HOSPITAL 7K 45
Rosslyn Ter. EH6: Edin 7D 12
Ross Open Air Theatre
   . . . . .3C 4 (3G 21)
Ross Pl. EH9: Edin 1K 33
   EH22: Newt 7D 42
Ross Rd. EH16: Edin 2K 33
Rothesay M. EH3: Edin 3D 20
Rothesay Pl. EH3: Edin 3E 20
   EH21: Muss 3F 25
Rothesay Ter. EH3: Edin 3E 20

Roull Gro. EH12: Edin 6F **19**
Roull Pl. EH12: Edin 6G **19**
Roull Rd. EH12: Edin 6F **19**
Rowallan Ct. EH12: Edin 4C **18**
   (off Craigievar Wynd)
Rowan Gdns. EH19: Bonn 7H **41**
Rowanhill Cl. EH32: Port S . .4H **15**
Rowanhill Dr. EH32: Port S . .4H **15**
Rowanhill Pk. EH32: Port S . .4G **15**
Rowanhill Way
   EH32: Port S 4H **15**
Rowan Tree Av. EH14: Cur . . .1G **37**
Rowan Tree Av. EH14: Cur . . .2G **37**
Rowantree Rd. EH22: May 6G **43**
Roxburgh Pl.
   EH8: Edin 5G **5** (4J **21**)
Roxburgh's Cl. EH1: Edin 4E **4**
Roxburgh St.
   EH8: Edin 5G **5** (4J **21**)
Roxy Art House, The 5G **5**
Royal Botanic Garden & Arboretum
   . . . . .7A **12**
Royal Cir. EH3: Edin . . .1B **4** (2F **21**)
Royal Commonwealth Pool . . .6K **21**
Royal Cres. EH3: Edin 1G **21**
ROYAL EDINBURGH HOSPITAL
   . . . . .1E **30**
Royal Elizabeth Yd.
   EH29: Kltn 4K **7**
Royal Forth Yacht Club 3J **11**
Royal Highland Showground
   . . . . .5E **16**
ROYAL HOSPITAL FOR
   SICK CHILDREN 6H **21**
ROYAL INFIRMARY OF EDINBURGH
   . . . . .3E **34**
Royal Lyceum Theatre 5B **4**
Royal Mile 4F **5**
Royal Observatory & Vis. Cen.
   . . . . .2H **33**
Royal Pk. Pl. EH8: Edin 2B **22**
Royal Pk. Ter. EH8: Edin 2B **22**
Royal Scots Greys Memorial . .3C **4**
Royal Scots Medway
   EH19: Bonn 1F **47**
Royal Scots Monument 3D **4**
Royal Scottish Academy
   . . . . .3D **4** (3G **21**)
Royal Society of Edinburgh . . .2D **4**
Royal Ter. EH7: Edin 1G **5** (2J **21**)
Royal Ter. M. EH7: Edin .1J **5** (2K **21**)
ROYAL VICTORIA HOSPITAL
   . . . . .1C **20**
Royston Mains Av.
   EH5: Edin 4G **11**
Royston Mains Cl.
   EH5: Edin 4H **11**
Royston Mains Cres.
   EH5: Edin 4G **11**
Royston Mains Gdns.
   EH5: Edin 4H **11**
Royston Mains Grn.
   EH5: Edin 4H **11**
Royston Mains Pl.
   EH5: Edin 4G **11**
Royston Mains Rd.
   EH5: Edin 4H **11**
Royston Mains St.
   EH5: Edin 4G **11**
Royston Ter. EH3: Edin 6A **12**
Rullion Grn. Av. EH26: Pen . . .7B **44**
Rullion Grn. Cres.
   EH26: Pen 7B **44**
Rullion Grn. Gro. EH26: Pen . .7B **44**
Rullion Rd. EH26: Pen 2A **50**
Ruskin Pl. EH22: May 1G **49**
Russell Gdns. EH12: Edin 4C **20**
Russell Pl. EH5: Edin 4A **12**
Russell Rd. EH11: Edin 4C **20**
   EH12: Edin 4C **20**
Rustic Cotts. EH13: Edin 5K **31**
Rutherford Dr. EH16: Edin . . .3B **34**
Ruthven Pl. EH16: Edin 3C **34**
Rutland Ct. EH3: Edin . .5A **4** (4F **21**)
Rutland Ct. La.
   EH3: Edin 5A **4** (4F **21**)
Rutland Pl. EH1: Edin 4A **4**
Rutland Sq. EH1: Edin . .4A **4** (3F **21**)

Rutland St. EH1: Edin . . .4A **4** (3F **21**)
Ryehill Av. EH6: Edin 7G **13**
Ryehill Gdns. EH6: Edin 6G **13**
Ryehill Gro. EH6: Edin 7G **13**
Ryehill Pl. EH6: Edin 6G **13**
Ryehill Ter. EH6: Edin 6G **13**

S

Saddletree Loan EH16: Edin . .2C **34**
St Albans Rd. EH9: Edin 1H **33**
St Andrew Pl. EH6: Leith 6F **13**
St Andrew Sq.
   EH2: Edin 2E **4** (2H **21**)
St Andrew Square Stop (NET)
   (Due to open 2011)
   . . . . .2E **4** (2H **21**)
St Andrew St. EH22: Dalk 2C **42**
St Annes EH22: Newt 1C **48**
St Anne's Av. EH18: Las 7E **40**
St Anne's Path EH18: Las 7E **40**
St Anthony La. EH6: Leith 5E **12**
St Anthony Pl. EH6: Leith 5E **12**
St Anthony St. EH6: Leith 5E **12**
St Bernard's Cres.
   EH4: Edin 1A **4** (2E **20**)
St Bernard's Row EH4: Edin . .1F **21**
St Catherine's Gdns.
   EH12: Edin 5J **19**
St Catherine's Mnr.
   EH12: Edin 5H **19**
   (off St Catherine's Gdns.)
St Catherine's Pl. EH9: Edin . .6J **21**
St Cecilia's Hall Mus. of Instruments
   . . . . .4G **5**
St Clair Av. EH6: Edin 7F **13**
St Clair Cres. EH25: Rosl 3A **46**
St Clair Pl. EH6: Edin 7F **13**
St Clair Rd. EH6: Edin 7F **13**
St Clair St. EH6: Edin 7F **13**
St Clair Ter. EH10: Edin 2D **32**
St Clement's Cres.
   EH21: Wall 4K **25**
St Clement's Gdns. Nth.
   EH21: Wall 4K **25**
St Clement's Gdns. Sth.
   EH21: Wall 4K **25**
St Clement's Ter. EH21: Wall . .4K **25**
St Colme St.
   EH3: Edin 3A **4** (2F **21**)
ST COLUMBA'S HOSPICE 4K **11**
St Cuthbert's Church 4B **4**
St David's Gdns. EH22: Dalk . .4C **42**
St David's Gro. EH22: Dalk . . .3C **42**
St David's Pl. EH3: Edin 4E **20**
St David's Ter. EH3: Edin 4E **20**
   EH22: Dalk 4B **42**
St Fillans Ter. EH10: Edin 2E **32**
St Germains Cnr.
   EH33: Tran 1H **27**
St Giles' Cathedral 4E **4** (3H **21**)
St Giles St. EH1: Edin . . .4E **4** (3H **21**)
St James Cen.
   EH1: Edin 2F **5** (2H **21**)
St James Pl.
   EH1: Edin 1F **5** (2H **21**)
St James's Gdns. EH26: Pen . . .3C **50**
St James's Sq. EH1: Edin 2F **5**
St James's Vw. EH26: Pen . . .3C **50**
St John's Av. EH12: Edin 5G **19**
St John's Church 4B **4**
St John's Cres. EH12: Edin . . .5H **19**
St John's Gdns. EH12: Edin . . .5G **19**
St John's Hill
   EH8: Edin 5H **5** (4J **21**)
St John's Rd. EH12: Edin 5E **18**
St John's Ter. EH12: Edin 5G **19**
St John St. EH8: Edin . . .4H **5** (3J **21**)
St Katharine's Brae
   EH16: Edin 6A **34**
St Katharine's Cres.
   EH16: Edin 6A **34**
St Katharine's Loan
   EH16: Edin 7B **34**
St Kentigern Mall
   EH26: Pen 3D **50**
St Kentigern Rd. EH26: Pen . .1B **50**

St Kentigern Way EH26: Pen . . .1D **50**
ST LEONARD'S 7J **5** (5K **21**)
St Leonard's Bank
   EH8: Edin 7J **5** (5K **21**)
St Leonard's Crag
   EH8: Edin 7J **5** (4K **21**)
St Leonard's Hill
   EH8: Edin 6H **5** (4J **21**)
St Leonard's La.
   EH8: Edin 7H **5** (5J **21**)
St Leonard's St.
   EH8: Edin 7H **5** (5J **21**)
St Margarets Pl. EH9: Edin . . .7G **21**
St Margaret's Rd. EH9: Edin . . .7F **21**
St Mark's La. EH15: Port 3H **23**
St Mark's Pl. EH15: Port 3H **23**
St Martin's La. EH33: Tran 2J **27**
St Mary's Episcopal Cathedral
   . . . . .3E **20**
St Mary's Episcopal Church . . .1C **42**
St Mary's Pl. EH15: Port 4J **23**
St Mary's Pl. La. EH15: Port . . .3H **23**
St Mary's RC Cathedral
   . . . . .1F **5** (2H **21**)
St Mary's St.
   EH1: Edin 4G **5** (3J **21**)
St Michael's Av.
   EH21: Muss 3E **24**
St Mungo's Vw. EH26: Pen 3D **50**
St Ninian's Dr. EH12: Edin . . .4F **19**
St Ninian's Rd. EH12: Edin . . .4F **19**
St Ninian's Row EH1: Edin 2F **5**
St Ninian's Ter. EH10: Edin . . .2D **32**
St Ninians Way EH21: Muss . . .2J **25**
St Patrick Sq.
   EH8: Edin 7G **5** (5J **21**)
St Patrick St. EH8: Edin 7G **5**
St Peter's Bldgs. EH3: Edin . . .5E **20**
St Peter's Pl. EH3: Edin 5E **20**
St Ringans Gdns.
   EH32: Pres 5D **14**
St Ronan's Ter. EH10: Edin . . .2E **32**
St Stephen Pl.
   EH3: Edin 1A **4** (1F **21**)
St Stephen's Ct. EH11: Edin . . .2E **30**
St Stephen St.
   EH3: Edin 1A **4** (1F **21**)
St Teresa Pl. EH10: Edin 7D **20**
St Thomas Rd. EH9: Edin 7H **21**
St Triduana's Rest EH7: Edin . .1C **22**
St Vincent Pl.
   EH3: Edin 1B **4** (1F **21**)
St Vincent St.
   EH3: Edin 1B **4** (1F **21**)
Salamanca Cres. EH26: Pen . . .6E **44**
Salamander Ct. EH6: Leith 5G **13**
Salamander Pl. EH6: Leith 5G **13**
Salamander St. EH6: Leith 5G **13**
Salamander Yards
   EH6: Leith 6H **13**
Salisbury Craigs 6K **5** (4K **21**)
Salisbury M. EH9: Edin 6K **21**
Salisbury Pl. EH9: Edin 6J **21**
Salisbury Rd. EH9: Edin 6K **21**
   EH16: Edin 6K **21**
Salisbury Vw. EH22: May 7F **43**
Salmond Pl. EH7: Edin 2A **22**
Salters Gro. EH22: Dalk 1E **42**
Salters Rd. EH22: Dalk 7F **25**
   EH21: Muss, Wall 6H **25**
   EH22: Dalk 2E **42**
   (not continuous)
Salters Ter. EH22: Dalk 2E **42**
Saltire Ct. EH1: Edin 5B **4**
Saltire Sq. EH5: Edin 3G **11**
Saltire St. EH5: Edin 3G **11**
Salt Preston Pl. EH32: Pres . . .5D **14**
Salvesen Cres. EH4: Edin 5D **10**
Salvesen Gdns. EH4: Edin 4E **10**
Salvesen Gro. EH4: Edin 4E **10**
Salvesen Ter. EH4: Edin 4E **10**
Samoa Ter. EH26: Pen 6E **44**
Sanderson's Gro.
   EH33: Tran 1H **27**
Sanderson's Wynd
   EH33: Tran 1H **27**
Sandford Gdns. EH15: Port . . .3G **23**
Sand Port EH6: Leith 4F **13**
Sandport Pl. EH6: Leith 4E **12**

Sandport St. EH6: Leith 4E **12**
Sandport Trad. Est.
   EH6: Leith 4E **12**
Sandport Way EH6: Leith 4E **12**
   (off Sandport Pl.)
Sauchiebank EH11: Edin 5C **20**
Saugh Cotts. EH22: Newt 2C **48**
SAUGHTON 1H **31**
Saughton Av. EH11: Edin 6A **20**
Saughton Cres. EH12: Edin . . .5K **19**
Saughton Gdns. EH12: Edin . . .5K **19**
Saughton Gro. EH12: Edin 5K **19**
SAUGHTONHALL 5K **19**
Saughtonhall Av. EH12: Edin . .5K **19**
Saughtonhall Av. W.
   EH12: Edin 5K **19**
Saughtonhall Cir.
   EH12: Edin 5A **20**
Saughtonhall Cres.
   EH12: Edin 5K **19**
Saughtonhall Dr. EH12: Edin . . .5K **19**
Saughtonhall Gdns.
   EH12: Edin 5A **20**
Saughtonhall Gro.
   EH12: Edin 5A **20**
Saughtonhall Pl. EH12: Edin . . .5K **19**
Saughtonhall Ter.
   EH12: Edin 5A **20**
Saughton Loan EH12: Edin . . .5K **19**
Saughton Mains Av.
   EH11: Edin 7H **19**
   (not continuous)
Saughton Mains Bank
   EH11: Edin 7J **19**
Saughton Mains Dr.
   EH11: Edin 1H **31**
Saughton Mains Gdns.
   EH11: Edin 1H **31**
Saughton Mains Gro.
   EH11: Edin 1J **31**
Saughton Mains Loan
   EH11: Edin 1H **31**
Saughton Mains Pk.
   EH11: Edin 7H **19**
Saughton Mains Pl.
   EH11: Edin 1H **31**
Saughton Mains St.
   EH11: Edin 7H **19**
Saughton Mains Ter.
   EH11: Edin 7H **19**
Saughton Pk. EH12: Edin 5K **19**
Saughton Rd. EH11: Edin 7H **19**
Saughton Rd. Nth.
   EH12: Edin 5G **19**
Saughton Sports Complex 6K **19**
Saughton Stop (NET)
   (Due to open 2011) 7G **19**
Saunders Ct. EH12: Edin 6F **19**
Saunders St.
   EH3: Edin 1A **4** (2F **21**)
Savile Pl. EH9: Edin 1K **33**
Savile Ter. EH9: Edin 1K **33**
Saw Mill Gdns. EH19: Bonn . . .1J **47**
Saw Mill Medway
   EH19: Bonn 1J **47**
Saw Mill Path EH19: Bonn 1J **47**
Saw Mill Rd. EH19: Bonn 1J **47**
Saxe Coburg Pl. EH3: Edin . . .1F **21**
Saxe Coburg St. EH3: Edin . . .1F **21**
Saxe Coburg Ter. EH3: Edin . . .1F **21**
   (off Saxe Coburg St.)
Scarlett Pk. EH21: Wall 3J **25**
Schaw Rd. EH32: Pres 5F **15**
School Brae EH4: Cram 4J **9**
   EH18: Las 4G **41**
School Grn. EH18: Las 4G **41**
School La. EH30: S Q'fry 1G **7**
   EH32: Cock 3G **15**
School Sq. EH33: Elph 7F **27**
School Wynd EH28: Rat 2D **28**
Schoolyard Ct. EH25: Rosl 3A **46**
SCIENNES 6J **21**
Sciennes EH9: Edin 6J **21**
Sciennes Gdns. EH9: Edin 6J **21**
Sciennes Hill Pl. EH9: Edin . . .6J **21**
Sciennes Ho. Pl. EH9: Edin . . .6J **21**
Sciennes Pl. EH9: Edin 6J **21**
Sciennes Rd. EH9: Edin 6H **21**
Scollon Av. EH19: Bonn 5J **41**

Scone Gdns. EH8: Edin 2C **22**
Scotch Malt Whisky Society . . .**5E 12**
(off Giles St.)
Scotch Whisky Heritage Cen.
. . . .**5D 4**
Scottish National War Memorial
. . . . .5C **4** (4G **21**)
Scotland St. EH3: Edin 1G **21**
Scotland St. La. E.
EH3: Edin 1H **21**
Scotland St. La. W.
EH3: Edin 1G **21**
Scotsman Bldgs. EH1: Edin . . .3F **5**
Scotstoun Av. EH30: S Q'fry . .2H **7**
Scotstoun Grn. EH30: S Q'fry . .2H **7**
Scotstoun Gro. EH30: S Q'fry . .2H **7**
Scotstoun Pk. EH30: S Q'fry . .3H **7**
Scottish American War Memorial
. . . . .4C **4**
Scottish Gallery 1C **4**
Scottish Mining Mus.
(Lady Victoria Colliery)
. . . . .2C **48**
Scottish National Gallery of
Modern Art 3C **20**
Scottish National Portrait Gallery
. . . . .1E **4**
Scottish Parliament . . .3J **5** (3K **21**)
Scottish Parliament Vis. Cen., The
. . . . .3K **5**
Scottish RU & Edinburgh Rugby
. . . . .5A **20**
Scott Monument 3E **4**
Scott Rd. EH26: Pen 7C **44**
Scotway Cen., The
EH22: Dalk 5K **35**
Seacot EH6: Edin 6H **13**
SEAFIELD
EH6 . . . . .6H **13**
EH25 . . . . .7H **39**
Seafield Av. EH6: Edin 6H **13**
Seafield Cl. EH25: Bil 7J **39**
Seafield Crematorium & Cemetery
EH6: Edin 6H **13**
Seafield Cres. EH25: Bil 7J **39**
Seafield Moor Rd.
EH10: Edin 3G **39**
EH25: Rosl 3G **39**
Seafield Pl. EH6: Edin 6H **13**
Seafield Rd. EH6: Edin 6H **13**
EH25: Bil 7H **39**
Seafield Rd. E.
EH15: Edin, Port
. . . . .6K **13** & 1F **23**
Seafield St. EH6: Edin 6J **13**
Seafield Way EH15: Edin 7K **13**
Seaforth Dr. EH4: Edin 1A **20**
Seaforth Ter. EH4: Edin 1A **20**
(off Queensferry Rd.)
EH19: Bonn 7F **41**
Sealcarr St. EH5: Edin 3H **11**
Seaport St. EH6: Leith 5F **13**
Seaview Cres. EH15: Port 4K **23**
Seaview Ter. EH15: Port 4K **23**
Second Gait EH14: Cur 4A **30**
Second St. EH22: Newt 2D **48**
(not continuous)
Semple St. EH3: Edin . . .6A **4** (4F **21**)
Seton Chapel (Buriel Vault)
formerly Collegiate Church
. . . . .4K **15**
Seton Ct. EH32: Port S 3J **15**
EH33: Tran 3G **27**
Seton Pl. EH9: Edin 6J **21**
EH32: Port S 3H **15**
Seton Sands Res. Cvn. Site
EH32: Port S 3K **15**
Seton Vw. EH32: Port S 4J **15**
Seton Wynd EH32: Port S 3J **15**
Seventh St. EH22: Newt 1D **48**
Shadepark Cres. EH22: Dalk . . .2D **42**
Shadepark Dr. EH22: Dalk . . .1D **42**
Shadepark Gdns.
EH22: Dalk 1D **42**
Shaftesbury Pk. EH11: Edin . . .7C **20**
Shandon Cres. EH11: Edin . . .7C **20**
Shandon Pl. EH11: Edin 7C **20**
Shandon Rd. EH11: Edin 7C **20**
Shandon St. EH11: Edin 7C **20**

Shandon Ter. EH11: Edin 7C **20**
Shandwick Pl.
EH2: Edin 4A **4** (4E **20**)
Shandwick Place Stop (NET)
(Due to open 2011)
. . . . .4A **4** (3E **20**)
Shank Av. EH23: Gore 7D **48**
Shanter Way EH16: Edin 3A **34**
Sharpdale Loan EH16: Edin . . .2B **34**
Shaw Pl. EH22: May 5F **43**
Shaws Ct. EH26: Mil B 5E **44**
Shaw's Cres. EH26: Mil B 5E **44**
Shaw's Pl. EH7: Edin 7D **12**
Shaw's Sq. EH1: Edin 1H **21**
(off Gayfield Sq.)
Shaw's St. EH7: Edin 7D **12**
Shaw's Ter. EH7: Edin 7D **12**
Sheriff Bank EH6: Leith 5E **12**
Sheriff Brae EH6: Leith 5E **12**
Sheriffhall (Park & Ride) . . .6J **35**
SHERIFFHALL JUNC. 7K **35**
Sheriffhall Mains Cotts.
EH22: Dalk 6K **35**
Sheriff Pk. EH6: Leith 5E **12**
Sherwood Av. EH19: Bonn . . .7J **41**
Sherwood Ct. EH19: Bonn . . .7J **41**
Sherwood Cres.
EH19: Bonn 7J **41**
Sherwood Dr. EH19: Bonn . . .7J **41**
Sherwood Gro. EH19: Bonn . . .7K **41**
Sherwood Ind. Est.
EH19: Bonn 6J **41**
Sherwood Loan EH19: Bonn . . .7J **41**
Sherwood Pk. EH19: Bonn . . .7J **41**
Sherwood Pl. EH19: Bonn . . .7J **41**
Sherwood Ter. EH19: Bonn . . .7J **41**
Sherwood Vw. EH19: Bonn . . .7J **41**
Sherwood Wlk. EH19: Bonn . . .7K **41**
Sherwood Way EH19: Bonn . . .7J **41**
Shore EH6: Leith 5F **13**
Shore Pl. EH6: Leith 5F **13**
Shore Rd. EH30: S Q'fry 1G **7**
Shorthope St. EH21: Muss . . .2E **24**
Shrub Mt. EH15: Port 2G **23**
Shrub Pl. EH7: Edin 7D **12**
Shrub Pl. La. EH7: Edin 7D **12**
Sienna Gdns. EH9: Edin 6J **21**
SIGHTHILL 2F **31**
Sighthill Av. EH11: Edin 2G **31**
Sighthill Bank EH11: Edin . . .2F **31**
Sighthill Ct. EH11: Edin 2F **31**
Sighthill Cres. EH11: Edin . . .3F **31**
Sighthill Dr. EH11: Edin 3F **31**
Sighthill Gdns. EH11: Edin . . .2F **31**
Sighthill Grn. EH11: Edin 2F **31**
Sighthill Gro. EH11: Edin 2G **31**
Sighthill Ind. Est.
EH11: Edin 1D **30**
Sighthill Loan EH11: Edin . . .2E **30**
Sighthill Neuk EH11: Edin . . .2F **31**
Sighthill Pk. EH11: Edin 2F **31**
Sighthill Ri. EH11: Edin 3F **31**
Sighthill Rd. EH11: Edin 3F **31**
Sighthill Rdbt. EH11: Edin . . .2F **31**
Sighthill Shop. Cen.
EH11: Edin 2F **31**
Sighthill St. EH11: Edin 3F **31**
Sighthill Ter. EH11: Edin 2F **31**
Sighthill Vw. EH11: Edin 2F **31**
Sighthill Wynd EH11: Edin . . .2F **31**
Silverburn Dr. EH26: Pen 1A **50**
SILVERKNOWES 6C **10**
Silverknowes Av. EH4: Edin . . .6B **10**
Silverknowes Bank
EH4: Edin 6C **10**
Silverknowes Brae
EH4: Edin 6C **10**
Silverknowes Ct. EH4: Edin . . .6C **10**
Silverknowes Cres.
EH4: Edin 6C **10**
Silverknowes Dell EH4: Edin . .6C **10**
Silverknowes Dr. EH4: Edin . . .6C **10**
Silverknowes Eastway
EH4: Edin 6C **10**
Silverknowes Gdns.
EH4: Edin 5C **10**
Silverknowes Grn.
EH4: Edin 6D **10**

Silverknowes Gro.
EH4: Edin 5C **10**
Silverknowes Hill EH4: Edin . . .6C **10**
Silverknowes Loan
EH4: Edin 6B **10**
Silverknowes Midway
EH4: Edin 6D **10**
Silverknowes Neuk
EH4: Edin 7D **10**
Silverknowes Parkway
EH4: Edin 5C **10**
Silverknowes Pl. EH4: Edin . . .4B **10**
Silverknowes Rd. E.
EH4: Edin 6C **10**
Silverknowes Rd. Sth.
EH4: Edin 7C **10**
Silverknowes Southway
EH4: Edin 6D **10**
Silverknowes Ter. EH4: Edin . .6B **10**
Silverknowes Vw. EH4: Edin . . .6D **10**
SILVERMILLS 1G **21**
Silvermills EH3: Edin 1F **21**
Simon Sq. EH8: Edin . . .6G **5** (4J **21**)
Simpson Loan
EH3: Edin 7D **4** (5G **21**)
Sinclair Cl. EH11: Edin 6C **20**
Sinclair Gdns. EH11: Edin 6C **20**
Sinclair Pl. EH11: Edin 6B **20**
Sir Harry Lauder Rd.
EH15: Edin, Port 2F **23**
Sir Walter Scott Pend
EH22: Pres 5D **14**
Sir William Fraser Homes
EH13: Edin 5J **31**
Sixth St. EH22: Newt 1C **48**
Skeltiemuir Av. EH19: Bonn . . .1G **47**
Skeltiemuir Ct. EH19: Bonn . . .1G **47**
Skeltiemuir Gro.
EH19: Bonn 1H **47**
Slaeside EH14: Bal 4E **36**
SLATEFORD 1A **32**
Slateford Gait EH11: Edin 7B **20**
Slateford Grn. EH14: Edin 6B **20**
Slateford Rd. EH11: Edin 2A **32**
EH14: Edin 1A **32**
Slateford Station (Rail) 1A **32**
Slater's Steps EH8: Edin 4H **5**
Sleigh Dr. EH7: Edin 1B **22**
Sleigh Gdns. EH7: Edin 1C **22**
Sloan St. EH6: Edin 7E **12**
Smeaton Gro. EH21: Muss . . .5F **25**
Smithfield St. EH11: Edin 6B **20**
Smith's Land EH30: S Q'fry . . .1G **7**
(off Hawthorn Bank)
Smith's Pl. EH6: Edin 6E **12**
Smithy Grn. Av. EH22: Dan . . .5K **35**
Society Rd. EH30: S Q'fry 1E **6**
Solicitors Bldgs. EH1: Edin . . .5F **5**
Somerset Pl. EH6: Leith 6F **13**
Somers Pk. EH33: Tran 3G **27**
Sommerville Gdns.
EH30: S Q'fry 3J **7**
Sour Howe EH10: Edin 7D **32**
Southbank EH4: Edin 6B **10**
Southbank Ct. EH4: Edin 6B **10**
Sth. Barnton Av. EH4: Edin . . .7B **10**
South Beechwood
EH12: Edin 5J **19**
Sth. Bri. EH1: Edin 4F **5** (3H **21**)
EH8: Edin 4F **5** (4J **21**)
Sth. Charlotte St.
EH2: Edin 3B **4** (3F **21**)
Sth. Clerk St. EH8: Edin 5J **21**
Sth. College St.
EH8: Edin 5F **5** (4H **21**)
South Cres. EH32: Pres 6E **14**
South Doors EH32: Cock 3G **15**
South E. Circus Pl. EH3: Edin . .1B **4**
Sth. Elixa Pl. EH8: Edin 3D **22**
Sth. Elphinstone Rd.
EH33: Elph 7F **27**
Sth. Ettrick Rd. EH10: Edin . . .7D **20**
SOUTHFIELD 5E **22**
Southfield Bank EH15: Edin . . .5F **23**
Southfield Farm Gro.
EH15: Port 4E **22**
Southfield Gdns. E.
EH15: Edin 4F **23**

Southfield Gdns. W.
EH15: Edin 4F **23**
Southfield Loan EH15: Edin . . .5F **23**
Southfield Pl. EH15: Port 3G **23**
Southfield Rd. E. EH15: Edin . .5F **23**
Southfield Rd. W.
EH15: Edin 5E **22**
Southfield Sq. EH15: Edin 5F **23**
Southfield Ter. EH15: Edin 5F **23**
Southfield Vs. EH15: Port 4G **23**
Sth. Fort St. EH6: Edin 5D **12**
Sth. Gayfield La.
EH1: Edin 1G **5** (1J **21**)
Sth. Gillsland Rd.
EH10: Edin 1D **32**
Sth. Grange Av. EH32: Pres . . .7C **14**
Sth. Gray's Cl.
EH1: Edin 4G **5** (3J **21**)
Sth. Gray St. EH9: Edin 7K **21**
Sth. Groathill Av. EH4: Edin . . .1A **20**
SOUTH GYLE 6D **18**
Sth. Gyle Access EH12: Edin . . .7E **18**
Sth. Gyle B'way. EH12: Edin . . .6B **18**
Sth. Gyle Cres. EH12: Edin . . .7C **18**
Sth. Gyle Cres. La.
EH12: Edin 7D **18**
Sth. Gyle Gdns. EH12: Edin . . .6D **18**
Sth. Gyle Ind. Est.
EH12: Edin 7D **18**
Sth. Gyle Loan EH12: Edin . . .6D **18**
Sth. Gyle Mains EH12: Edin . . .6D **18**
Sth. Gyle Pk. EH12: Edin 6D **18**
Sth. Gyle Rd. EH12: Edin 6D **18**
(not continuous)
South Gyle Station (Rail) . . .6D **18**
Sth. Gyle Wynd EH12: Edin . . .6E **18**
SOUTHHOUSE 7B **34**
Southhouse Av. EH17: Edin . . .7B **34**
Southhouse Brae EH17: Edin . .7B **34**
Southhouse B'way.
EH17: Edin 1B **40**
Southhouse Cl. EH17: Edin . . .1B **40**
Southhouse Cres.
EH17: Edin 7B **34**
Southhouse Crossway
EH17: Edin 1B **40**
Southhouse Dr. EH17: Edin . . .7B **34**
Southhouse Gdns.
EH17: Edin 1B **40**
Southhouse Gro. EH17: Edin . .1B **40**
Southhouse Loan
EH17: Edin 7B **34**
Southhouse Pl. EH17: Edin . . .7B **34**
Southhouse Rd. EH17: Edin . . .7A **34**
Southhouse Sq. EH17: Edin . . .1B **40**
Southhouse Ter. EH17: Edin . . .7C **34**
Southhouse Wlk. EH17: Edin . .7B **34**
Sth. Lauder Rd. EH9: Edin 7J **21**
Sth. Laverockbank Av.
EH5: Edin 4B **12**
Sth. Lawlawn Ct. EH4: Edin . . .6B **10**
Sth. Learmonth Av.
EH4: Edin 2D **20**
Sth. Learmonth Gdns.
EH4: Edin 2D **20**
SOUTH LEITH 5F **13**
Sth. Lorimer Pl. EH32: Cock . . .4G **15**
Sth. Lorne Pl. EH6: Edin 7E **12**
Sth. Maybury EH12: Edin 5C **18**
South Mdw. Wlk.
EH9: Edin 7C **4** (5G **21**)
Sth. Mellis Pk. EH8: Edin 3E **22**
Sth. Morton St. EH15: Port . . .4J **23**
(not continuous)
Sth. Oswald Rd. EH9: Edin . . .1G **33**
Sth. Oxford St. EH8: Edin 6K **21**
South Pk. EH6: Newh 4C **12**
South Parrotshot EH15: Edin . .6H **23**
Sth. Quarry Av. EH23: Gore . . .6G **49**
Sth. Quarry Blvd.
EH23: Gore 6F **49**
Sth. Quarry Brae EH23: Gore . .6F **49**
Sth. Quarry Cres.
EH23: Gore 6G **49**
Sth. Quarry Dr. EH23: Gore . . .6G **49**
Sth. Quarry Gdns.
EH23: Gore 6G **49**
Sth. Quarry M. EH23: Gore . . .6G **49**
Sth. Quarry Pk. EH23: Gore . . .6F **49**

Sth. Quarry Pl.—Tay St.

Sth. Quarry Pl. EH23: Gore 6F **49**
Sth. Quarry Ter. EH23: Gore . . .6F **49**
Sth. Quarry Vw. EH23: Gore . . .6G **49**
Sth. Quarry Wlk. EH23: Gore . . .6F **49**
Sth. Quarry Way EH23: Gore . . .6G **49**
SOUTH QUEENSFERRY 1G **7**
Sth. St Andrew St.
EH2: Edin 2E **4** (2H **21**)
Sth. St David St.
EH2: Edin 2E **4** (3H **21**)
South Scotstoun
EH30: S Q'fry 3H **7**
Sth. Seton Pk. EH32: Port S . . .4G **15**
SOUTH SIDE 7G **5** (5J **21**)
Sth. Sloan St. EH6: Edin 7E **12**
(not continuous)
South Steil EH10: Edin 3C **32**
South St. EH21: Muss 2D **24**
EH22: Dalk 2C **42**
Sth. Trinity Rd. EH5: Edin 5A **12**
South Vw. EH32: Pres 6E **14**
Soutra Ct. EH16: Edin 6B **34**
Spalding Cres. EH22: Dalk 2D **42**
Spa Pl. EH15: Port 2G **23**
Spartans FC 6H **11**
Speedwell Av. EH22: Dan 4G **35**
Spencer Pl. EH5: Edin 4A **12**
Spence St. EH16: Edin 6K **21**
Spey St. EH7: Edin 7D **12**
Spey St. La. *EH7: Edin 7D 12*
(off Spey St.)
Spey St. M. EH7: Edin 7D **12**
Spey Ter. EH7: Edin 7D **12**
Spier's Pl. EH6: Leith 5E **12**
Spinney, The EH17: Edin 6D **34**
Spittalfield Cres.
EH8: Edin 7H **5** (5J **21**)
Spittal St. EH3: Edin 6B **4** (4F **21**)
Spittal St. La.
EH3: Edin 5C **4** (4G **21**)
Spottiswoode Rd. EH9: Edin . . .6G **21**
Spottiswoode St. EH9: Edin . . .6G **21**
Springfield EH6: Edin 6E **12**
Springfield Bldgs. EH6: Edin . . .6E **12**
Springfield Cres.
EH30: S Q'fry 1E **6**
Springfield La. EH6: Edin 6E **12**
Springfield Lea
EH30: S Q'fry 1E **6**
Springfield Pl. EH23: Gore 7F **49**
EH25: Rosl 2A **46**
EH30: S Q'fry 1E **6**
Springfield Rd. EH30: S Q'fry . . .1E **6**
Springfield St. EH6: Edin 6E **12**
Springfield Ter. EH30: S Q'fry . . .1E **6**
Springfield Vw. EH30: S Q'fry . . .1E **6**
Spring Gdns. EH8: Edin 2A **22**
Springvalley Gdns.
EH10: Edin 1E **32**
Springvalley Ter. EH10: Edin . . .1E **32**
Springwell Pl. EH11: Edin 5D **20**
Springwell Ter. *EH30: S Q'fry . . .1G 7*
(off Hopetoun Rd.)
Springwood Pk. EH16: Edin 4B **34**
Spruce Wlk. *EH20: Loan 6K 39*
(off Nivensknowe Pk.)
Spylaw Av. EH13: Edin 5H **31**
Spylaw Bank Rd.
EH13: Edin 5H **31**
Spylaw Ho. EH13: Edin 6J **31**
Spylaw Pk. EH13: Edin 5H **31**
Spylaw Rd. EH10: Edin 7D **20**
Spylaw St. EH13: Edin 6J **31**
Square, The EH22: Dan 4H **35**
EH22: Newt 1D **48**
EH26: Pen 3D **50**
EH29: Kltn 2B **16**
Stable La. EH10: Edin 7E **20**
Stafford St. EH3: Edin . . .4A **4** (3E **20**)
Stair Pk. EH12: Edin 4A **20**
EH33: Tran 1F **27**
Standingstane Rd.
EH30: Dalm 3K **7**
Stanedykehead EH16: Edin 6K **33**
Stanhope Pl. EH12: Edin 4C **20**
Stanhope St. EH12: Edin 4C **20**
Stanley Av. EH25: Bil 7J **39**
Stanley Pl. EH7: Edin 2A **22**
Stanley Rd. EH6: Newh 4B **12**
Stanley St. EH15: Port 4G **23**
Stanwell St. EH6: Edin 6E **12**
Stapeley Av. EH7: Edin 1E **22**
Starbank Rd. EH5: Edin 4B **12**
Stark's Cotts. EH13: Edin 5C **32**
Station Brae EH15: Port 3G **23**
Station Loan EH14: Bal 2E **36**
Station Rd. EH12: Edin 5G **19**
EH20: Loan 5C **40**
EH21: Muss 3E **24**
EH22: Dalk 3A **42**
EH22: Newt 7C **42**
EH23: Gore 7E **48**
EH25: Rosl 2A **46**
EH28: Rat S 5C **16**
EH29: Kltn 2B **16**
EH30: Dalm, S Q'fry 1H **7**
EH32: Pres 7E **14**
Station Ter. EH29: Kltn 2B **16**
Station Vw. EH30: S Q'fry 2J **7**
Stead's Pl. EH6: Edin 6E **12**
Steele Av. EH22: May 7H **43**
Steel's Pl. EH10: Edin 1F **33**
Steil Gro. EH33: Tran 3H **27**
Steils, The EH10: Edin 3C **32**
STENHOUSE 7J **19**
Stenhouse Av. EH11: Edin 6J **19**
Stenhouse Av. W.
EH11: Edin 6J **19**
Stenhouse Cotts. EH11: Edin . . .7J **19**
Stenhouse Cres. EH11: Edin . . .7J **19**
Stenhouse Cross EH11: Edin . . .7J **19**
Stenhouse Dr. EH11: Edin 7H **19**
Stenhouse Gdns. EH11: Edin . . .7J **19**
Stenhouse Gdns. Nth.
EH11: Edin 7J **19**
Stenhouse Gro. EH11: Edin 7J **19**
Stenhouse Mill Cres.
EH11: Edin 1K **31**
Stenhouse Mill La.
EH11: Edin 1K **31**
Stenhouse Mill Wynd
EH11: Edin 1K **31**
Stenhouse Pl. E. EH11: Edin . . .7J **19**
Stenhouse Pl. W. EH11: Edin . . .7J **19**
Stenhouse Rd. EH11: Edin 1J **31**
(not continuous)
Stenhouse St. E. EH11: Edin . . .7J **19**
Stenhouse St. W.
EH11: Edin 7H **19**
Stenhouse Ter. EH11: Edin 7K **19**
Stennis Gdns. EH17: Edin 5C **34**
Stevenlaw's Cl.
EH1: Edin 4F **5** (3H **21**)
Stevenson Av. EH11: Edin 6A **20**
Stevenson Dr. EH11: Edin 7J **19**
Stevenson Gro. EH11: Edin 6A **20**
Stevenson La. EH22: Newt 2D **48**
Stevenson Pl. EH18: Las 7D **40**
Stevenson Rd. EH11: Edin 6A **20**
EH26: Pen 6E **44**
Stevenson Ter. EH11: Edin 6A **20**
Stewart Av. EH14: Cur 2G **37**
Stewart Clark Av.
EH30: S Q'fry 2H **7**
Stewart Cres. EH14: Cur 1G **37**
Stewartfield EH6: Edin 6C **12**
Stewart Gdns. EH14: Cur 1G **37**
Stewart Gro. EH22: Dan 4G **35**
Stewart Pl. EH14: Cur 2G **37**
EH29: Kltn 1B **16**
Stewart Rd. EH14: Cur 2G **37**
Stewart's Melville FP RFC 6K **11**
Stewart Ter. EH11: Edin 6B **20**
EH30: S Q'fry 1F **7**
(not continuous)
Stills Gallery 4F **5** (3H **21**)
Stirling Rd. EH5: Edin 4A **12**
EH29: Kltn 1A **16**
Stobhill Rd. EH22: Newt 2D **48**
EH23: Gore 6F **49**
(Hunter Sq.)
EH23: Gore 2D **48**
(Lingerwood Wlk.)
STOBS MILLS 7E **48**
STOCKBRIDGE 1F **21**
Stone Av. EH22: May 7F **43**
Stone Cres. EH22: May 7F **43**
Stone Pl. EH22: May 1F **49**
STONEYBANK 4D **24**
Stoneybank Av. EH21: Muss . . .4C **24**
Stoneybank Ct. EH21: Muss . . .3C **24**
Stoneybank Cres.
EH21: Muss 4D **24**
Stoneybank Dr. EH21: Muss . . .3C **24**
Stoneybank Gdns.
EH21: Muss 3C **24**
(not continuous)
Stoneybank Gdns. Nth.
EH21: Muss 3C **24**
Stoneybank Gdns. Sth.
EH21: Muss 4D **24**
Stoneybank Gro.
EH21: Muss 4D **24**
Stoneybank Pl. EH21: Muss . . .4D **24**
Stoneybank Rd. EH21: Muss . . .4D **24**
Stoneybank Ter.
EH21: Muss 4D **24**
Stoney Cft. Rd. EH30: S Q'fry . . .1G **7**
Stoneyflatts EH30: S Q'fry 1F **7**
Stoneyflatts Cres.
EH30: S Q'fry 1F **7**
Stoneyflatts Pk. EH30: S Q'fry . . .2F **7**
Stoneyhill Av. EH21: Muss 3C **24**
Stoneyhill Ct. EH21: Muss 3C **24**
Stoneyhill Cres.
EH21: Muss 3C **24**
Stoneyhill Dr. EH21: Muss 3C **24**
Stoneyhill Farm Rd.
EH21: Muss 3D **24**
(not continuous)
Stoneyhill Gdns.
EH21: Muss 3C **24**
Stoneyhill Gro. EH21: Muss . . .3C **24**
Stoneyhill Pl. EH21: Muss 3C **24**
Stoneyhill Ri. EH21: Muss 3C **24**
Stoneyhill Rd. EH21: Muss 3C **24**
Stoneyhill Steading
EH21: Muss 3D **24**
Stoneyhill Ter. EH21: Muss 3C **24**
Stoneyhill Wynd
EH21: Muss 3C **24**
Stoneypath EH14: Edin 3K **31**
Strachan Gdns. EH4: Edin 1J **19**
Strachan Rd. EH4: Edin 1J **19**
STRAITON 4A **40**
Straiton (Park & Ride) 3A **40**
STRAITON JUNC. 2A **40**
Straiton La. EH15: Port 3H **23**
Straiton Mains EH20: Loan 4A **40**
Straiton Pk. EH20: Loan 4A **40**
Straiton Pk. Cvn. Pk.
EH20: Loan 4K **39**
Straiton Pk. Way
EH20: Loan 4A **40**
Straiton Pl. EH15: Port 2H **23**
Straiton Pl. Loan EH15: Port 3H **23**
Straiton Pond Local Nature Reserve
. . . . .3C **40**
Straiton Rd. EH17: Edin 1A **40**
EH20: Loan 4A **40**
(not continuous)
Straiton Vw. EH20: Loan 4A **40**
Strathalmond Ct. EH4: Cram 7G **9**
Strathalmond Grn.
EH4: Cram 7G **9**
Strathalmond Pk.
EH4: Cram 1B **18**
Strathalmond Rd.
EH4: Cram 1B **18**
Strathearn Pl. EH9: Edin 7F **21**
Strathearn Rd. EH9: Edin 7G **21**
Strathesk Gro. EH26: Pen 1E **50**
Strathesk Pl. EH26: Pen 1E **50**
Strathesk Rd. EH26: Pen 1E **50**
Strathfillan Rd. EH9: Edin 7G **21**
Straun Wynd EH32: Pres 5F **15**
Strawberry Bank EH22: Dalk . . .4A **42**
Stuart Ct. EH12: Edin 3D **18**
Stuart Cres. EH12: Edin 3D **18**
Stuart Grn. EH12: Edin 3D **18**
Stuart Pk. EH12: Edin 3D **18**
Stuart Sq. EH12: Edin 3D **18**
Stuart Wynd EH12: Edin 3D **18**
Succoth Av. EH12: Edin 3B **20**
Succoth Ct. EH12: Edin 3B **20**
Succoth Gdns. EH12: Edin 3B **20**
Succoth Hgts. EH12: Edin 3B **20**
Succoth Pk. EH12: Edin 3A **20**
Succoth Pl. EH12: Edin 3B **20**
Suffolk Rd. EH16: Edin 1K **33**
Suffolk Rd. La. EH16: Edin 1K **33**
Sugarhouse Cl. EH8: Edin 4H **5**
Summer Bank EH3: Edin 1G **21**
Summerfield Gdns.
EH6: Edin 6G **13**
Summerfield Pl. EH6: Edin 6G **13**
Summerhall EH9: Edin 5J **21**
Summerhall Pl. *EH9: Edin 6J 21*
(off Summerhall)
Summerhall Sq. EH9: Edin 6J **21**
Summerlee EH32: Pres 6C **14**
Summer Pl. EH3: Edin 7A **12**
Summerside Pl. EH6: Newh . . .5C **12**
Summerside St. EH6: Newh . . .5C **12**
Summertrees Ct. EH16: Edin . . .3B **34**
SUNBURY 3D **20**
Sunbury M. EH4: Edin 3D **20**
Sunbury Pl. EH4: Edin 3D **20**
Sunbury St. EH4: Edin 3D **20**
Sunnybank EH7: Edin 2B **22**
Sunnybank Pl. EH7: Edin 2B **22**
Sunnybank Ter. *EH7: Edin 2A 22*
(off Lwr. London Rd.)
Sunnyside EH7: Edin 1A **22**
Suntrap 2A **30**
Surgeon's Hall EH8: Edin 5G **5**
Sutherland St. EH12: Edin 4C **20**
Suttieslea Cres. EH22: Newt . . .7E **42**
Suttieslea Dr. EH22: Newt 7E **42**
Suttieslea Pl. EH22: Newt 7E **42**
Suttieslea Rd. EH22: Newt 7E **42**
Suttieslea Wlk. EH22: Newt 7E **42**
Swallow La. EH22: Dalk 2F **43**
Swan Cres. EH23: Gore 5E **48**
Swanfield EH6: Edin 5E **12**
Swan Rd. EH33: Tran 3G **27**
Swan Spring Av. EH10: Edin . . .5D **32**
SWANSTON
EH10, Boghall 2E **38**
EH10, Fairmilehead 7E **32**
Swanston Av. EH10: Edin 7E **32**
Swanston Cres. EH10: Edin 7E **32**
Swanston Dr. EH10: Edin 1F **39**
Swanston Gdns. EH10: Edin . . .7E **32**
Swanston Grn. EH10: Edin 7E **32**
Swanston Gro. EH10: Edin 1F **39**
Swanston Loan EH10: Edin 7E **32**
Swanston Muir EH10: Edin 7C **32**
Swanston Pk. EH10: Edin 7E **32**
Swanston Pl. EH10: Edin 7E **32**
Swanston Rd. EH10: Edin 7D **32**
Swanston Row EH10: Edin 7E **32**
Swanston Ter. EH10: Edin 7F **33**
Swanston Vw. EH10: Edin 7E **32**
Swanston Way EH10: Edin 7E **32**
Swinton Pl. EH20: Loan 6K **39**
Sycamore Av. EH32: Port S 4H **15**
Sycamore Gdns. EH12: Edin . . .5F **19**
Sycamore Path *EH20: Loan 6K 39*
(off Nivensknowe Pk.)
Sycamore Rd. EH22: May 7G **43**
Sycamore Ter. EH12: Edin 5G **19**
Sydney Pk. EH7: Edin 1E **22**
Sydney Pl. EH7: Edin 1E **22**
Sydney Ter. EH7: Edin 1E **22**
Sylvan Pl. EH9: Edin 6H **21**
Syme Cres. EH10: Edin 4C **32**
Syme Pl. EH10: Edin 4C **32**
Syme Rigg EH10: Edin 4C **32**

T

Tait Dr. EH26: Pen 2D **50**
Tait St. EH22: Dalk 2C **42**
Talbot Rice Gallery 5F **5** (4H **21**)
Talisman Pl. EH16: Edin 3B **34**
Tanfield EH3: Edin 7B **12**
Tantallon Pl. EH9: Edin 6H **21**
Tartan Weaving Mill & Exhibition
. . . . .4D **4**
Tarvit St. EH3: Edin 7B **4**
Taylor Gdns. EH6: Leith 5E **12**
Taylor Pl. EH7: Edin 2A **22**
EH22: Dalk 3E **42**
Tay St. EH11: Edin 6D **20**

Telfer Subway EH11: Edin 5D 20
Telferton EH7: Edin 2F 23
Telford Cotts. EH26: Pen . . .3D 50
  (off Beach Pl.)
Telford Dr. EH4: Edin 7G 11
Telford Gdns. EH4: Edin 7G 11
Telford Gro. EH4: Edin 6G 11
Telford March EH4: Edin 7G 11
Telford Pl. EH4: Edin 7G 11
Telford Rd. EH4: Edin 1K 19
Templar's Cramond
  EH4: Cram 6H 9
Templeland Gro. EH12: Edin . . .4F 19
Templeland Rd. EH12: Edin . . .4E 18
Temple Pk. Cres.
  EH11: Edin 6D 20
Tennant St. EH6: Edin 6E 12
Tenth St. EH22: Newt 7D 42
Terrars Cft. EH8: Edin 7J 5
Terregles EH26: Pen 1B 50
Teviotbank Ho. EH16: Edin . . .1G 35
Teviotdale Pl. EH3: Edin 7A 12
Teviot Gro. EH26: Pen 7D 44
Teviot Pl. EH1: Edin 6E 4 (4H 21)
The . . . .
  Names prefixed with 'The' for
  example 'The Avenue' are
  indexed under the main name
  such as 'Avenue, The'
Third Gait EH4: Cur 5A 30
Third St. EH22: Newt 2C 48
  (not continuous)
Thirlestane La. EH9: Edin 7G 21
Thirlestane Rd. EH9: Edin 6G 21
Thistle Ct. EH2: Edin 2D 4
Thistle Pl. EH11: Edin 6E 20
Thistle St. EH2: Edin . . .2C 4 (2G 21)
Thistle St. Nth. E. La.
  EH2: Edin 2D 4 (2G 21)
Thistle St. Nth. W. La.
  EH2: Edin 2C 4 (2G 21)
Thistle St. Sth. E. La.
  EH2: Edin 2D 4 (2G 21)
Thistle St. Sth. W. La.
  EH2: Edin 2C 4 (2G 21)
Thomson Cres. EH14: Cur 7D 30
  EH32: Port S 3G 15
Thomson Dr. EH14: Cur 7D 30
Thomson Gro. EH14: Cur 7D 30
Thomson Rd. EH14: Cur 7D 30
Thomson's Ct. EH1: Edin 5D 4
  EH8: Edin 3K 5
Thorburn Gro. EH13: Edin 6A 32
Thorburn Rd. EH13: Edin 6K 31
Thorburn Ter. EH26: Pen 3C 50
Thornhall Cotts. EH22: Dalk . . .1D 42
Thornton Rd. EH24: Rose 5D 46
Thorntree Cres. EH32: Pres . . .6F 15
Thorntreeside EH6: Edin 7F 13
Thorntree St. EH6: Edin 6E 12
Thornville Ter. EH6: Edin 7F 13
Thornybank EH22: Dalk 1E 42
Thornybank Ind. Est.
  EH22: Dalk 1F 43
Thorny Bauk
  EH3: Edin 7B 4 (5F 21)
Thornybauk EH3: Edin 6B 4 (5F 21)
  (not continuous)
Thornyhall EH22: Dalk 1E 42
Threipmuir Av. EH14: Bal 5E 36
Threipmuir Gdns. EH14: Bal . . .5E 36
Threipmuir Pl. EH14: Bal 5E 36
Timber Bush EH6: Leith 4F 13
  (not continuous)
Timmins Ct. EH28: Rat 2D 28
Tinto Pl. EH6: Edin 6D 12
Tipperlinn Rd. EH10: Edin 7E 20
Toddshill Rd. EH29: Kltn 2A 16
Tolbooth Wynd EH6: Leith 5F 13
TOLL CROSS 6B 4 (4F 21)
TOLL CROSS JUNC. 7B 4
Tollhouse Gdns. EH33: Tran . . .4H 27
Toll Ho. Gro. EH33: Tran 3H 27
Toll Ho. Neuk EH33: Tran 4H 27
Torduff Rd. EH13: Edin 7H 31
Torphichen Pl. EH3: Edin 4E 20
Torphichen St. EH3: Edin 4E 20
Torphin Bank EH13: Edin 7H 31
Torphin Rd. EH13: Edin 7H 31

Torrance Pk. EH4: Edin 2E 18
Torrence Medway
  EH26: Mil B 5E 44
Torsonce Rd. EH22: Dalk 3B 42
Toscana Ct. EH16: Dan 4G 35
Tourist Info. Cen.
  Edinburgh 3F 5 (3H 21)
  Edinburgh Airport 3F 17
  Musselburgh Service Area
  . . . . .6D 24
  Newtongrange 2C 48
  Penicuik 1E 50
Toward Ct. EH12: Edin 4C 18
  (off Craigievar Wynd)
Tower Pl. EH6: Leith 4F 13
Tower St. EH6: Leith 4F 13
Tower Wharf EH6: Leith 4F 13
Tower Wynd EH6: Leith 4F 13
Trafalgar La. EH6: Leith 5C 12
Trafalgar St. EH6: Leith 5D 12
TRANENT 2H 27
Tranent By-Pass EH33: Tran . . .1D 26
Tranent St. EH33: Elph 7F 27
Traprain Ter. EH20: Loan 6C 40
Traquair Pk. E. EH12: Edin 5H 19
Traquair Pk. W. EH12: Edin . . .5G 19
Traverse Theatre 5B 4 (4F 21)
Trelawney Ter. EH26: Pen 6E 44
Trench Knowe EH10: Edin 7E 32
Tressilian Gdns. EH16: Edin . . .3A 34
Trinity Ct. EH5: Edin 5A 12
Trinity Cres. EH5: Edin 3A 12
Trinity Gro. EH5: Edin 4A 12
Trinity Mains EH5: Edin 5A 12
Trinity Pk. Ho. EH5: Edin 5A 12
Trinity Rd. EH5: Edin 4A 12
Trinity Way EH5: Edin 5A 12
Tron Church 4F 5
  (off Hunter Sq.)
Tron Sq. EH1: Edin 4F 5
Trotter Haugh EH9: Edin 1H 33
Trunk's Cl. EH1: Edin 4G 5
Tryst Pk. EH10: Edin 7D 32
Tunnel, The EH14: Edin 3J 31
Turlies, The EH13: Edin 5J 31
Turner Av. EH14: Bal 2D 36
Turner Pk. EH14: Bal 2D 36
Turnhouse Farm Rd.
  EH12: Edin A 2J 17
Turnhouse Rd.
  EH12: Edin, Edin A 2H 17
Turret Gdns. EH32: Pres 7D 14
Tweeddale St. EH1: Edin 4G 5
Tweedsmuir Ho. EH16: Edin . . .1F 35
Tyler's Acre Av. EH12: Edin . . .6G 19
Tyler's Acre Gdns.
  EH12: Edin 6G 19
Tyler's Acre Rd. EH12: Edin . . .6G 19
Tynecastle 6C 20
Tynecastle La. EH11: Edin 6C 20
Tynecastle Ter. EH11: Edin 6C 20
Tytler Ct. EH8: Edin 2A 22
Tytler Gdns.
  EH8: Edin 2K 5 (2K 21)

Ulster Cres. EH8: Edin 3C 22
Ulster Dr. EH8: Edin 3D 22
Ulster Gdns. EH8: Edin 4D 22
Ulster Gro. EH8: Edin 4D 22
Ulster Ter. EH8: Edin 4D 22
Union Pk. EH19: Bonn 6H 41
Union Pl. EH1: Edin 1G 5
Union St. EH1: Edin 1F 5 (1H 21)
University of Edinburgh
  King's Buildings 2J 33
Upper Bow EH1: Edin . . .4E 4 (3H 21)
Upper Broomieknowe
  EH18: Las 6G 41
Up. Coltbridge Ter.
  EH12: Edin 3C 20
Upper Craigour EH17: Edin 3E 34
Up. Craigour Way
  EH17: Edin 3D 34
Up. Cramond Ct. EH4: Cram . . .6J 9
Upper Damside EH4: Edin 3D 20

Up. Dean Ter.
  EH4: Edin 1A 4 (2E 20)
Up. Gilmore Pl.
  EH3: Edin 7A 4 (5F 21)
Up. Gilmore Ter. EH3: Edin 5F 21
Up. Gray St. EH9: Edin 6J 21
Up. Greenside La.
  EH1: Edin 1G 5 (2J 21)
Upper Gro. Pl. EH3: Edin 5E 20
Upper Hermitage EH6: Edin . . .6F 13
Usher Hall 5B 4

V

Valleyfield Rd. EH26: Pen . . .3D 50
Valleyfield St.
  EH3: Edin 7B 4 (5F 21)
Valleyfield Vw. EH26: Pen . . .3D 50
Vanburgh Pl. EH6: Edin 6F 13
Vancluse Pl. EH6: Edin 3C 50
Vandeleur Av. EH7: Edin 1E 22
Vandeleur Gro. EH7: Edin 2E 22
Vandeleur Pl. EH7: Edin 1E 22
Veitch's Sq. EH4: Edin 1F 21
Vennel EH1: Edin 5D 4 (4G 21)
Vennel, The EH30: S Q'fry 1H 7
Ventnor Pl. EH9: Edin 7A 22
Ventnor Ter. EH9: Edin 7K 21
Vernon Cotts. EH15: Port 3H 23
  (off Bellfield St.)
Vexhim Pk. EH15: Edin 6H 23
Victoria Gdns. EH22: Newt 7B 42
Victoria Pk. Neuk
  EH6: Newh 5C 12
Victoria Quay EH6: Leith 4E 12
Victoria Rd. EH22: Newt 7B 42
Victoria St. EH1: Edin . . .5E 4 (4H 21)
  EH24: Rose 4D 46
Victoria Ter. EH1: Edin 5D 4
  EH21: Muss 2G 25
Victor Pk. Ter. EH12: Edin 4F 19
Viewbank Av. EH19: Bonn 5K 41
Viewbank Dr. EH19: Bonn 5J 41
Viewbank Rd. EH19: Bonn 5H 41
Viewbank Vw. EH19: Bonn 5J 41
Viewcraig Gdns.
  EH8: Edin 4H 5 (3J 21)
Viewcraig St.
  EH8: Edin 4H 5 (4J 21)
Viewfield EH19: Bonn 5K 41
Viewfield Rd. EH14: J Grn 5G 31
VIEWFORTH 5E 20
Viewforth EH3: Edin 5E 20
  EH10: Edin 6E 20
  EH11: Edin 5E 20
  EH32: Port S 3H 15
Viewforth Gdns. EH10: Edin . . .6F 21
  EH33: Tran 1G 27
Viewforth Pl. EH30: S Q'fry 2G 7
Viewforth Rd. EH30: S Q'fry . . .1G 7
Viewforth Sq. EH10: Edin 6E 20
Viewforth Ter. EH10: Edin 6E 20
  EH33: Tran 2G 27
Viewpark Gdns. EH19: Bonn . . .5H 41
Villa Dean EH24: Rose 5C 46
Villa Rd. EH30: S Q'fry 1G 7
Violet Ter. EH11: Edin 6C 20
Vivian Ter. EH4: Edin 7C 10
Vogrie Cres. Sth.
  EH23: Gore 6F 49
Vogrie Pl. EH23: Gore 6F 49
Vogrie Rd. EH23: Gore 7F 49
Vorlich Cres. EH26: Pen 7E 44
Vue Cinema
  Edinburgh 1G 5 (2J 21)
  Leith 3E 12

W

Waddell Pl. EH6: Edin 6E 12
Wadingburn La. EH18: Las 4F 41
Wadingburn Rd. EH18: Las 5E 40
Wakefield Av. EH7: Edin 1F 23
Walker Cres. EH22: Dalk 4K 41
Walker Dr. EH30: S Q'fry 1F 7
Walker Pl. EH18: Las 7E 40

Walkers Ct. EH14: Edin 4G 31
Walkers Rigg EH14: Edin 3G 31
Walker St. EH3: Edin 3E 20
Walkers Wynd EH14: Edin 3G 31
Walker Ter. EH11: Edin 4E 20
Wallace Av. EH21: Wall 4J 25
Wallace Cres. EH21: Wall 3J 25
  EH25: Rosl 2A 46
Wallace Pl. EH33: Tran 1G 27
WALLYFORD 4K 25
Wallyford Ind. Est.
  EH21: Wall 4A 26
Wallyford Station (Rail) 3K 25
Wallyford Toll EH21: Muss 2K 25
Walter Scott Av. EH16: Edin . . .3B 34
  (not continuous)
Wanless Ct. EH21: Muss 2F 25
Warden's Cl. EH1: Edin 5E 4
WARDIE 4J 11
Wardie Av. EH5: Edin 5K 11
Wardieburn Dr. EH5: Edin 4J 11
Wardieburn Pl. E. EH5: Edin . . .4J 11
Wardieburn Pl. Nth.
  EH5: Edin 4J 11
Wardieburn Pl. Sth.
  EH5: Edin 4J 11
Wardieburn Pl. W.
  . . . . .4H 11
Wardieburn Rd. EH5: Edin 4H 11
Wardieburn St. E. EH5: Edin . . .4J 11
Wardieburn St. W.
  EH5: Edin 4H 11
Wardieburn Ter. EH5: Edin 4H 11
Wardie Cres. EH5: Edin 4J 11
Wardie Dell EH5: Edin 4K 11
Wardie Fld. EH5: Edin 4J 11
Wardie Gro. EH5: Edin 4J 11
Wardie Ho. La. EH5: Edin 4K 11
Wardie Pk. EH5: Edin 5K 11
Wardie Rd. EH5: Edin 5K 11
Wardie Sq. EH5: Edin 4K 11
Wardie Steps EH5: Edin 4K 11
Wardlaw Pl. EH11: Edin 6C 20
Wardlaw St. EH11: Edin 6C 20
Wardlaw Ter. EH11: Edin 6C 20
Wardrop's Ct.
  EH1: Edin 4E 4 (3H 21)
Warrender Pk. Cres.
  EH9: Edin 6F 21
Warrender Pk. Rd.
  EH9: Edin 6G 21
  (not continuous)
Warrender Pk. Ter.
  EH9: Edin 6G 21
Warrender Swimming Cen. . . .7G 21
WARRISTON 6B 12
Warriston Av. EH3: Edin 6B 12
Warriston Cres. EH3: Edin 7B 12
Warriston Dr. EH3: Edin 6A 12
Warriston Farm Rd.
  EH14: Cur 6J 29
Warriston Gdns. EH3: Edin 6A 12
Warriston Gro. EH3: Edin 6A 12
Warriston Pl. EH3: Edin 7B 12
  (off Inverleith Row)
Warriston Rd. EH3: Edin 7B 12
  EH7: Edin 5B 12
Warriston's Cl. EH1: Edin 4E 4
Warriston Ter. EH3: Edin 6A 12
Washington La. EH11: Edin 5D 20
Washington St. EH11: Edin 5D 20
Waterfall Wlk. EH22: Dalk 3D 42
Waterfront Av. EH5: Edin 4G 11
Waterfront B'way.
  EH5: Edin 4G 11
Waterfront Gait EH5: Edin 4F 11
Waterfront Pk. EH5: Edin 4F 11
Waterloo Bank EH26: Pen 3D 50
Waterloo Pl.
  EH1: Edin 2F 5 (2H 21)
  EH33: Elph 6F 27
Waterloo Rd. EH33: Tran 4H 27
Water of Leith Vis. Cen. 2A 20
Water of Leith Walkway
  EH3: Edin 1F 21
  (off Malta Ter.)
Water's Cl. EH6: Leith 5F 13
  (off Shore)
Water St. EH6: Leith 5F 13

Watertoun Rd. EH9: Edin 1J 33
Watson Cres. EH11: Edin 6D 20
Watsonian FC 1C 32
Watson's Bldgs. EH4: Edin ..6C 10
Watson St. EH26: Pen 2C 50
Watt Gro. EH22: May 1G 49
Watt Pk. EH22: Newt 2D 48
Watt's Cl. EH21: Muss 2D 24
Wauchope Av. EH16: Edin ...7E 22
Wauchope Cres. EH16: Edin .7E 22
Wauchope Ho. EH16: Edin ...1F 35
Wauchope Pl. EH16: Edin ...7E 22
      (not continuous)
Wauchope Rd. EH16: Edin ...7F 23
Wauchope Sq. EH16: Edin ...7F 23
Wauchope Ter. EH16: Edin ..7E 22
Waugh Path EH19: Bonn 5K 41
Waulkmill Dr. EH26: Pen 3D 50
Waulkmill Loan EH14: Cur ...2G 37
Waulkmill Rd. EH26: Pen 3D 50
Waulkmill Vw. EH26: Pen 3D 50
Waverley Bri.
      EH1: Edin 3E 4 (3H 21)
Waverley Ct. EH19: Bonn ...6J 41
Waverley Cres. EH19: Bonn .6J 41
Waverley Dr. EH19: Bonn 6J 41
Waverley Pk. EH8: Edin 2A 22
      EH19: Bonn 6J 41
      EH22: May 7F 43
Waverley Pk. Ter. EH8: Edin .2A 22
Waverley Pl. EH7: Edin 2A 22
Waverley Rd. EH19: Bonn ...6J 41
      EH22: Dalk 3B 42
Waverley Steps EH1: Edin ...3F 5
Waverley St. EH22: May 1F 49
Waverley Ter. EH19: Bonn ...6J 41
      EH22: May 7F 43
Weavers Knowe Cres.
      EH14: Cur 7B 30
Webster's Land EH1: Edin ...5C 4
Wedderburn Ct. EH21: Muss ..5F 25
Wedderburn Ho.
      EH21: Muss 5F 25
Wedderburn Ter.
      EH21: Muss 4F 25
Wee Brae EH18: Las 4G 41
Weir Ct. EH11: Edin 2F 31
      (off Sighthill Bank)
      EH22: Dalk 3A 42
Weir Cres. EH22: Dalk 3A 42
Well Ct. EH4: Edin 3E 20
Wellflats Rd. EH29: Kltn 2B 16
Wellhead Cl. EH30: S Q'fry ..2J 7
Wellington Cotts.
      EH22: Dalk 7B 24
Wellington Pl. EH6: Leith 6F 13
Wellington St.
      EH7: Edin 1J 5 (1K 21)
Well Wynd EH33: Tran 2H 27
Wemyss Gdns. EH21: Wall ...3A 26
Wemyss Pl.
      EH3: Edin 2B 4 (2F 21)
      EH32: Port S 3G 15
Wemyss Pl. M.
      EH3: Edin 2A 4 (2F 21)
Werberside M. EH4: Edin 6H 11
Wesley Cres. EH19: Bonn ...6K 41
W. Adam St.
      EH8: Edin 5G 5 (4J 21)
W. Annandale St. EH7: Edin ..7C 12
West App. Rd. EH3: Edin 5B 20
      EH11: Edin 6A 4 (5B 20)
Westbank EH4: Edin 6B 10
Westbank Loan EH15: Port ..2G 23
Westbank Pl. EH15: Port 2G 23
Westbank St. EH15: Port 2G 23
W. Barton Ter. EH4: Edin 2B 20
West Bow EH1: Edin ...5E 4 (4G 21)
W. Bowling Grn. St.
      EH6: Edin 5D 12
W. Brighton Cres.
      EH15: Port 3G 23
W. Bryson Rd. EH11: Edin ..6D 20
Westburn Av. EH14: Edin 4E 30
Westburn Gro. EH14: Edin ...4E 30
Westburn Middlefield
      EH14: Edin 4E 30
Westburn Pk. EH14: Edin 4F 31
W. Cairn Cres. EH26: Pen ...1C 50

W. Caiystane Rd.
      EH10: Edin 6E 32
W. Camus Rd. EH10: Edin ...6E 32
W. Carnethy Av. EH13: Edin ..7J 31
W. Castle Rd. EH10: Edin 6E 20
W. Catherine Pl. EH12: Edin ..4C 20
West Cherrybank EH6: Newh ..4B 12
West Coates EH12: Edin 4C 20
W. Colinton Ho. EH13: Edin ..6J 31
W. College St.
      EH1: Edin 5F 5 (4H 21)
West Ct. EH4: Edin 2A 20
      EH16: Edin 1E 34
WEST CRAIGS 5B 18
W. Craigs Av. EH12: Edin ...5B 18
W. Craigs Cres. EH12: Edin ..4B 18
W. Craigs Ind. Est.
      EH12: Edin 4B 18
West Cft. EH28: Rat 2E 28
W. Cromwell St. EH6: Leith ..4E 12
West Crosscauseway
      EH8: Edin 7G 5 (5J 21)
WEST END 4A 4
West End EH2: Edin ...4A 4 (3F 21)
West End Pl. EH11: Edin 5D 20
Wester Broom Av.
      EH12: Edin 6E 18
Wester Broom Dr.
      EH12: Edin 6E 18
Wester Broom Gdns.
      EH12: Edin 6E 18
Wester Broom Gro.
      EH12: Edin 6E 18
Wester Broom Pl.
      EH12: Edin 5E 18
Wester Broom Ter.
      EH12: Edin 6E 18
Wester Cl. EH6: Newh 3C 12
      (off Newhaven Pl.)
Wester Coates Av.
      EH12: Edin 4C 20
Wester Coates Gdns.
      EH12: Edin 4C 20
Wester Coates Pl.
      EH12: Edin 3C 20
Wester Coates Rd.
      EH12: Edin 4C 20
Wester Coates Ter.
      EH12: Edin 4C 20
Wester Drylaw Av. EH4: Edin .7E 10
Wester Drylaw Dr.
      EH4: Edin 7D 10
Wester Drylaw Pk.
      EH4: Edin 7F 11
Wester Drylaw Pl. EH4: Edin .7E 10
Wester Drylaw Row
      EH4: Edin 7F 11
WESTER HAILES 4F 31
Wester Hailes Cen.
      EH14: Edin 4G 31
Wester Hailes Pk.
      EH14: Edin 4G 31
Wester Hailes Rd.
      EH11: Edin 3E 30
      EH14: Edin 3E 30
Wester Hailes Station (Rail)
      ....4F 31
Wester Hill EH10: Edin 4C 32
WESTER MILLERHILL 5K 35
Western Cnr. EH14: Edin 4K 19
Western Gdns. EH12: Edin ...4A 20
WESTERN GENERAL HOSPITAL
      ....1C 20
Western Harbour Breakwater
      EH6: Newh 2C 12
Western Harbour Dr.
      EH6: Newh 3C 12
Western Harbour Midway
      EH6: Newh 2C 12
Western Harbour Pl.
      EH6: Newh 2C 12
Western Harbour Ter.
      EH6: Newh 2C 12
Western Harbour Vw.
      EH6: Newh 2C 12
      (not continuous)
Western Harbour Way
      EH6: Newh 2C 12
Western Pl. EH12: Edin 4A 20

Western Ter. EH12: Edin 4A 20
Wester Row EH14: Cur 3A 30
Wester Steil EH10: Edin 3C 32
W. Fairbrae Cres.
      EH11: Edin 1G 31
W. Fairbrae Dr. EH11: Edin ..1G 31
West Ferryfield EH5: Edin 5J 11
Westfield Av. EH11: Edin 6A 20
Westfield Bank EH22: Dalk ...4A 42
Westfield Ct. EH11: Edin 6A 20
      EH22: Dalk 4A 42
Westfield Dr. EH22: Dalk 4A 42
Westfield Gro. EH22: Dalk ...4A 42
Westfield Pk. EH22: Dalk 4A 42
Westfield Rd. EH11: Edin 6B 20
Westfield St. EH11: Edin 6B 20
Westgarth Av. EH13: Edin ...6K 31
W. Gorgie Parks EH14: Edin ..7A 20
W. Gorgie Pl. EH14: Edin 1A 32
W. Grange Gdns. EH9: Edin ..1H 33
W. Granton Access
      EH5: Edin 6G 11
      EH5: Edin 4G 11
W. Granton Rd. EH5: Edin ...4F 11
Westhall Gdns. EH10: Edin ...6F 21
W. Harbour Rd. EH5: Edin ...3H 11
      EH32: Cock 3F 15
W. Holmes Gdns.
      EH21: Muss 2D 24
Westhouses Av. EH22: May ..1G 49
Westhouses Rd. EH22: May ..1G 49
Westhouses St. EH22: May ..1G 49
W. Ingliston Cotts.
      EH28: Ing 5D 16
Westland Cotts. EH17: Edin ..7E 34
West Loan EH32: Pres 6D 14
W. Loan Ct. EH32: Pres 6D 14
W. Lorimer Pl. EH32: Cock ...4F 15
W. Mains Rd. EH9: Edin 2J 33
W. Maitland St. EH12: Edin ...4E 20
West Mayfield EH9: Edin 7K 21
W. Mill Bank EH13: Edin 6J 31
W. Mill Ct. EH18: Las 4G 41
W. Mill La. EH4: Edin 3E 20
W. Mill Rd. EH13: Edin 6H 31
Westmill Rd. EH18: Las 5G 41
Westmill Wynd EH18: Las ...5G 41
W. Montgomery Pl.
      EH7: Edin 1K 21
Westmost Cl. EH6: Newh 3B 12
      (off Pier Pl.)
W. Newington Pl. EH9: Edin ..6J 21
W. Nicolson St.
      EH8: Edin 6G 5 (4J 21)
W. Norton Pl.
      EH7: Edin 1K 5 (2K 21)
WESTPANS 1K 25
West Pk. Pl. EH11: Edin 5C 20
W. Parliament Sq. EH1: Edin ..4E 4
W. Pilton Av. EH4: Edin 6F 11
W. Pilton Bank EH4: Edin 5F 11
W. Pilton Brae EH4: Edin 5G 11
W. Pilton Cres. EH4: Edin 5E 10
W. Pilton Crossway
      EH4: Edin 5F 11
      (not continuous)
W. Pilton Dr. EH4: Edin 5F 11
W. Pilton Gdns. EH4: Edin ...5F 11
W. Pilton Grn. EH4: Edin 5F 11
W. Pilton Gro. EH4: Edin 5F 11
      (not continuous)
W. Pilton Lea EH4: Edin 5F 11
W. Pilton Loan EH4: Edin 5F 11
W. Pilton March EH4: Edin ...4G 11
W. Pilton Pk. EH4: Edin 5G 11
W. Pilton Ri. EH4: Edin 5F 11
W. Pilton Rd. EH4: Edin 5G 11
W. Pilton St. EH4: Edin 5F 11
W. Pilton Ter. EH4: Edin 6F 11
W. Pilton Vw. EH4: Edin 6F 11
W. Pilton Way EH4: Edin 5F 11
West Port EH1: Edin ...6C 4 (4G 21)
      EH3: Edin 6C 4 (4G 21)
W. Powburn EH9: Edin 1J 33
W. Preston St. EH8: Edin 6J 21
West Princes Street Gdns.
      ....4B 4 (3F 21)
West Register House 3A 4

W. Register St.
      EH2: Edin 2E 4 (2H 21)
W. Register St. La. EH2: Edin ..2E 4
W. Relugas Rd. EH9: Edin ...1H 33
W. Richmond St.
      EH8: Edin 6G 5 (4J 21)
W. Savile Gdns. EH9: Edin ...1J 33
W. Savile Rd. EH16: Edin 1K 33
W. Savile Ter. EH9: Edin 1J 33
West Seaside EH32: Pres 6C 14
W. Shore Bus. Cen.
      EH5: Edin 3F 11
W. Shore Rd. EH5: Edin 4E 10
W. Shore Rd. Trad. Est.
      EH5: Edin 3F 11
Westside Plaza EH14: Edin ...4F 31
W. Silvermills La. EH3: Edin ..1F 21
W. Stanhope Pl. EH12: Edin ..4C 20
      (off Stanhope Pl.)
West St. EH26: Pen 3C 50
West Ter. EH30: S Q'fry 1G 7
      (off High St.)
West Tollcross
      EH3: Edin 7B 4 (5F 21)
West Werberside EH4: Edin ..6H 11
West Windygoul EH33: Tran ..3F 27
W. Windygoul Gdns.
      EH33: Tran 4F 27
West Winnelstrae EH5: Edin ..6J 11
West Woods EH4: Edin 7H 11
Westpans Health Club 7H 11
Wheatfield Gro. EH20: Loan ..5A 40
Wheatfield Loan EH20: Loan ..4B 40
Wheatfield Pl. EH11: Edin 6B 20
Wheatfield Rd. EH11: Edin ...6B 20
Wheatfield St. EH11: Edin 6C 20
Wheatfield Ter. EH11: Edin ...6B 20
Wheatfield Wlk. EH20: Loan ..5A 40
Wheatsheaf La. EH22: Dalk ..1C 42
Whinny Loan EH21: Wall 4B 26
      EH33: Tran 4B 26
Whin Pk. EH32: Cock 4F 15
Whin Pk. Ind. Est.
      EH32: Cock 4F 15
Whins Pl. EH15: Port 3G 23
WHITECRAIG 7G 25
Whitecraig Av. EH21: Whit ...7G 25
Whitecraig Cres.
      EH21: Whit 7G 25
Whitecraig Gdns.
      EH21: Whit 7G 25
Whitecraig Gdns. E.
      EH21: Whit 7G 25
Whitecraig Rd. EH21: Whit ...7G 25
Whitecraig Ter. EH21: Whit ...7G 25
White Dales EH10: Edin 7G 33
Whitedales EH10: Edin 1K 19
White Hart St. EH22: Dalk ...2C 42
      (off Buccleuch St.)
Whitehead Gro.
      EH30: S Q'fry 2H 7
WHITEHILL 4H 43
Whitehill Av. EH21: Muss 3C 24
      (not continuous)
Whitehill Bus. Cen.
      EH22: Dalk 3G 43
Whitehill Dr. EH22: Dalk 3F 43
Whitehill Farm Rd.
      EH21: Muss 4C 24
Whitehill Gdns. EH21: Muss ..4C 24
Whitehill Gro. EH22: Dalk ...3F 43
Whitehill Lodge EH22: Dalk ..3F 43
      (off Whitehill Dr.)
Whitehill Pl. EH24: Rose 4D 46
Whitehill Rd. EH15: Edin 1J 35
      EH21: Dalk, Muss 1J 35
      EH22: Dalk 1J 35
      EH24: Rose 5D 46
Whitehill St. EH21: Edin 7K 23
White Horse Cl. EH8: Edin ...3J 5
Whitehouse Loan EH9: Edin ..6F 21
Whitehouse Rd. EH4: Cram ..6H 9
Whitehouse Ter. EH9: Edin ...7G 21
Whitelea Cres. EH14: Bal 5E 36
Whitelea Rd. EH14: Bal 5E 36
White's Cl. EH22: Dalk 2C 42
Whitingford EH6: Edin 5C 12

Whitson Cres. EH11: Edin 6K 19
Whitson Gro. EH11: Edin 6K 19
Whitson Pl. E. EH11: Edin 6K 19
Whitson Pl. W. EH11: Edin 6K 19
Whitson Rd. EH11: Edin 6J 19
Whitson Ter. EH11: Edin 6K 19
Whitson Wlk. EH11: Edin 6J 19
Whitson Way EH11: Edin 6K 19
Whyte Pl. EH7: Edin 2A 22
Wilfrid Ter. EH8: Edin 2C 22
WILKIESTON 6A 28
Wilkieston Rd. EH28: Rat ...3B 28
William Black Pl.
    EH30: S Q'fry 2H 7
Williamfield Sq.
    EH15: Edin 3G 23
William Jameson Pl.
    EH15: Port 2G 23
William St. EH3: Edin ...4A 4 (3E 20)
William St. Nth. E. La.
    EH3: Edin 3E 20
        (off Melville St.)
William St. Nth. W. La.
    EH3: Edin 3E 20
        (off Melville St.)
William St. Sth. E. La.
    EH3: Edin 3E 20
        (off William St.)
William St. Sth. W. La.
    EH3: Edin 4E 20
        (off William St.)
Willow Av. EH19: Bonn 7H 41
Willowbank Row EH6: Newh ..4C 12
WILLOWBRAE 4C 22
Willowbrae Av. EH8: Edin ...3C 22
Willowbrae Gdns. EH8: Edin ..3D 22
Willowbrae Rd. EH8: Edin ...2C 22
Willow Pk. EH10: Edin 7D 20
Willow Path EH20: Loan 5J 39
        (off Nivensknowe Pk.)
Willow Rd. EH22: May 7G 43
Willow Tree Pl. EH14: Bal ...2F 37
Wilson Av. EH22: Dalk 2E 42
    EH32: Pres 6D 14
Wilson Rd. EH23: Gore 5F 49
Wilson's Cl. W. EH22: Dalk ...2C 42

Wilson's Ct. EH8: Edin 3H 5
Wilsons Pk. EH15: Port 2H 23
Wilson St. EH26: Pen 2C 50
Wilson Wlk. EH33: Tran 3G 27
Wilton Rd. EH16: Edin 2K 33
WINCHBURGH 7A 6
Windmill Cl. EH8: Edin 7G 5
Windmill La.
    EH8: Edin 7F 5 (5J 21)
Windmill Pl. EH8: Edin 6G 5
Windmill St.
    EH8: Edin 7F 5 (5H 21)
Windsor Cres. EH26: Pen 1E 50
Windsor Dr. EH26: Pen 1E 50
Windsor Gdns. EH21: Muss ...2G 25
Windsor Pk. EH21: Muss 2H 25
Windsor Pk. Dr. EH21: Muss ..2H 25
Windsor Pk. Pl. EH21: Muss ..2H 25
Windsor Pk. Ter.
    EH21: Muss 2H 25
Windsor Pl. EH15: Port 3H 23
Windsor Pl. La. EH15: Port ...3H 23
Windsor Rd. EH26: Pen 1E 50
Windsor Sq. EH26: Pen 1E 50
Windsor St.
    EH7: Edin 1H 5 (1J 21)
Windsor St. La.
    EH7: Edin 1H 5 (1J 21)
Windsor Ter. EH26: Pen 1E 50
Windygoul Cres.
    EH33: Tran 3H 27
Windy Wynd EH21: Muss 4F 25
Winton Ct. EH32: Cock 3G 15
    EH33: Tran 4J 27
Winton Dr. EH10: Edin 1F 39
Winton Gdns. EH10: Edin 1G 39
Winton Gro. EH10: Edin 7F 33
    EH33: Tran 4J 27
Winton Loan EH10: Edin 1G 39
Winton Pk. EH10: Edin 1F 39
    EH32: Cock 4G 15
Winton Ter. EH33: Tran 2H 27
Winton Ter. EH10: Edin 1F 39
Winton Way EH33: Tran 4H 27
Wishart Av. EH19: Bonn 5K 41

Wishart Pl. EH22: Dalk 3A 42
Wishaw Ter. EH7: Edin 2B 22
Wisp, The EH16: Dan, Edin ..4G 35
    EH16: Edin 7G 23
    EH22: Edin 7G 23
Wisp Grn. EH16: Edin 7H 23
Witholm EH22: Dalk 4G 43
Wolrige Rd. EH16: Edin 4A 34
Wolseley Cres. EH8: Edin ...2C 22
Wolseley Gdns. EH8: Edin ...2C 22
        (off Scone Gdns.)
Wolseley Pl. EH8: Edin 2C 22
        (off London Rd.)
Wolseley Ter. EH8: Edin 2C 22
Wolsey Av. EH19: Bonn 7J 41
Woodbine Gdns. EH32: Pres ..6D 14
Woodbine Ter. EH6: Edin 7F 13
Woodburn Av. EH22: Dalk ...2E 42
Woodburn Bank EH22: Dalk ..2E 42
Woodburn Dr. EH22: Dalk ...2D 42
Woodburn Gdns. EH22: Dalk ..2E 42
Woodburn Gro. EH22: Dalk ...3E 42
Woodburn Loan EH22: Dalk ..2E 42
Woodburn Medway
    EH22: Dalk 3E 42
Woodburn Pk. EH22: Dalk ...2E 42
Woodburn Pl. EH10: Edin 1F 33
    EH22: Dalk 3E 42
Woodburn Rd. EH22: Dalk ...2D 42
Woodburn St. EH22: Dalk ...2E 42
Woodburn Ter. EH10: Edin ...1F 33
    EH22: Dalk 3F 43
Woodburn Vw. EH22: Dalk ...3F 43
Woodend Pk. EH25: Rosl 3K 45
Woodfield Av. EH13: Edin ...6H 31
    EH25: Bil 7H 39
Woodhall Av. EH14: J Grn ...6F 31
Woodhall Bank EH13: Edin ...7H 31
Woodhall Ct. EH14: J Grn ...7F 31
Woodhall Dr. EH14: J Grn ...6F 31
Woodhall Gro. EH13: Edin ...7H 31
Woodhall Mill Brae
    EH14: J Grn 6G 31
Woodhall Rd. EH13: Edin 6H 31
    EH14: J Grn 7F 31

Woodhall Ter. EH14: J Grn ...6F 31
Woodlands Gro.
    EH15: Edin 5E 22
Woodrow EH23: Gore 5D 48
Woods Ct. EH19: Bonn 6H 41
Woodside Dr. EH26: Pen 2D 50
Woodside Gdns.
    EH21: Muss 2G 25
Woodside Ter. EH15: Port ...4J 23
Woodstock Pl. EH16: Edin ...3B 34
Woodville Ter. EH6: Edin 7F 13
Woolmet Cres. EH22: Dan ...4H 35
World's End Cl. EH1: Edin ...4G 5
Wright's Ho's. EH10: Edin ...6F 21
Writers' Mus. & Makars Court, The
    ....4E 4
Wyvern Pk. EH9: Edin 7H 21
Wyvis Pk. EH26: Pen 7E 44

Y

Yardheads EH6: Leith 5E 12
Yarrow Ct. EH26: Pen 7E 44
Yeaman La. EH11: Edin 5D 20
Yeaman Pl. EH11: Edin 5D 20
Yewlands Cres. EH16: Edin ..5B 34
Yewlands Gdns.
    Pl.EH16: Edin 5B 34
York Bldgs. EH4: Edin 2B 20
        (off Queensferry Rd.)
York La. EH1: Edin 1F 5 (2H 21)
York Pl. EH1: Edin 1E 4 (2H 21)
York Rd. EH5: Edin 4A 12
Young Av. EH33: Tran 3H 27
Young St.
    EH2: Edin 3B 4 (3F 21)
Young St. Nth. La.
    EH2: Edin 3B 4 (2F 21)
Young St. Sth. La.
    EH2: Edin 3B 4 (3F 21)

Z

Zetland Pl. EH5: Edin 4A 12

The representation on the maps of a road, track or footpath is no evidence of the existence of a right of way.

The Grid on this map is the National Grid taken from Ordnance Survey® mapping with the permission of the Controller of Her Majesty's Stationery Office.

SAFETY CAMERA INFORMATION

Safety camera locations are publicised by the Safer Roads Partnership who operate them in order to encourage drivers to comply with speed limits at these sites. It is the driver's absolute responsibility to be aware of and to adhere to speed limits at all times.

By showing this safety camera information it is the intention of Geographers' A-Z Map Company Ltd., to encourage safe driving and greater awareness of speed limits and vehicle speed. Data accurate at time of printing.

Printed and bound in the United Kingdom by Gemini Press Ltd., Shoreham-by-Sea, West Sussex
Printed on materials from a sustainable source